SCHOOL PROFESSIONALS WORKING WITH CHILDREN WITH COCHLEAR IMPLANTS

SCHOOL PROFESSIONALS WORKING WITH CHILDREN WITH COCHLEAR IMPLANTS

Patricia M. Chute, Ed.D.
Mary Ellen Nevins, Ed.D.

PLURAL
PUBLISHING
INC.
SAN DIEGO
OXFORD
BRISBANE

5521 Ruffin Road
San Diego, CA 92123

e-mail: info@pluralpublishing.com
Website: http://www.pluralpublishing.com

Copyright © by Plural Publishing, Inc. 2006

Typeset in 11/13 Garamond by Flanagan's Publishing Services, Inc.
Printed in the United States of America by Edwards Brothers Malloy
17 16 15 14   7 6 5

For permission to use material from this text, contact us by
Telephone: (866) 758-7251
Fax: (888) 758-7255
e-mail: permissions@pluralpublishing.com

Library of Congress Cataloging-in-Publication Data:

Chute, Patricia M.
    School professionals working with children with cochlear implants/
    Patricia M. Chute, Mary Ellen Nevins.
        p. ; cm.
    Includes bibliographical references.
    ISBN-13: 978-1-59756-013-9 (softcover)
    ISBN-10: 1-59756-013-8 (softcover)
    1. Teachers of the deaf. 2. Hearing impaired children–Education.
  3. Cochlear implants.   I. Nevins, Mary Ellen. II. Title.
    [DNLM: 1. Cochlear Implants. 2. Child. 3. Mainstreaming (Education)
      HV 2431 C564s 2006]
  HV2430.C48 2006
  371.91'2–dc22

                                                    2006001246

CONTENTS

PREFACE ix

CHAPTER 1 The Winds of Change:
Fifteen Years of Cochlear
Implantation After FDA Approval 1

CHAPTER 2 The Zone of Cochlear Implant
Performance 17

CHAPTER 3 Characteristics of Educational
Programs that Support Children
with Cochlear Implant 41

CHAPTER 4 Building Collaborative Teams:
Whose Job Is It Anyway? 55

CHAPTER 5 The Mapping Process and Beyond 69

CHAPTER 6 Developing Auditory Skills:
Thinking Outside the "Box" 83

CHAPTER 7 Clear Speech: The Possible Dream 103

CHAPTER 8 Auditory Access and Literacy
Development 117

CHAPTER 9 Supporting Communication
with Sign 131

CHAPTER 10 Special Populations with
Cochlear Implants 147

CHAPTER 11   **Listening in Noisy Classrooms: Room Acoustics, FMs, and Other Assistive Devices**   **165**

CHAPTER 12   **Listening with Two Ears: Bilateral Cochlear Implants and Cochlear Implants and Hearing Aids**   **179**

CHAPTER 13   **Social Development and the Cochlear Implant**   **193**

CHAPTER 14   **A Glimpse into the Future**   **201**

REFERENCES   **211**

APPENDIX A   **Organizational Resources and Web Sites Providing Information on Deafness or Cochear Implants in Children**   **221**

APPENDIX B   **Sample Daily Log**   **225**

APPENDIX C   **FM Manufacturer Resources**   **227**

INDEX   **229**

DEDICATION

To Amy L. Popp, Au.D.

It seems only right that we dedicate this book to you.

You are a colleague, a collaborator, a confidante,
and a computer whiz.

You have been a referee, a negotiator,
an arbitrator, and a savior.

But most of all, you have been a friend.

PREFACE

It is with a great deal of amazement that we reflect on our more than 25 years of experience as speech and hearing professionals. We have been fortunate to witness the birth and growth of a new field: cochlear implantation. Through the years we have attempted to chronicle this extraordinary process through our writing. Our first book, *Children with Cochlear Implants in Educational Settings* (1996) answered an immediate need for information about the new technology in a reader-friendly text. *The Parents' Guide to Cochlear Implants* (2002) was written expressly for parents to help them become better consumers of implant technology. This, our third book in a rather modest trilogy, represents our commitment to the continuing education of school professionals. It is an outgrowth of the many conversations we have had with educational audiologists, speech-language pathologists, and teachers across the country. It tackles many of the new questions that have arisen as the field has evolved including: What is implant success? Who is qualified to work with a child with a cochlear implant? How many implants does a child need? Is there a place for implantation in children with cognitive deficits?

From the vantage point of having had experience with profoundly deaf children using traditional hearing aids, we welcome the advances of the field of implantation. We believe so strongly in this technology that we want to ensure that those who come after us will have the knowledge and skills to help children reach their fullest potential with their implants. School-based professionals have a vital role to play; consider this your playbook! We encourage you to join us in this journey and invite you to share in our amazement.

Chapter 1

THE WINDS OF CHANGE

Fifteen Years of Cochlear Implantation After FDA Approval

Not since the advent of hearing aid technology has an innovation come along that has had the impact of the cochlear implant on deaf society. Today, it is difficult to conceptualize that hearing aids, which grew out of the rehabilitation efforts following World War II, were once hailed as one of the greatest medical achievements of its time (Alpiner, Hansen, & Kaufman, 2003). Thousands of individuals returning from the war with noise-induced hearing loss were afforded this new technology. The effectiveness of these first-generation hearing instruments was considered remarkable and permitted many hard-of-hearing adults to function in a hearing society by maintaining spoken language communication. The excitement surrounding hearing aids found its way into schools for deaf children and a generation of children with mild-to-moderate hearing losses benefited from this technology as well. Unfortunately, the limitations of these devices made sound inaccessible for the majority of those classified with severe-to-profound deafness. As a result, individuals with this degree of hearing loss would continue to struggle to develop spoken language skills or rely on sign language as their main mode of communication. The restrictions that manual communication placed on its users affected every aspect of daily life including educational access, employment opportunities, and interaction with the general public. Methodologies that developed speechreading and kinesthetic approaches to speech production were able to assist a small segment of the profoundly deaf to integrate into the hearing world but this was accomplished only with great struggle on the part of the deaf individual. It would take another three decades before technology was developed to fulfill the promise made by the hearing aid industry to all individuals with hearing loss.

Thus, the cochlear implant created a wind of change that would ultimately be felt by deaf individuals and the professionals with whom they work. These changes can be seen in the technology as well as in the way we teach, train, and support deaf children today. Not only has the cochlear implant evolved, but treatment paradigms have been rethought, educational institutions have been restructured, and professional training has been re-engineered to meet the needs of this new population of deaf individuals. No doubt, more change will come. However, in an attempt to view cochlear implants within a larger social context, it is necessary to consider not only the device itself, but its effect on the children who receive it as well as the speech and hearing professionals working in the educational system that provide services to implant recipients.

TECHNOLOGIC CHANGES

In the 1960s, early attempts were made to develop auditory systems that might provide better acoustic signals to the profoundly deaf population. To accomplish this goal, researchers began to investigate the utility of direct electrical stimulation to the cochlea. The first-generation cochlear implant systems, developed in California in the mid-1970s, took advantage of innovations in microsurgical techniques (Clark, 1975; House & Urban, 1973). Single-channel devices designed by the House Ear Institute (formerly known as the Walt Disney Rehabilitation Research Institute) were implanted initially in adults and subsequently in children. The objective of electrical stimulation was to bypass the damaged (or missing) hair necessary for the transmission of auditory signals to the brain. In individuals with profound deafness, traditional amplification was not sufficient to stimulate these hair cells. By directly exciting the residual neural elements in the cochlea, implant recipients were able to hear sound and some of its basic features. Studies of adult users of single-channel implants were encouraging in that they demonstrated improvements in auditory abilities. Early implant recipients were able to detect environmental sounds and a wide range of tonal signals that afforded users access to conversational speech. Detection of speech permitted implant users to process timing and intensity cues that assisted them in speech reading (Bilger, Black, & Hopkinson, 1977). Speech understanding through the implant alone, however, was not possible. Nonetheless, in 1982, the U.S. Food and Drug Administration (FDA) approved the single-channel implant for use in postlinguistically deafened adults, thereby paving the way for studies in children.

While the single-channel implant was being developed in the United States, other researchers in Australia, Europe, and the United States were investigating the use of multichannel cochlear implants (Clark, 1995). It was believed that multiple-electrode stimulation would provide more information to the cochlea so that speech understanding through listening alone would be possible. In the early 1980s, the Nucleus Cochlear Implant System, developed and manufactured in Australia, was introduced in a nationwide clinical trial in the United States. This device showed great promise as many of the adult recipients were able to understand some speech (40%) without the use of lipreading (Clark, Busby, & Roberts, 1987). The FDA approved this device for use in postlinguistically deafened adults in 1986. Pediatric trials began as the adult study was coming to a close, and in 1990, the Nucleus-22 implant became the first cochlear implant system to receive approval from the FDA for use in children (Clark, Busby, & Dowels, 1992).

Although several research laboratories in Europe were studying other types of designs, these products were not distributed in the United States. Cochlear Corporation (now known as Cochlear Americas) manufactured the Nucleus system and was the sole producer of cochlear implants in the United States for several years. It was not until 1993 when Advanced Bionics Corporation (formerly known as Minimed Technologies) began clinical investigations into a new implant that would be known as the Clarion. This device would later receive FDA approval for use, first in adults (1995) and subsequently in children (1996). In 1997, a third manufacturer, Med El, would enter the U.S. marketplace to investigate its device known as the Combi 40+. Med El technology was a result of research that had been developed in laboratories in Innsbruck, Austria and had received widespread use throughout Europe. At the present time, the U.S. Food and Drug Administration authorizes distribution from only three manufacturers of cochlear implant systems despite the fact that numerous other systems are available in Europe. These three companies, Cochlear Americas, Advanced Bionics, and Med El, distribute implants both in the United States and in worldwide markets.

Changes in cochlear implant technology over the past 25 years can be categorized into three main areas: electrode/receiver design, speech processing, and external hardware. With each successive change, performance has increased and greater numbers of potential candidates have considered implantation an option. In many cases, recipients have been able to take advantage of newer technology without additional surgery. However, in some cases, when internal components have advanced, this has not been possible.

ADVANCES IN ELECTRODE/RECEIVER DESIGN

The earliest version of cochlear implant systems utilized a single-ball electrode implanted 6 mm into the cochlea. When the number of electrode sites increased, research demonstrated better performance. Thus, internal receivers with multiple electrode contacts were developed. The type of electrode contact advanced from single-ball to banded, half-banded, or plate electrodes. The type of electrode contact and the number of contacts varies from manufacturer to manufacturer with no known "magic number" of electrode sites required. Electrode arrays have gone from being straight, to coiled, to incorporating a device known as a "positioner" in order to bring the contacts closer to the sites to be stimulated. Along with the modifications in electrode array design, there have been numerous changes in the surgical tools utilized by the implant surgeon to make the insertion easier and less traumatizing to the cochlear structures. The "brains" of the internal receiver have also changed. These receiver/stimulators now differ in the way the electrodes are grounded, the type of materials that are used to encase the microchip inside, the design of the antenna, and the access to the internal magnet. All these alterations have resulted in improved performance and better reliability.

CHANGES IN SPEECH PROCESSING STRATEGIES

As the goal of the cochlear implant is to provide the best quality signal, the methods used to extract acoustic information, process it, and deliver it to the electrodes are the essence of its function. During the early days of single-channel devices, information was delivered to one electrode, which limited processing to basic detection and timing information. First generation multichannel devices implemented processing strategies that coded the fundamental frequency (F_0) with the second formant (F_2). These strategies evolved over time and subsequently also delivered first formant information (F_1). Later, additional high-frequency information was provided to enhance perception. All these changes resulted in better outcomes for implant recipients; however, this was only the beginning of performance enhancements that were yet to come. Coding strategies today include more sophisticated designs such as continuous interleaved sampling (CIS), spectral peak (SPEAK), advanced combined encoders (ACE), high resolution, and N of M (Clark, 2004). The good news for the professional working in the implant field and the recipient who receives one of the devices is that performance increases have been documented with all these strategies with no one strategy being the best for every recipient. Unfortunately, given the present technology, there is no way of determining during the preimplantation period which strategy might be the best for an individual recipient. This is a challenge that still faces the industry.

EXTERNAL HARDWARE MODIFICATIONS

Perhaps one of the greatest changes that affected acceptance of cochlear implants within the community of candidates was the evolution that occurred in the external device worn by the recipient. The early units were very large, bulky, body-worn devices that required as many as three AA batteries and had components that could easily break. Body processors are still available today for very young and elderly recipients but are more stylish in appearance and more durable for daily use. Initially, the early speech processors had limited memory such that only one program could be stored and accessed. Not until the introduction of the Clarion device in 1993 did a body-worn processor have sufficient memory to store more than one program. Today, all cochlear implants have multiple-program storage capability.

In 1998, when Cochlear Americas introduced the first behind-the-ear speech processor, the next generation of implants was introduced. This effectively transformed implantation by offering a device that resembled the more commonly accepted technology in hearing aids. With this major change in the cosmetics of the device, potential candidates who had been reluctant to abandon their behind-the-ear (BTE) hearing aids were now more inclined to consider the option of implantation. BTE models have continued to evolve and have become modular so that even an infant can use them. They are more efficient with battery power, incorporate tele-coils, and interface better with assistive technology for FM systems. For a more complete description of the devices presently available, the reader is directed to the Web sites for each of the manufacturers listed (see Appendix A).

Much like hearing aid technology, cochlear implant technology has evolved substantially over a relatively short period of time. Products made in the late 1980s and early 1990s have been replaced or upgraded to reflect the latest research in auditory perception. Interestingly, however, the parameters that drove early implant research in auditory perception have expanded to include related areas of study. At first, studies concerning the safety and efficacy of cochlear implant systems were developed to measure a variety of auditory behaviors. Although this is still true today, there has been expanded interest in related areas of performance such as speech production, language development, educational achievement, reading ability, communication methodology, and social interaction. In other words, there has been a heightened awareness in measuring the effects that the new auditory perception has on the growth and development of children who receive these devices. This has taken the research from the medical facilities into the educational facilities that provide service to these children. The resulting impact on the speech and hearing professional in the school has been, and continues to be, the new emphasis in the field.

Although many studies of auditory perception continue to be the backbone of outcome measures and are necessary as new technology evolves, a variety of new professionals initially thought to be extraneous to implantation have become actively involved in both the research and the dispensing of services to those with implants. These professionals including speech-language pathologists (especially those working in the schools), educational audiologists, teachers of deaf children, mainstream teachers, psychologists, social workers, and early interventionists have all become active participants in the process of managing habilitation and studying implant performance.

IMPACT OF IMPLANTATION ON THE FIELD OF AUDIOLOGY

The audiologist remains one of the key professionals in dispensing auditory devices to children who are deaf and hard of hearing. However, the knowledge and skills required by audiologists now entering the field far surpasses those of audiologists of 20 years ago. Changes in hearing aid technology aside, the audiologist who works with children with cochlear implants must be specifically trained in mapping or programming these instruments. Programming cochlear implants requires specialized equipment and a thorough knowledge of each of the different implant systems. It requires experience coupled with an in-depth understanding of acoustics and speech processing. It can only be fully mastered by training under the supervision of another audiologist with expertise in this area. At the present time, there are no programs that train audiologists in mapping as part of their graduate degree.

Assessment procedures that are integral to measuring performance both pre and postimplantation have also changed substantially over the years. New tests have been developed to determine degree and type of benefit. Although the majority of these tests have utilized standard equipment, some of the more sophisticated protocols require additional technology that may not be available in every setting. A great deal of the change in assessment has occurred as a direct result of the improved benefits reported anecdotally by parents. In an effort to capture this information, test procedures were developed to assess auditory abilities in children with more residual hearing and those of younger ages. Additionally, as children began to demonstrate ceiling effects on many of the standard audiological batteries, newer ones embedded in noise were developed. As more children receive bilateral implants, test protocols continue to evolve and will no doubt require additional methodologies to measure some of the more subtle changes in performance.

As the number of children implanted continues to grow, the pressure on the audiologic community will also increase. This pressure extends not only to audiologists in medical settings, but also to those in private practice and in schools. Training professionals who are already active in the field of audiology but are inactive in the area of cochlear implantation will require a huge effort. These professionals should not be overlooked as practicing audiologists bring with them a wealth of knowledge and experience in working with populations of individuals with hearing loss. Present day graduate students in university programs must also have coursework and clinical experience so they can begin their careers with the skills required. This challenge will only be met with the cooperation of university programs, cochlear implant manufacturers, and the national organizations that oversee the field.

IMPACT OF IMPLANTATION ON THE FIELD OF SPEECH-LANGUAGE PATHOLOGY

The role of the speech-language pathologist (SLP) has undergone a multiplicity of changes to adapt to implant technology. Historically, the speech pathologist in the medical setting was the main personnel member involved in the collection of baseline measures to assess progress with implants. Many of the same professionals dispensed (re)habilitative services to implant recipients both young and old. Although this remains true today, the number of school-age children implanted has made the school speech-language pathologist a pivotal person in the overall treatment of children with implants.

Prior to the availability of implantation, the majority of deaf children were educated in schools for the deaf, self-contained classrooms, or, in limited numbers, mainstream classes. Because of this, the district, school-based speech-language pathologist in general education settings rarely serviced children with profound hearing loss. However, as the number of children implanted has increased, more of them are finding their way into mainstream education settings and into the therapy rooms of the school speech-language pathologist. Not unlike the changes in audiology, modifications in assessment paradigms for the evaluation of children with implants have also occurred. This has required SLPs to learn new protocols and methods of measurement to monitor performance over time. Additionally, for SLPs with some experience with populations of children with hearing loss, there has been a growing need to re-examine previously employed techniques to determine their utility with this population. The overall result is that many SLPs must either revisit existing knowledge and skills to determine how they must be adapted for this population or, if their exposure to children with implants has been limited, learn entirely new ones.

As newborn hearing screening has successfully identified babies with hearing loss at birth, the SLP working in early intervention must be aware of candidacy issues for those with profound deafness. As one of the main providers of service to infants and toddlers with hearing aids, the progress (or lack of progress) these children make with traditional amplification must be monitored so that parents can be advised of the technology as early as possible. This relatively new role for the SLP requires new knowledge in the area of cochlear implant performance to properly counsel parents of deaf children.

IMPACT OF IMPLANTATION ON THE FIELD OF EDUCATION

The classroom teacher, trained in methodologies of service delivery that focused on manual communication, is not sufficiently prepared to encourage the spoken-language learning made possible by the cochlear implant. Although some programs trained teachers in auditory/oral approaches, the number of profoundly deaf children who could functionally develop language with this method was extremely limited. Teacher education programs experienced vast pendular swings in training teachers, resulting in a philosophic rift between those that emphasized spoken language and those that

represented manual trends. The clash between the Deaf community and the hearing world became more pronounced as hearing
aid technology failed to provide the auditory input for profoundly
deaf children to succeed orally as a group.

The skepticism regarding implantation grew when, during the
early studies of single-channel implants, poor selection of candidates resulted in greater numbers of nonusers of the device. This
supported the belief of teachers at schools for deaf children that the
implant was another failed piece of technology for children with
profound hearing loss. Even though technology continued to evolve,
mistakes were made in the implantation of congenitally deaf adolescents who had little desire to use audition and spoken language
to communicate. As the rift grew wider, the National Association for
the Deaf (NAD) issued a position paper in 1990 condemning implantation. Teachers in schools for the deaf using ASL saw the implant
as an intrusion into Deaf culture with very little promise.

Teachers in oral classrooms, however, had a very different
impression. These teachers began to observe rapid changes in their
implanted students. Thus, oral programs across the United States
experienced a rebirth as parents flocked to them to meet their children's educational and auditory needs. Existing programs found
they had complete classes with only cochlear implant recipients
enrolled. New programs began to develop as the demand for this
type of educational environment increased. Some of these programs
were housed in medical facilities with cochlear implant centers.
Others developed regionally in response to parental pressure for
auditory/oral education.

For the child who was in a simultaneous communication setting, teachers struggled with the implanted child in a classroom of
children with greater functional degrees of hearing loss. Teaching
children with implants so that they have access to audition to hone
their listening skills while providing them with sign language to
add to their academic development still creates challenges for the
classroom teacher today. Data regarding children in classrooms that
utilize some form of manual communication indicate poorer
speech production in these children, thus adding to the confusion
for parents. However, many of these implanted children rely on
sign language as the primary vehicle of content instruction and,
thus, it cannot be eliminated. The debate continues as to how

to best integrate the various modalities for maximizing listening and learning.

The last and probably the most critical teacher to feel the effects of implantation has been the mainstream classroom teacher. Traditionally, students with hearing loss functioning with hearing aids were educated either in mainstream classes or in special classes within a public school. As a group, districts saw only a handful of these children over time, and, in some cases, never enrolled a child with hearing loss. When cochlear implants were first being studied, research indicated that children entered the mainstream approximately 3 to 4 years postimplantation (Nevins & Chute, 1996; Niparko, Cheng, & Francis, 2000). Although this trend continues, it is important to note that more children are being implanted between the first and second year of life. This would effectively provide them with access to mainstream education environments as early as kindergarten. In many cases, parents are mainstreaming their deaf child with a cochlear implant as early as preschool. This will require a new approach from districts across the country as general education teachers are faced with this ever growing group of children.

The cochlear implant, therefore, has created sweeping changes in the education of deaf children that can be felt in every aspect of classroom instruction. In schools for the deaf, there is a growing trend to incorporate children with implants in preschool classes. This has important implications for school philosophy and mission on which teachers will need to come to consensus. Although the NAD has not supported implantation unequivocally, their revised position statement, issued in 2000, did recognize implantation as one of many alternatives available for deaf children. In 2000, the Laurent Clerc National Deaf Education Center at Gallaudet University established a cochlear implant education center to provide services for children with implants in its preschool with the intention of providing a model for other deaf schools to follow. For the first time, in a very long time, there seems to be open dialogue between groups who, in the past, found discussion difficult.

For schools that use an approach supported with sign language in some way, the challenges remain the same. Teachers must learn to balance the utilization of sign language for instruction with sufficient opportunities for listening to and producing spoken language. Meeting the individual goals for each child must be a clear part of the process, taking into account the factors that influence cochlear implant performance.

The influx of children with cochlear implants has placed pressure on the auditory oral training programs to produce more teachers with experience in educating children using this methodology. Private funding has become available for the development of auditory oral schools that can also be used as training grounds for the next generation of teachers. How these schools will fit into the framework of education of the deaf is still unclear as children with implants enter mainstream classes at younger ages.

Finally, mainstream teachers must now add another component to the myriad challenges that face them daily. Classrooms are now filled with children with a variety of learning challenges from English as a second language, to reading disorders and learning disabilities. Children who are deaf and use cochlear implants may also present with some of these and other challenges as well. Regardless, teachers must be aware of the auditory needs of children with implants and attend to them to ensure their success.

All four groups of teachers, then, will require professional development to accommodate this growing group of children. In addition to professional development, however, training programs must also become proactive in the process so that those graduating are able to work effectively in the field. Clearly, because the classroom teacher spends the bulk of the school day with the child with an implant, this professional, and the training he or she brings to the process, will ultimately prove to be the catalyst for success.

CHANGES FOR OTHER PROFESSIONALS

Psychologists, social workers, and the early interventionist case manager have also seen changes in children who are deaf and have now received cochlear implants. The role that these professionals played prior to implantation was often as a referral source or advisor. These roles have not changed intrinsically but functionally. Psychologists who treated children with profound deafness were often seen solely as evaluators and developed tests to overcome the limitations in verbal output. Now, these children can be viewed more within the context of the hearing child and the psychologist can begin to treat them as such. Similarly, social workers, especially those who provide information and counseling to parents of children with hearing loss in early intervention, must acquire updated information to provide the best service. As more children with multiple disabilities access implantation, it becomes evident that the roles both these professionals play will continue to change. The parents' dependence on these qualified individuals as resources makes it critical for these experts to remain current about options for children with hearing loss.

The early interventionist (EI) trained in deafness will also be responsible for disseminating unbiased information about communication choices available in the language-learning years. To provide important information to parents during a very critical time, it is vital for these specialists to be well versed in candidacy requirements for implantation. Historically, the early interventionist was an individual with a breadth of knowledge in overall child development but only an overview of presenting challenges to normal development. Because deafness represents a low-incidence group, the early interventionist may have had limited exposure to this group of children and their special needs. Additionally, deafness was often not identified until the child aged out of the years covered under early intervention. With newborn hearing screening, however, EI professionals must now be knowledgeable about hearing loss and its effects on communication and education. For this reason, as cochlear implantation has become more prevalent in this young population, it becomes even more important for the early interventionist to be aware of the latest technology.

CHANGES IN POPULATION OF COCHLEAR IMPLANT RECIPIENTS

The population of implant recipients in the United States and throughout the world has increased as awareness of the technology has become more widespread and improved outcomes have been publicized. As of December 2004, data from the manufacturers indicate more than 65,000 recipients worldwide with approximately one-third located in the United States (personal communication,

Cochlear Americas, 2005). Although the number of adult recipients is slightly greater than the number of children implanted, this is due to the manner in which cochlear implants were first investigated (adults studies preceded pediatric studies). This ratio is expected to change markedly as more states adopt Universal Newborn Hearing Screening, thereby setting the stage for early implantation. Estimates in the United States of children with severe-to-profound bilateral sensorineural hearing loss note approximately 45,000 children in this classification. Presently only 22% of these children are receiving cochlear implants. As implant awareness increases and newborn hearing-screening programs are organized to assist in identifying potential candidates, this percentage is expected to increase to more than 50% within the next 2 to 3 years. (personal communication, Cochlear Americas, 2005).

In addition to the number of children being identified at birth, the increase in the cochlear implant population is also a direct result of the changing candidacy criteria with respect to functional hearing level. More children with residual hearing (but limited benefit from their hearing aids) are now receiving these devices. Changes in audiologic criteria have occurred over the past decade, so that children no longer need to be profoundly deaf but can now be severely-to-profoundly deaf. The resulting increase in children who potentially can access this technology will create a domino effect for the professionals involved. Harnessing the energy of speech and hearing professionals responsible for the treatment of children with hearing loss will remain a challenge.

As cochlear implantation continues to evolve, there is no doubt that more professionals will be needed to deliver services to children with this device. For very young children, who represent the largest growing segment of implant recipients, the focus of intervention will be very different from treatment previously implemented. Preparing professionals to maximize the auditory potential of this device in the development of speech and spoken language is the responsibility of a consortium of individuals and entities: university level instructors, experienced service providers, and the manufacturers. The pressure placed on the speech and hearing professional in the delivery of services for this population will also grow. If the educational needs of children with cochlear implants are to be met so that "no child is left behind," then it is important for school professionals to be well prepared to meet this challenge.

SUMMARY

Cochlear implantation is here to stay. It has replaced the hearing aid as the treatment of choice for the severely-to-profoundly deaf. For that reason, its effects will be felt in much the same manner as those created by hearing aids decades ago. When hearing aids were first introduced, the field of audiology was born, the role of the speech pathologist grew, and the teachers in regular education were included as extended members on the intervention team. We are at the threshold of a new era of change that will influence all the professional fields associated with treating children with hearing loss. Children with implants now have access to opportunities never before imagined. For professionals working in the school, this change should be viewed as a welcome one in which there is plenty to learn and much to do.

This book is a direct result of conversations with school professionals who are ready, willing, and able to bring their present knowledge and specialized skills to the task of effecting change in the education of deaf children. It is meant to act as a reference for those who are in graduate programs in the field as well as a resource for those already in practice. This resource cannot answer all questions (many are still unanswerable) but it can provide the school professional with a framework within which a comprehensive intervention plan is developed.

Chapter 2

THE ZONE OF COCHLEAR IMPLANT PERFORMANCE

School professionals providing services to children with cochlear implants are often in a quandary regarding the wide range of performance that these children might demonstrate. Most often, these are professionals who have "inherited" a child at some point during the implant process and were not involved during the initial days of that child's candidacy. Even if a therapist is working with a child during the evaluation period, he or she is often extraneous to the process and thus lacks an understanding of the relationship of candidacy to performance. The more a school professional knows about a child at the preimplant stage, the greater the understanding of the process and the rate of progress postimplantation. School professionals rarely have an extensive history of working with children with implants. What they often do have is experience with: children who have language disorders but not hearing loss, children with lesser degrees of hearing loss, or children with profound hearing loss using hearing aids. Thus, expectations for benefit with implants are based on publications, presentations, and an internal belief system that may not be in line with the true potential for the child.

To be successful working in schools, the speech and hearing professional requires a framework within which performance can be better understood to drive habilitation. Overall trends in implantation identify several areas of growth that will directly affect educational professionals. First, a changing demographic exists in which more children are being implanted at younger ages. In addition, children with disabilities and those from more culturally, linguistically, and economically diverse populations are also accessing implantation. Educationally, there are a wider variety of classroom settings that support this new technology as parents of these children seek academic environments to meet their family needs. Furthermore, there are auditory, language, speech, and educational characteristics of implant recipients that have been documented since the early days of implantation. Reviewing these trends and characteristics allows the reader to have a perspective that views performance differences between and among children from a vantage point that begins with candidacy.

AUDITORY PERFORMANCE

Auditory performance with cochlear implants has received the greatest amount of attention as the device is an auditory prosthesis and auditory performance is critical to its existence. General outcomes identified through controlled research with a multitude of child populations overwhelmingly support the use of a cochlear implant for the pediatric population (Kirk, 2000; Osberger et al., 1991; Staller et al., 1991). Of note, research has demonstrated that children implanted at young ages have greater potential for benefit (Waltzman, 2000). Additionally, children with shorter durations of deafness also perform better than those implanted with longer durations (Fryauf-Bertschy et al., 1992). Regardless of which group the child represents, it is important for the child to have been exposed to auditory stimuli via hearing aids as this will contribute to more positive outcomes. Children with less hearing loss and who subsequently lose access to audition have also demonstrated better outcomes postimplantation (Cowan et al., 1997; Fisher & Kalberer, 2000; Zwolan et al., 1997). Similarly, children with progressive hearing losses will have listening experiences that contribute to success with the implant (Harker et al., 1999).

LANGUAGE DEVELOPMENT

As the body of research on auditory performance grew, more studies regarding the effect of the implant on spoken language evolved (Robbins 1999; Robbins et al., 1999; Shopmeyer et al., 2000). With 90% of deaf children born to hearing parents (Quigley & Kretschmer, 1982), many families prefer to raise their deaf child with a communication modality similar to their own. Thus, developing spoken language skills became a driving force for parents to seek implantation for their children. Studies have supported the use of implants for language growth and have demonstrated that receptive skills for this group progress at a faster rate than deaf, unimplanted children of hearing parents. Additionally, investigators have reported that increased levels of syntactic complexity are reached earlier with implanted children (Robbins, 2000). Early gains in communication initiations and successful participation in conversation have resulted as the child's ability to use language to address his or her wants and needs develops. As prosodic features can be accessed auditorily in a more natural manner, implant recipients have demonstrated the ability to communicate intent nonlinguistically (Robbins, 2000). Caution for expecting these results in every child who receives an implant must be taken, as a variety of factors contribute to implant success.

SPEECH PRODUCTION

Auditory input from the cochlear implant provides access to an acoustic signal that allows the recipient to hear and produce suprasegmental cues (Robbins, 2000; Robbins et al., 1995). These appear early in postimplant habilitation and contribute to emerging productive performance. The implant also permits more natural voice production as the child is able to access greater amounts of frequency, intensity, and timing information. The availability of second formant information contributes to increased accuracy in vowel production along with improvements in the less visible features of consonant production such as place, manner, and voicing. Overall, children who are implanted early and/or have shorter durations of deafness enjoy a high degree of intelligibility (Svirsky & Chin, 2000; Waltzman et al., 1997). Children who begin the process with long durations of deafness and unintelligible speech will never reach the same levels of intelligibility that children implanted early will demonstrate. This forecast of speech outcome should not preclude implantation but should be understood by the parents and child as they enter the process so that expectations can be adjusted accordingly.

EDUCATIONAL ACHIEVEMENT

As the spoken language skills of children with implants have increased commensurate with their good auditory performance, more children are mainstreamed at younger ages. In fact, children implanted early, on average, will enter the mainstream classroom after 3 to 4 years of implant use (Nevins & Chute, 1996; Niparko et al., 2000). Additionally, children with implants demonstrate better reading skills than their deaf unimplanted counterparts (Spencer et al., 1997). Research that has controlled for educational environment reports better overall outcomes when children are educated in auditory-oral classrooms (Osberger et al., 2000a). Again, the results of educational achievement will be driven by the larger auditory factors noted above.

OVERALL PERFORMANCE OUTCOMES

Implant "success" is the goal for children who use these devices. However, what constitutes success may differ from child to child in much the same way it does for hearing children. At the two extremes of a performance continuum are optimal or maximal "success" and "failure." Failure, in this sense, is not meant to include mechanical failure. Operationally, it is defined as a child who no longer chooses to wear the implant despite its proper functioning. At the other end of the continuum is what is considered maximal success. Characteristics of optimal implant use include: open-set speech recognition (the ability to understand speech using audition alone), achievement of age-appropriate spoken language skills, and educational competence similar to hearing age-mates. Although a large number of children reach these maximal goals, an even larger number of children perform somewhere between these two extremes. They can and should be considered successful.

Children who obtain some open-set speech recognition and require the support of speech reading for more demanding communication interactions are certainly considered successful users of their cochlear implants. However, some children require speech reading continuously to maximize their benefit with the device. These children, too, are considered successful users. In some cases, the implant recipient may have access to a wider range of communication partners due to improvements in speech production and continue to flourish with implant use. Auditory awareness from the implant may assist a child in recognizing speaker changes during conversation. With this ability, attention can be switched quickly to participate more fluidly in the exchange. Finally, for some children, the implant allows a better auditory connection to the environment often resulting in more manageable behaviors. All these children can be considered successful in their use of the cochlear implant. Quite simply, there is continuous wear time even if performance is not at the upper limit.

For this reason, performance can fall within a *zone* with the two extremes of maximal success and failure at either end. The *zone of cochlear implant performance* can be conceptualized into two distinct regions: the physiologic zone and the intervention zone. In understanding the zone and its regions, the speech and hearing professional is better able to consider a child's responses with the implant to plan and evaluate habilitation more effectively.

THE PHYSIOLOGIC ZONE

The physiologic zone can be conceptualized as representing the functional anatomy of the ear and central processing system. It is characterized by what is commonly referred to as "neural survival" within the inner ear and the ability to sort and manage the signal once it reaches the higher centers. It is probably the most critical aspect of hearing and it remains the area about which we have the least knowledge. Traditional hearing tests can give professionals only a very small glimpse of this portion of the zone. There are other tests that can provide some insight; however, professionals are unable to make predictions about postimplant performance with respect to these factors.

Neural survival is that aspect of cochlear physiology that represents the number of potential sites of excitation in the cochlea. Deafness leaves the cochlea with limited potential as the normal physiology is compromised due to the lack of hair cells. The extent of the damage is virtually impossible to assess because of the complexity of how we hear. Problems related to limited neural survival in the cochlea make the implant less effective from the initial point of stimulation of the auditory system. With reduced capability of the auditory nerve, the electrical signal being sent will either be substantially truncated or not be sent at all. Although there are some potential signs of this prior to implantation, it cannot be predicted with 100% accuracy. The cochlear implant can bypass damaged or missing hair cells but there must still be some residual neural elements to stimulate to begin transmission to the brain. Children with residual hearing have better populations of these elements and, therefore, perform in a manner that is somewhat more predictable. (Although the reader will soon learn there are numerous other factors that will contribute to this predictability.) The converse, however, is not true. Children with very limited or no hearing preimplantation may still perform well, but specifying expectations for performance become more complex. Thus, determining "neural survival," the most important contributing factor to implant performance, presently eludes professionals. Ironically, even if identifying cochlear neural survival becomes possible, there are even greater challenges to the signal once it leaves the cochlea.

Processing sound as it exits the end organ of hearing can be compromised even for individuals with perfectly normal cochleas. School professionals routinely see children identified with auditory processing disorders (APD) more regularly than they see children with implants. The results of the various treatments for hearing children with APD have gradations of success, thereby making the deaf child with a cochlear implant and a central processing problem a complete enigma. With no method to identify these children at the preimplant juncture, professionals are often left with many questions about performance after implantation.

The physiologic zone, therefore, encompasses an area that is not under the control of the experts in the field or the recipients of the device. When there are problems in the physiologic zone, *no amount of habilitation will override its effects.* This may color the belief systems of professionals who remain skeptical about implantation. However, it should be remembered that, despite the lack of knowledge concerning the important aspects of auditory perception, overall results with cochlear implants remain impressive.

THE INTERVENTION ZONE

The three components that make up the intervention zone include: candidacy, device management, and habilitation. As these areas are, in large part, under the control of the parent, professional, and recipient, it is here where we will focus our attention when discussing performance. Children will enter this portion of the zone based on their innate abilities identified at the time of candidacy. Progress within the zone will be influenced by the quality of services that are provided as the child negotiates the academic and therapeutic process. Here, issues of device management and habilitation will drive ultimate outcomes.

The intervention zone is the region in which the school-based speech-language professional has the greatest impact. It is an area that requires continual reassessment as the child travels along the continuum to attain maximal benefit from the device. What works best for one implant recipient may differ substantially from what works best with another. No single approach is the sole route to success. It is the responsibility of the speech-language pathologist, audiologist, educator, and parent to ensure that the child has every opportunity to find his or her best route.

WORKING WITHIN THE ZONE

The schematic in Figure 2–1 is provided as a frame of reference to better understand the performance continuum. As noted earlier, the two extremes of performance include failure and maximal success. These are noted at the end of each arrowed portion of Figure 2–1.

Children who enter the zone at a point along the continuum, close to success, will achieve maximal performance with the implant if physiologic and intervention factors are not limiting. Children who enter the zone distant from success and make limited movement

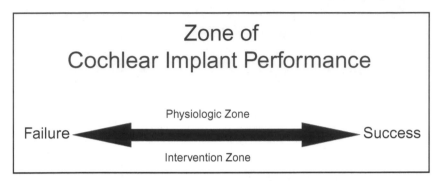

Figure 2–1. The Zone of Cochlear Implant Performance

along the continuum may choose to disengage from the process and cease to wear their implants (Figure 2-2).

Children may enter the zone at the same point but some will progress a short distance and others longer distances (Figure 2-3).

Regardless of the distance traveled, implant recipients can be considered successful implant users as long as they are making some movement within the zone. An individual child's zone can be conceptualized as beginning at the point of entry and ending at the point of anticipated maximal performance. Figure 2-4 demonstrates two different children and their zone profiles.

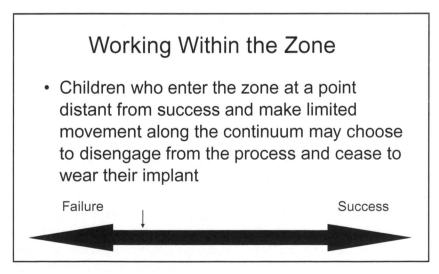

Figure 2–2. Distance from Success in the Zone

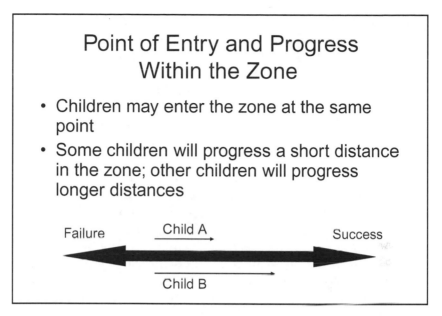

Figure 2–3. Point of Entry and Progress within the Zone

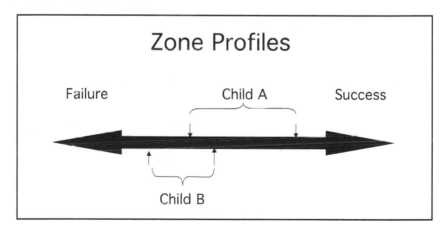

Figure 2–4. Zone Profiles of Two Implant Recipients

The speed with which a child progresses within the zone can be classified as rapid, slow, or none at all. Children who progress rapidly will have positive physiologic and intervention zone profiles; those who progress slowly will have questionable profiles in one or both areas. Slow progress may be accelerated with mediation in the intervention zone if that is where the problem is located. Intervention zone issues include those that were present at the time of candidacy, the management of the device, and the habilitation program in effect. For children who show no progress, there may be a combination of both physiologic and intervention issues that negatively affect performance. With these children, even the best intervention plan may not succeed due to overriding physiologic factors. These would include limited neural survival and/or auditory processing disorders.

In the auditory processing literature, it is documented that children may fail to comprehend auditory stimuli even in the presence of normal hearing (Bellis, 2003). Auditory processing disorders, as a group, often come with concomitant speech and language delays. For this reason, the deaf child who has an auditory processing problem and receives a cochlear implant will make poor use of the implant due to the presence of central issues. Unfortunately, these issues are often identified after auditory access is provided. Remediation for this group of children should include a comprehensive approach that combines, audition, speech reading, and, in some cases, sign language to support overall development.

To operate effectively within the zone, several aspects can be addressed by professionals working in the field of implantation. Because a child's point of entry into the zone drives progress and ultimate outcome, there are aspects of preimplant circumstances that can be mediated by the cochlear implant team and the parents. These are issues present at the time of candidacy.

Candidacy Factors Influencing Point of Entry into the Zone

Although the most basic factor that is assessed during cochlear implant candidacy is related to a child's hearing ability with traditional amplification, it should not be the only factor evaluated during this period. A multiplicity of issues contributing to outcomes with a cochlear implant require consideration at the time of candidacy. They include:

- age at implantation
- duration of deafness

- structure of the cochlea

- use of residual hearing

- presence and sophistication of a formal language system

- presence of a second language in the home

- presence of disabilities

- family structure and support

- expectations of the parents and the child

- educational environment

- availability of support services.

In exploring each of these areas identified at the time of candidacy, the school-based personnel working with children postimplantation may have a better appreciation for the differences that may be seen in performance.

Age at Implantation and Duration of Deafness

The two factors of age at implantation and duration of deafness define the entry point into the zone and are considered non-negotiable at the time of candidacy. In other words, these are not factors that can be changed with remediation. Studies have shown that younger children with a shorter duration of deafness will perform better than children who are implanted at an older age with a longer duration of deafness (Fryauf-Bertschy et al., 1992: Kirk, 2000; Waltzman 2000). That is not to imply that older, congenitally deaf children cannot receive cochlear implants; it merely marks the initial point of entry into the zone as farther from the success point. These children are often successful users but require longer use of the implant before all the benefits are seen. For older children with short durations of deafness (as in the case of hearing children who might be deafened from disease or trauma after the age of 5), the greatest potential for benefit has been noted (Osberger & Fisher, 1998).

Relative to issues of age at implantation and duration of deafness, their effects on point of entry into the zone may be ameliorated through careful counseling and, in some cases, preimplant training. Preimplant training is often effective when dealing with adolescents seeking implants. Many times these teens are left outside the process as their parents drive the decision-making. Because congenitally deafened teenagers represents the largest group of nonusers of the device, it is important to ensure that any adolescent entering the zone has a complete understanding of the commitment and slow progress that may occur (Kirk, 2000; Miyamoto et al., 1994). The teenage recipient (and his or her family) requires counseling regarding the anticipated slow rate of progress given the preimplant profile. In addition, a teen must be made aware that the sound of an implant will be vastly different from that of a hearing aid. Because the implant provides more high-frequency information, the teenage listener may initially find these sounds bothersome rather than helpful. High-frequency information is foreign to recipients who have only had limited input in the low-frequency portion of the cochlea. Listening to this type of sound may be considered obtrusive by some and may lead to early negative feelings toward the implant. This, coupled with slow progress, may result in the recipient disassociating from the implant. It is for this reason that caution should be taken when considering congenitally deaf adolescents for implantation.

Exercising the same level of caution will not be necessary for congenitally deaf children with shorter durations of deafness. Children who are born deaf and implanted at young ages (especially within the first year or two of life) represent some of the best performers with cochlear implants. Professionals working with children with implants should have a clear understanding of the interplay of the critical factors of age at implantation and duration of deafness in order to tailor therapeutic approaches appropriately.

Structure of the Cochlea

Cochlear anatomy will contribute to the point of entry into the zone and is also a non-negotiable factor. Children with abnormal cochleas will enter the continuum at a point farther from success than a child with normal cochlear anatomy. As this condition cannot be changed, some issues must be addressed at the time of candidacy to more precisely counsel parents and recipients regarding expected performance. For candidates with ossified (bony) cochleas (generally secondary to meningitis), the additional bone in the cochlea may prevent a full insertion of the electrode array, thereby restricting the number of electrodes that can ultimately be stimulated. Additionally, even with a portion of the array inserted, ossification may limit the quantity and quality of electrical stimulation.

Malformed cochleas also can restrict implant function. These anatomical malformations are often referred to as "Mondini" deformities. They include a large group of compromised features of the normal cochlea, which structurally has 2½ turns. In Mondini deformities, there may be less than the normal number of turns or there may be what is known as a "common cavity," which has no turns at all. Because the cochlea is malformed, neural elements are likely to be abnormal, thereby making the electrical stimulation less than adequate. These malformations are accompanied by other aberrations that affect cranial nerves that lie close to the auditory nerve (VIII N). Children with Mondini deformities may have inadvertent stimulation of the facial nerve (VII N) due to the abnormalities of the VIII N. This may reduce the number of electrodes that can be inserted and the amount of current that can be sent to the electrodes. Some children with Mondini abnormalities have performed quite well; however, some demonstrate limited performance. Careful counseling at the time of preoperative evaluation is crucial for this group so that parents (and the child, if appropriate) can fully understand performance expectations appropriate to the child's profile.

Use of Residual Hearing

As outcomes of cochlear implantation have improved steadily with progress in technology, more children with residual hearing are seeking the device. This has been one of the major changes in the field of implantation over the past two decades. Children who use traditional amplification and demonstrate some open-set speech recognition ability (30%) can now be considered candidates for implantation. These children often enter the implant process with relatively good spoken language ability and substantial auditory perception. Most often, the reason for their limited discrimination is lack of access to high-frequency information necessary to perceive consonants. As a result, these children will enter the zone at a point of entry closer to success and will often progress in a more rapid fashion. To mediate the point of entry into the zone, the educational audiologist at the school should ensure that the child's hearing aids and FM systems are properly fitted and working within specifications. Parents should ensure maximal wear time of hearing aids as well as maintain an active role in the habilitative process. Generally, once implanted, children with residual hearing are able to use their previous knowledge of sound to decode the new signals from the implant. Often, they represent some of the best performers.

Presence and Sophistication of a Formal Language System

For children to make proper use of the cochlear implant, they must have a formal language system (or one that is emerging). Although sign language skills can be considered in the total language assessment picture, this system must be one that is accompanied by spoken English. Children whose language age and chronological age differ by more than 3 to 4 years are often poor users of the cochlear implant (Nevins & Chute, 1996). This occurs due to a mismatch of the new auditory representations of language and the child's own impoverished language base supported largely through visual representation. Likewise, children who have been exposed only to American Sign Language (ASL) will be unable to make the transition to spoken language with the same ease as a child who has used spoken language continuously. For these children, there is serious question regarding their appropriateness as candidates and, in some centers, they are not recommended for implantation. Finally, there must be a motivation on the part of the implant recipient to produce spoken language in order for it to evolve.

Children who enter the zone with poor spoken language skills will enter at a greater distance from success and move more slowly across the continuum. Movement through the zone may require a change in communication modality to make progress. For children using simultaneous communication, an auditory-oral emphasis within this approach or a switch to an auditory/oral environment will be necessary to see the types of performance changes that reflect maximal usage (Cowan et al,, 1997; Osberger et al., 2000b). This may not be a realistic goal for all children who fit this profile and addressing language and educational needs will override any change in communication modality. In cases in which a child is losing ground educationally due to placement in an auditory-only environment, it may be necessary to move to one that includes a simultaneous communication approach. However, as noted previously, children with marked delays in language should not enter the zone at all.

Generally, studies that have assessed the development of spoken language skills after implantation have demonstrated that children in auditory-oral environments that value spoken language perform best (Moog & Geers, 1998; Robbins, 2000). Although spoken language development may not be an achievable goal for every child who receives an implant, improved auditory perception and continued movement across the continuum still identifies many children as successful users.

Presence of a Second Language in the Home

With the growing diversity of cultures in the United States, it is not uncommon for children seeking implants to come from homes in which the language spoken is not English. As this trend continues, it is important to increase the number of speech and hearing professionals who are fluent in additional languages. For children receiving implants at young ages (during the language-learning years), the presence of a second language in the home may cause a slight delay in the emergence of both languages. The child's entry point into the zone, therefore, will be slightly farther from success than if only spoken English were used. Parents, however, are encouraged to use the language they speak most naturally when conversing with their child. In other words, when parents are not fluent in English, they are unable to be effective language models in English. It is best to have the child exposed to correct grammar and articulation, regardless of which language is spoken. Movement along the continuum may be a bit slower, but will evolve in a manner similar to hearing children who speak English as a second language. However, as the age at implantation and the duration of deafness increase, the overall results may be compromised.

Presence of Disabilities

Research indicates that approximately 38% of children who have hearing loss will also have an additional disability (Dayton, 1970). These can be as mild as traditional myopia and be remediated by wearing glasses or be as involved as deficits that are cognitive in nature. Noncognitive deficits can include a variety of disabilities such as low muscle tone, blindness, or mild cerebral palsy, to name a few. Some cognitive deficits result in behaviors that severely restrict the child's ability to function and often include more organic brain issues. Whether the disability is cognitive or noncognitive in nature, it will affect the child's point of entry into the zone, with the cognitive deficits making the entry point farther from success than the noncognitive ones.

As with many outcomes already discussed, performance of children with noncognitive disabilities will often be related to age at implantation and the duration of deafness. Regardless, there is often some delay in progress noted initially with this group of children (Chute, 2001). Children with cognitive deficits may experience very limited benefit from the device. Movement along the zone's continuum will most definitely be influenced by the age at implantation and can be facilitated through the therapeutic approaches that are put in place at that time. Children who present with other disabilities have a better chance of benefit if implanted at a young age than those who are implanted when they are older. In fact, for children with cognitive deficits, implantation should not be considered once the child is past the language-learning years. In these cases, children may find the sound from the implant more of an intrusion than an enhancement. On average, children with disabilities require more therapy. Additional services include: occupational therapy, physical therapy, and behavioral therapy, to name a few. It may also be necessary to expand the cochlear implant team and recruit experts in the areas of challenge to ensure that the child is receiving the best approach to his or her hearing loss and other disability. However, as long as the child wears the device every day and is able to make even small amounts of progress, he or she should be considered a successful cochlear implant user. School professionals working with these children must recognize that progress may be extremely slow, especially during the initial stages of habilitation.

Family Structure and Support

American families, as a rule, have become more stressed in recent years as economic, educational, and societal pressures have mounted.

The importance of the family in the (re)habilitation of anyone with a disability is paramount to the process. For the deaf child seeking a cochlear implant, it is no different. Family structure these days can range from the very traditional to the more nontraditional that is reflected in single parents, alternative lifestyle parents, and foster parents. Regardless of family type, family structure and support will define the child's entry point into the zone. Extended family members, such as grandparents, step-parents, and caregivers should be considered an integral part of the process. The resources available to any given family may substantially affect a child's performance with the device. Recent studies have shown a correlation between income and cochlear implant outcomes (Miyamoto, 2005; Stern et al., 2005). Families challenged by economic issues, health problems, or caring for elderly parents may have limited resources. These may affect the child's overall performance with the implant.

Mediating the point of entry into the zone for families with challenges may require additional counseling by the implant team as well as networking with other parents and professionals. The role of the social worker for families with limited resources should not be overlooked. When school personnel are aware of the challenges facing these families, the pace of progress that a child is making will be contextualized.

Expectations of Parent and Child

The decision for implantation, whether made only by the parents or by both the parents and the child, brings with it a wide range of expectations. Many expectations are realistic and many are not. Unrealistic expectations (which are often seen in adolescent implant recipients) may set the stage for limited use or nonuse. Recall that nonuse is the only category identified as "failure" when considering the zone. Parents and children with unrealistic expectations should not gain entry to the process until they have a clearer understanding of the implant's potential in light of their child's profile. On the other hand, limited expectations may predispose the child for reduced achievement with the implant. This may become a self-fulfilling prophecy that can lead to nonuse. Adolescents, especially, may display frustration when experiencing a delay in material benefit and reject the implant. In some cases, professionals with prior negative experiences or attitudes toward implantation may contribute to this result as well.

To mediate the point of entry into the zone and facilitate progress through it, counseling and networking can be of great benefit. Here the Internet has become an invaluable resource, allowing parents and recipients to correspond freely about their experiences. It is important, however, that the Internet not be the only support system for the child or parent as there are often comments that incite rather than quell concerns. Support from school-based professionals who follow the child on a daily basis becomes essential for those who experience frustration with slow progress. Contact with the implant center can assist parents and users in obtaining information and referrals when needed.

Educational Environment

The classroom environment in which a child with a cochlear implant is placed contributes to the performance outcomes that are measured. Programs that value audition and spoken language will be most conducive to success. Conversely, programs that emphasize sign language with minimal opportunities for use of spoken language will limit performance. School personnel with little information or experience with children with implants may also hamper performance. Children who enter the zone from programs that do not value audition or spoken language skills will enter at a point farther from success than those who are in programs that promote them. In fact, children who are in ASL programs that have no intention of adapting the educational environment should not enter the zone.

Mediating the point of entry into the zone to assist in maximizing the benefit from the implant requires dissemination of information to school personnel regarding implantation as a process of which they are a part. Professional development related to cochlear implants, both within and outside the school district, should be in place. In some circumstances, changing school placement may be a consideration if the school is unable to meet the educational and therapeutic needs of the child. These measures will help facilitate movement within the zone to attain the best possible outcome.

Availability of Support Services

The role that therapeutic intervention plays in the overall benefit from implantation cannot be overstated. Children who have access to therapists that provide comprehensive speech, language, and auditory services make better progress than those who do not. When a child is enrolled in intensive therapy (especially during the early periods following implantation), there is greater potential to perform at high levels.

To mediate the point of entry into the zone, the cochlear implant team or the parent should identify personnel experienced in working with children with hearing loss. Ultimately, professionals who have worked directly in the field are preferred. But, given the paucity of trained therapists in this area, those with general experience with children who have hearing loss can adapt easily. Parents may also need to negotiate for increased services as the child enters the implant process. Additional meetings with special education administrators may be necessary to ensure that the child's Individualized Family Service Plan (IFSP) or Individualized Educational Plan (IEP) reflects changes in type and amount of services as a function of implantation.

PROGRESS THROUGH THE ZONE'S CONTINUUM

Once the child enters the implant process, progress is encouraged within the intervention zone. This requires an understanding of the factors that contribute to movement along the continuum of performance. Addressing these factors involves the cooperation of the school, the cochlear implant team, and the family. Areas in the intervention zone that can be influenced include device management and habilitation. Matters of device management consist of wear time, duration of implant use, proper functioning of the implant, and the appropriate adjustment of the device (known as mapping).

Device Management

Progress through the zone will be more effective if the child wears his or her device all waking hours every day (Meyer et al., 1998). Cumulatively, as the child continues to wear the device over time, long-term use will also contribute to improved performance. Children who use their implants only at school or only at home will not have sufficient exposure to spoken language to make appropriate gains. In some cases, parents and school personnel may have to implement a "wear program" to increase implant use. These programs may take the form of behavioral management schedules for a very young child or behavioral contracts in teenagers. Each group requires a specified plan to increase wear time. Therapeutic approaches that foster success will help to reinforce use in children who may be limiting their wear time.

In addition to time spent wearing the device, the implant must be monitored for proper functioning. The internal receiver stability should be checked regularly by the implant center. External hardware must be adequately maintained by parents, professionals, and the child (when appropriate). If the device is not fully functioning, then movement through the zone will be seriously compromised.

To ensure that the device is optimally operational, school personnel should make certain that the child is seen for regular mapping sessions. Quality and timely mapping leads to better performance. School professionals working with children with implants should try to observe the mapping process at the cochlear implant center or review one of the videos that are available through the manufacturers. They should also be prepared to work cooperatively with the implant center to communicate information about auditory/speech behaviors that can assist with the mapping. Mapping is discussed in greater detail in chapter 5.

In addition to a properly set device, the device must be properly maintained. The educational audiologist, speech-language pathologist, and teacher should be knowledgeable in basic troubleshooting of the implant. They should know how to perform daily checks of the equipment and how to manipulate the function control settings. This is especially necessary for professionals working with very young children or children who have just been "switched-on." Knowledge of appropriate device settings will also facilitate better performance. Communication with the cochlear implant center is the best means of ensuring cooperation and collaboration among professionals.

Habilitation

The habilitation factors that influence progress within the zone include the amount and quality of family input, the presence of a second language in the home, the educational environment, and the availability of support services. School personnel must be integrally involved to move the child efficiently along the continuum. In some cases, it may be difficult to control all these variables; however, an understanding of them will assist the habilitationist in monitoring performance of the child.

Parents who are active participants in providing children with the necessary auditory, speech, and language stimuli will contribute to the success of their child's overall development. Assuming the role of "therapist" may be a challenge for some parents, who may require guidance by professionals on how to create opportunities for listening and speaking during everyday home activities. Immediate and extended family members may also contribute to a positive attitude toward listening and speaking. Providing videos, networking, or workshops for family members may assist the school professional in reaching the auditory-speech goals for the child in a more efficient manner. For a child who is capable of certain behaviors in the therapy room but has little carryover into the everyday world, the role of the parent and caregiver becomes even more important.

Parents who speak a language other than English provide a rich language model for their native tongue. Children with a second language may demonstrate growth in the home language in the area of Basic Interpersonal Communication Skills (BICS) and develop English in the area of Cognitive and Academic Language Proficiency (CALP) (Cummins, 1984). In this case, overall language growth may be initially delayed. Family input is crucial to the development of listening and speaking skills and parents should be encouraged to use their native language in the home rather than attempt to speak a substandard version of English. Traditional parent/child exchanges (singing songs or family-centered activities) should be capitalized on to build early speech and language skills. Educational personnel should focus on developing school language in English knowing that the use of the home language may compromise the speed of development of English; but both languages will emerge.

School personnel must be aware of the fact that communication modality will affect the development of spoken language skills and that these skills can be more readily developed in classrooms that value audition and spoken language as the major communication tool. A climate that emphasizes auditory learning as opposed to auditory training will contribute to natural spoken language development. The opportunity for numerous quality turns in meaningful conversational exchanges will foster the simultaneous development of language and content. School professionals can assist in mediating progress through the zone in a variety of ways. Teachers in simultaneous communication programs must be prepared to provide a linguistically correct model of spoken English during their classroom day. They must also challenge the child in the classroom with auditory-only presentations and encourage the best speech production from the child during educational exchanges. Through these types of activities, the school professional is able to bring the child along the zone's continuum in a fluid manner.

Central to what occurs in the classroom are the support services available to the child through the school district. Children who receive auditory-speech language services more frequently have a better foundation for skill development than children who receive therapy in a less intense manner. Personnel supporting intervention must be experienced in the development of spoken language skills through the use of audition. As the quality of the service and the number of sessions decreases, the potential for maximizing performance decreases. This is especially true during the early period following implantation. With long-term device use, the need and content for these sessions can be re-evaluated.

In mediating performance along the zone's continuum, professionals might consider "frontloading" services for a child immediately after implantation. Additionally, school personnel should seek out continuing education opportunities to sharpen their proficiency in the area of assessment and development of auditory skills. Professionals in schools should establish networks with others for collaborative work so that updates in technology and performance expectations can be shared. A knowledgeable professional will be better able to monitor performance to ensure movement along the continuum.

ZONE BENCHMARKS

The concept of the zone is a framework for professionals that allows them to consider factors that contribute to success with a cochlear implant. Throughout this chapter, there has been discussion about entry points into the zone and progress along the continuum. The question remains regarding an operational definition of "progress." By now the reader should realize that progress for one child is not the same as progress for another. However, the school professional, especially one who is just beginning to work with children with implants, requires some information on how to chart a child's progress. In understanding that each child brings with him or her factors that contribute to performance, there should still be a logical progression of outcomes as the child makes his or her way across the continuum. This progress is couched in the stages of auditory development and is delineated from the lowest level of detection to the highest level of comprehension. In between these two extremes lies pattern perception, segmental recognition in closed sets, segmental recognition in open sets, and finally comprehension.

Children can demonstrate performance characteristics that are considered appropriate in any of these categories depending on the duration of implant use and many of the other factors already discussed. To chart a child's progress, therefore, the school professional will be required to obtain, either on his or her own or in conjunction with the cochlear implant team, baseline performance measures. These will occur first with hearing aids at the preoperative point and then immediately after switch-on. Assessment should continue as therapy is monitored to ensure that the child is moving along the continuum in the proper direction. For most children, unless they have a considerable amount of residual hearing, the most basic level of detection can be met relatively quickly. However, remember that children with disabilities may not demonstrate this skill for some time. Again, movement along the continuum will be determined by the entry point and the other factors associated with the child. Once detection has been mastered, the ability to perceive patterns will develop. For some children, this may be the endpoint for their journey along the continuum due to the confounding issues that were brought to implantation. In these cases, additional methods of communication from speech reading to sign language should be considered. For the vast majority of children, however, the ability to perceive segmental differences in words is an attainable goal. These will begin in closed sets and eventually progress to open sets. Unfortunately, there is no single time line that can be provided to the school-based professional to use as a yardstick. Continual progress coupled with daily wear time is an indicator of implant benefit.

Working productively in the zone is the essence of Chapters 6, 7, and 8 and will not be reviewed here. However, the importance of proper intervention and how it relates to performance is the cornerstone of good cochlear implant outcomes. To keep pace within the zone professionals must continually update their knowledge through networking and attendance at regional, statewide, and national meetings and workshops specific to implantation.

SUMMARY

The conceptualization of a zone of implant performance presents the school professional with an easy method of viewing children with implants and how they perform. The role that the speech and hearing professional can play to move a child along the zone's continuum is facilitated by an understanding of each child's strengths and weaknesses on entering the zone at the time of candidacy. The success of any one child should be determined not relative to the larger population of implanted children but within the context of an individual's amount of "value added" or progress along the continuum. Any progress, no matter how small nor how slow, should be considered indicative of success.

Chapter 3

CHARACTERISTICS OF EDUCATIONAL PROGRAMS THAT SUPPORT CHILDREN WITH COCHLEAR IMPLANTS

With more than 17,500 pediatric cochlear implant recipients in the United States, all educational settings will have growing numbers of children with implants on their rolls. Among these are state schools for deaf children, private schools for deaf children, regional programs for students with hearing loss, district-level small instruction classrooms for students with hearing loss, and general education or mainstream settings. Meeting the needs of children with cochlear implants requires a conscious commitment to creating an educational environment that will allow a child to take the fullest advantage of the auditory potential of the device. Over the years, "competition" between and among agencies that provide services to children with hearing loss, especially those using implant technology, has occurred. Some tout programming for children with cochlear implants despite the fact that teachers are neither knowledgeable nor skilled in the development and/or maintenance of auditory skills. Although children with implants make gains with their devices, they still present with educational needs and challenges that must be met in their respective school environments.

Whether the label assigned to the setting in which a child with an implant is placed is "school for the deaf" or "regional program" or "mainstream setting," providing support to children with implants is critical to any individual child's success with the device. Direct experience with hundreds of children with implants in schools and indirect experience with many more have led to the creation of a list of characteristics that can be observed in educational settings that support children with implants. Although this list is not exhaustive, it will certainly serve as a starting point for providing a best-practice educational context. Programs that have many, if not all, of the characteristics outlined, will be more likely to meet the needs of children with implants than programs with fewer of the characteristics. Some of these are more challenging to observe in particular settings. School-based professionals are encouraged to consider how their own programs fare with regard to these and, when necessary, develop strategies for improving the environment to provide maximum support for the child with a cochlear implant.

Among the various social, academic, and physical features of schools and programs that are welcoming to the child with the implant are the following outward signs that may indicate a school's ability to meet the comprehensive needs of an implant recipient. These 10 characteristics listed in Figure 3–1 are elaborated on in the following discussion.

DISPLAYS UNCONDITIONAL ACCEPTANCE OF A CHILD WITH A COCHLEAR IMPLANT

Many programs identify themselves as especially designed to meet the needs of children using cochlear implants. Most often these programs have an underlying auditory/oral communication philosophy and specialize in working with young children with implants to

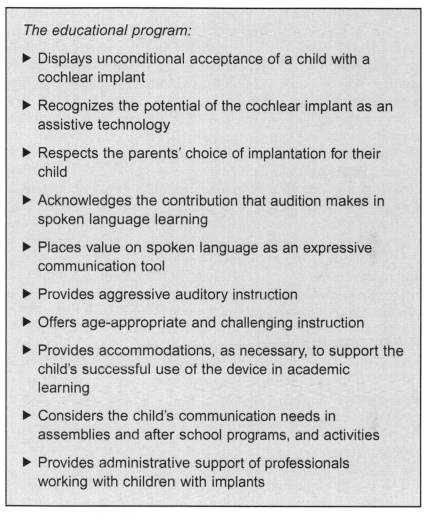

The educational program:

▶ Displays unconditional acceptance of a child with a cochlear implant

▶ Recognizes the potential of the cochlear implant as an assistive technology

▶ Respects the parents' choice of implantation for their child

▶ Acknowledges the contribution that audition makes in spoken language learning

▶ Places value on spoken language as an expressive communication tool

▶ Provides aggressive auditory instruction

▶ Offers age-appropriate and challenging instruction

▶ Provides accommodations, as necessary, to support the child's successful use of the device in academic learning

▶ Considers the child's communication needs in assemblies and after school programs, and activities

▶ Provides administrative support of professionals working with children with implants

Figure 3–1. Characteristics of Educational Programs that Support Children with Cochlear Implants

prepare them for later mainstream placement. School professionals in these settings can easily identify "unconditional acceptance" as a part of their school's mission. The commitment of the staff to assist a child in maximizing benefit from the device is unquestionable. In contrast, in other educational settings, especially environments in which there has been a commitment to direct communication via

ASL or another sign system, professionals experience the obvious dissonance between building language through manual communication and building it through spoken communication. Cochlear implant technology and the child who uses it are on the periphery of these schools' culture. Children with implants and the teachers and speech-language pathologists who work with them, are definitely in the minority in these settings. One has only to look at history to see how minority groups are often treated by the majority. Pressure to meet the needs of the many (children requiring visual communication) may result in failing to meet the needs of the few (students requiring auditory/oral communication). Furthermore, as children age, visible differences between implant users and those who do not use assistive technology may be enough for some students to isolate the child who is different from the majority group. Efforts to find commonalities and not differences between and among students must be undertaken to create an atmosphere of acceptance for students with implants in what otherwise might be considered an unreceptive environment. This is no less important when a child is being educated in a mainstream environment.

The challenges of integrating a child with hearing loss into the mainstream have been identified over the years. Acceptance of any child with special needs in the general education classroom carries with it certain responsibilities for both the teacher and the student. The goal of mainstream education is both academic and social in nature. Parents placing children with cochlear implants have the same goals in mind. Acceptance of these children leads to a positive self-image and the development of self-esteem. No cochlear implant professional would deny the fact that underlying all decisions about implantation is the tacit assumption that this technology will improve the quality of life for the individual who receives it. Accommodations that support a child with an implant are that child's right, not a special favor. Schools that agree to provide services, but only in a miserly manner, may be adhering to the letter of the law but not its spirit. Districts charged with providing services to a student with a cochlear implant are directed to meet the child's needs, not simply dole out resources parsimoniously. An accounting of services provided for the child with an implant may yield a glimpse into the acceptance level of the receiving district or school for that child.

RECOGNIZES THE POTENTIAL OF OF THE COCHLEAR IMPLANT AS ASSISTIVE TECHNOLOGY

There is no longer any question that, for individuals with severe to profound hearing loss, cochlear implant technology is the device of choice for ameliorating its effects. Although there have been and will continue to be improvements in implants, the hardware and software currently available are sophisticated enough to allow for auditory percepts previously unavailable via hearing aids. Therefore, schools that provide services to children with severe-to-profound hearing loss should routinely make recommendations that parents consider cochlear implants for their children classified with that degree of hearing loss. The device is no longer experimental or investigational; withholding information about its efficacy based on "moral" or "ethical" grounds can itself be labeled "unethical." When spoken language development is an identified parental goal, information dissemination regarding cochlear implant candidacy is the responsibility of the service provider, not a choice.

When a school program accepts a child with a cochlear implant, it must do so with the knowledge of the concomitant responsibilities of device management. Generally speaking, the younger the child with an implant, the greater the responsibility for active device monitoring by program professionals. One individual should be designated as the "point person" in providing daily equipment checks, although all individuals working with the child should have basic knowledge of implant components and their functioning. It would be wise to have a protocol in place for what to do if the implant does not seem to be working. Spare batteries and replacement cords may be part of the troubleshooting kit that is assembled and stored with the professional designated as device manager.

RESPECTS THE PARENTS' CHOICE OF IMPLANTATION FOR THEIR CHILD

Parents who choose implantation for their child often do so after great consideration and reflection. Experience suggests that no parent makes this choice without believing that they are offering the child the best possible option for future communication and academic and social success. More immediately, most hearing parents want their child to have direct access to the family experience, using the spoken language of the home. Choosing implantation provides the child with auditory information that will support this goal.

Like many decisions that parents make for their children, the passing of time validates or contradicts the earlier choice. Because there is no way to predict the future, professionals should support the parents as the responsible guardians of the child's well-being and respect the decisions they have made. In cases in which children with implants fail to "thrive" auditorily, it is counterproductive to question the original decision for implantation in light of current performance. When informed decisions are made initially, there can be no second guessing or recriminations later on. Respect for parents should not be contingent on the performance outcomes of the child with a cochlear implant. Professionals who support parents will affirm their right to continue to make choices for their child with hearing loss.

ACKNOWLEDGES THE CONTRIBUTION THAT AUDITION MAKES IN SPOKEN LANGUAGE LEARNING

Humans are uniquely able to communicate complex thoughts through the intricate arrangements of speech sounds to form meaningful words, phrases, and sentences. The physiology of the human body allows for both the reception of speech sounds and their production, with some notable exceptions. Individuals with peripheral hearing loss are unable to perceive the sounds of spoken language; those with central processing issues may receive the sounds but cannot interpret them. The inability to perceive sounds often results in an inability to produce them. However, there is ample evidence of individuals with hearing loss who use alternative methods to receive speech (through speech reading) and produce it (through visual, tactile, and kinesthetic means) for communicative purposes.

Because the majority language of our culture, English, is a spoken language, it makes intuitive sense that the most direct route for learning it is to take advantage of the natural hardwiring of human physiology. When peripheral hearing loss can be ameliorated (as through hearing aids or cochlear implants), then reception and processing of intricate speech sound patterns will result in comprehension of spoken language. Utilizing alternative methods for processing spoken language, such as speech reading, manual forms of communication, or print, may become less necessary depending on the degree to which the technology compensates for peripheral loss. Educational programs committed to developing English (or other spoken) language skills may wish to consider that spoken language is the "natural language" of humans with auditory access. Whether auditory access is available through the natural physiology or in spite of it, surrounding a child with spoken English is the most efficient course to its development.

PLACES VALUE ON SPOKEN LANGUAGE AS AN EXPRESSIVE COMMUNICATION TOOL

The other side of the listening coin is speaking. Children with auditory access should have speech capability commensurate with their peripheral hearing (whether uncomplemented or complemented by technology) unless there are other motor or neurologic issues that preclude the use of speech as an expressive tool. When listening is seen as a skill separate from speaking, the temptation exists to build auditory skills without productive accountability. Often, the needs and wants of children with hearing loss are anticipated and accommodated without requiring their verbal communication. This sets a precedent for the nonverbal use of language. As a rule, unconventional, nonverbal communication (e.g., gestures or home signs—an idiosyncratic manual representation that is used within the home only) will limit exchanges with those unfamiliar with a child's idiosyncratic system. Conventional, nonverbal communication (as in formal sign language), will limit the number of partners with whom a child can converse, as knowledge of sign language is a prerequisite to successful interaction. Children who use cochlear implants have the potential for auditory access that will provide a foundation for spoken language understanding, and production. When spoken communication is not only valued but also encouraged, the environment can be said to be supportive of a child with a cochlear implant.

PROVIDES AGGRESSIVE AUDITORY INSTRUCTION

If a child is to develop auditory skills in educational programs where concept and content development are identified priorities, efforts that go beyond simply providing auditory input will be necessary. Classrooms in which teachers are also using sign communication, talking while teaching provides some, but not focused, auditory input. This is seldom sufficient for a child with a cochlear implant to continue to learn through listening. Auditory instruction suggests that the classroom teacher provides purposeful listening opportunities that practice acquired auditory skills. This will necessitate some auditory-only exchanges between the teacher and the child with an implant. In addition, classroom teachers charged with aggressive auditory instruction should also attempt to develop new listening skills through the repetition and review of content that has previously been mastered (for a complete discussion of auditory skill development see chapter 6). These strategies are similar whether the child is in a classroom that uses sign communication or oral communication in a small instruction classroom, or a mainstream educational setting.

OFFERS AGE-APPROPRIATE AND CHALLENGING INSTRUCTION

One of the principal reasons parents choose mainstream education for their children with cochlear implants is to have access to a rigorous academic curriculum. Often schools for the deaf or regional programs for children with hearing loss have only a small number of children with sufficient language skills to support grade-level instruction in the content areas. Regional programs do not often have the "critical mass" of students to offer classes across the continuum of curricular challenge. These small instruction programs have generally committed to adapted curriculum presentation supported by instructional strategies advantageous to children with hearing loss. What is needed by children who successfully use cochlear implant technology is access to challenging subject matter that is presented using instructional strategies that support auditory learning. Instructional plans for children with cochlear implants, regardless of their placement, should include high standards in the area of academic achievement as well as developing and maintaining the auditory skills that will sustain learning.

PROVIDES ACCOMMODATION, AS NECESSARY, TO SUPPORT THE CHILD'S SUCCESSFUL USE OF THE DEVICE IN ACADEMIC LEARNING

Under the mantle of IDEA, children with hearing loss have a right to placement in the least restrictive environment (LRE). Ironically, in the field of deafness, it has been argued that the least restrictive environment is one that allows full and direct communication access, as in schools and programs especially designed for children with hearing loss. More often than not, this interpretation of IDEA is used to preclude the placement of children with hearing loss in district "special" classrooms that are not specifically designed to accommodate deaf children. For many children with implants, a traditional definition of the term least restrictive environment (i.e., general education classroom) applies. In circumstances in which a child is recommended for mainstream or general education placement, it is incumbent on the receiving school or district to offer support to a child by providing physical adaptations, assistive devices, or additional services to ensure success.

Throughout this book, we have referenced some of the accommodations that are generally provided to children with cochlear implants in mainstream settings. Physical adaptations such as noise-absorbing materials to create a better listening environment will benefit all children in the classroom, not only the child with an implant. Assistive devices such as personal FM systems to enhance listening in noisy classrooms are also recommended for children with implants in general education settings. Services that may be required by the child with an implant in the mainstream may be considered either indirect or direct. Indirect services are offered to children at high levels of academic and language functioning and are best served through consultation by a teacher of deaf children with the general classroom teacher. This is not to preclude direct services by other providers.

Direct academic support by a teacher of children who are deaf may be provided in either a pull-out or collaborative team-teaching model. Sometimes this intervention is designed to preteach, at other times sessions may be designated for review of material already presented in the classroom. In some cases, "replacement" instruction may be offered. For example, children who are having difficulty accessing grade-level instruction in reading in the classroom may be provided the opportunity to read at their own individual instructional level in a one-on-one session. In this way, academic learning time (the amount of time that a child actively participates in a challenging, but appropriate instructional activity) can be ensured. Ongoing speech, language, and auditory intervention by a certified speech-language pathologist or audiologist will likely be a part of related services identified on the IEP. This professional may take the lead in providing intensive, individual auditory and spoken language development. Monitoring by an educational audiologist will allow the school to track implant function, provide the annual assessments that drive instruction, and conduct the triennial evaluations that determine continued eligibility. Access to an educational interpreter or tutor note-taker, may also be required to support academic learning in the general education classroom. Specialized instructional materials, such as captioned videos or DVDs, may also be written into the IEP to assist in meeting a child's outlined goals and learning outcomes. These are especially important services to provide in the general education environment.

CONSIDERS THE CHILD'S COMMUNICATION NEEDS IN ASSEMBLIES AND AFTER SCHOOL PROGRAMS AND ACTIVITIES

Children who have options and choices may have greater opportunities to find skills and abilities at which they can excel. With a consideration of the multiple intelligences of all learners (Gardner, 1983), accommodations for children who use cochlear implants in nonacademic activities as well as those driven by language and content must be provided. This may be as simple as making preferential seating available in an all-school assembly on space exploration or as complex as locating interpreter services during a wrestling match at an away meet. Unfortunately, providing accommodations to a child with identified needs often comes as an afterthought, once the requirements of the many are addressed. This practice may result in a not-so-subtle message communicated to the child with an implant: it is an imposition to arrange for the special accommodations that will allow you to participate fully. Send this message often enough and a child will choose nonparticipation and disengage from the activity. Schools that provide a supportive environment for children with implants will not allow this to occur.

PROVIDES ADMINISTRATIVE SUPPORT OF PROFESSIONALS WORKING WITH CHILDREN WITH IMPLANTS

Years of experience suggest that, when administrators support authentic professional development, school personnel will often take more personal responsibility for the acquisition of knowledge and skills to assist them in providing services to children with implants. Over the years, the responsibility for providing information about implants and working with the children who receive them has shifted dramatically as the device is more readily accessible to children of all income strata. Initially, hospital cochlear implant centers took the lead in educating the school-based speech and hearing community because there was not widespread need for this information. Isolated and one-on-one exchange of knowledge and development of skills was a practical approach to continuing education for the few speech and hearing professionals in schools who required it. Educational consultants and school liaisons with cochlear implant centers provided much of this training (when it was available) in the first decade and a half of implantation. As the number of children with implants continues to grow and access the educational system, it is no longer economically feasible for implant centers to provide the same type of professional development service delivery once considered best practice. Today, Directors of State Departments of Education, district special education administrators, and even school principals are recognizing that it is the responsibility of the education agency to locate and support quality professional development for its school personnel to meet the needs of their students with hearing loss. In addition, the implant manufacturers have begun to acknowledge the important role of the school-based professional in maximizing the potential of the cochlear implant as a tool for learning. Each has developed literature, resources, or tool kits especially for teachers, speech-language pathologists, and audiologists in schools. The utility of online professional development continues to be explored by manufacturers, especially to support professionals in rural areas or those who have limited resources for training from their local education agency.

Beyond building knowledge and skills through continuing education administrative support acknowledges the important role that collaboration plays in helping a child benefit from the auditory potential of the cochlear implant. Scheduling that allows for common planning or case review time indicates that the administrator responsible for time management supports activities that are not considered instructional, face-to-face services. Encouraging networking with other speech and hearing professionals through the granting of release time for observation in other school programs is another indicator of administrative backing.

In the best of all possible worlds, having all 10 characteristics make a school a more attractive placement for a child with a cochlear implant. However, the realities of life dictate that we may not always get what we want. Schools may have several of the more important characteristics and commit to developing others later on. Clearly, some characteristics that carry more weight must be in place to meet minimal requirements. Those that focus on the role of audition and spoken language should be at the top of the list. School professionals must evaluate their own program's ability to meet the needs of children with cochlear implants and take responsibility for developing their program beyond what is considered minimally acceptable.

SUMMARY

No single education environment can meet the varied social, emotional, academic, and auditory needs of all children who utilize cochlear implant technology. Thus, any of the placement options available to children with hearing loss may be called on to assume the responsibility of meeting as many of an implant recipient's needs as possible. To that end, certain characteristics of educational programs can be identified as being supportive of a child with an implant; programs that have more of these characteristics may help a child achieve better outcomes overall than programs that have fewer of them. Teachers, speech-language pathologists, and educational audiologists fortunate to work in environments that are supportive of their own professional development needs will be better equipped to provide quality instruction to the child with a cochlear implant. We challenge all educational programs to critically examine their own efforts to meet the needs of students with implants and the professionals with whom they work.

Chapter 4

BUILDING COLLABORATIVE TEAMS

Whose Job Is It Anyway?

The concept of a multidisciplinary approach to providing services to children with hearing loss has been well supported in the literature. For a comprehensive discussion of this topic, the reader is directed to Luetke-Stahlman and Luckner (1991). Once the presence of a hearing loss has been confirmed, additional personnel join the audiologist to form a team that includes, at the very least, a speech-language pathologist and a teacher of deaf children. Interestingly, the technology breakthrough represented by the cochlear implant created the impetus for the medical and educational communities to form a partnership unheard of in the past. The unique habilitative needs of an implant recipient after surgery allowed these two institutions to begin a dialogue to bridge the cultural gap that had long existed between hospitals and schools. With each institution focused on the goal of providing substantial auditory benefit to profoundly deaf children, the commonality of their goals blurred the lines of territoriality as the medical and educational communities joined forces. Because the notion of hospital-school collaboration is a relatively recent one, it must be acknowledged that some medical communities (as well as school communities) have had limited success in creating an interinstitutional collaborative team. Suffice it to say that it is always beneficial when an implant recipient receives services from a medical facility that respects the contributions of educational professionals; a school community that strives to reach out to the medical centers responsible for surgery and device management to invite open communication between the two.

A number of professionals who provide services to children with cochlear implants are from the speech and hearing community. Sometimes these individuals are hospital-based; others are school-based personnel. Additional professionals who see a child with an implant may be engaged in private practice; regardless of the personal affiliation of any of the child's team, it is key for these professionals to work collaboratively and not competitively. There is little utility in comparing performance outcomes by the child in one setting to another, especially when it is implied that services in one are superior to the other. When speech and hearing professionals work cooperatively and seek out strategies and techniques to encourage the child's best performance across settings, it is more likely that overall outcomes will improve. Sometimes a "competition approach" unwittingly develops between private practice and school-based professionals. Private practice SLPs are providing a service for fees with therapy sessions that are generally longer and more auditorily focused. More often, they do not have the multiplicity of assessment and instructional issues that face school personnel. Even within a school setting, there can be competition between the speech-language pathologist and classroom teacher. The classroom teacher may feel that the SLP has an advantage in postimplant habilitation because of the individualization of the "pull-out" session. Regardless, when the question is posed: "Whose job is it anyway?" (to help a child use the implant to achieve the highest possible outcomes for listening, language, and speech development) the answer is: "It's everybody's job." Each professional on the team has the general responsibility to help a child maximize the potential of the cochlear implant but also has specific responsibilities for which he or she is accountable. A closer look at the responsibilities of the school-based professional on any child's collaborative team may lead to a better understanding of how individual roles may be defined.

SCHOOL-BASED SPEECH-LANGUAGE PATHOLOGIST

Among the responsibilities generally assigned to the school-based speech-language pathologist is the assessment of speech and language skills for the purpose of informing intervention. For children with implants, the SLP may also be charged with the task of assessing auditory skills using particular instruments designed for this purpose or through ongoing diagnostic therapy that will identify a child's strengths and weaknesses. The comprehensive picture of a child's skills and abilities that emerges from assessment enables the SLP to design and implement an intervention plan that encourages continuing development of listening skills, the vocabulary and syntax of English, and speech intelligibility. However, the school-based speech-language pathologist is the individual on the collaborative team who may serve in the greatest number of different roles. Children with cochlear implants may be found in placements ranging from special schools for deaf children who use implants to general education settings when mainstream placement for the child has been determined. At the former placement, the collegiality that exists between and among administration, faculty, and staff may make the workplace a stimulating one with all professionals operating under the same set of assumptions and working toward a common goal. On the other end of the placement continuum, SLPs in a general education setting may find themselves charged with a variety of additional roles. These include case manager, child advocate, device specialist, liaison with the implant center team as well as the family, and consultant to the classroom teacher(s). This leaves the SLP with little time for the critical auditory, speech, and language tasks normally assigned to this professional.

As case manager, the school-based SLP becomes the "go to" professional, especially when addressing the challenges awaiting children with implants in mainstream settings. Catapulted from novice to expert on the technology of the cochlear implant and the children who use them, many SLPs in mainstream settings are expected to hit the ground running after the child with an implant is assigned to their caseload. SLPs who find themselves as the sole individual responsible for children with cochlear implants should seek support through organizations affiliated with deafness and children who use implants. Finding a "mentor" or another SLP who has had experience in such a mainstream setting, may provide invaluable assistance in negotiating for and providing appropriate services to these children. Organizations such as AG Bell and the Network of Educators of Children with Cochlear Implants (see Appendix A) may be able to provide information and access to other professionals who will assist novice SLPs as they begin to work with implant recipients. One thing is certain, however; once a child with a cochlear implant enters an educational system, a number of additional professionals will "need to know" about the child's skills and abilities. Therefore, SLPs in mainstream settings should make sure that they organize and catalogue all of the information distributed to teachers in year one, because the likelihood is great that the process will begin anew the following year with a new classroom teacher. Even when individuals attend a general in-service presentation, adult learning literature tells us that, unless there is the need for the direct application of the information, attention to, and recall of, the material is not of sufficient importance to warrant a commitment to fully process what is being presented.

Balancing the need to provide one-on-one auditory, speech, and language intervention directly with the necessity of offering indirect service through consultation to classroom (and other "specials") teachers is a dilemma that faces many SLPs in mainstream settings. With only so many hours allotted to any particular child, the struggle to find the right combination of direct and indirect services may be daunting. One recommendation for getting the most out of therapy, while at the same time modeling strategies for the classroom teacher that encourage listening and language development, calls for the SLP to go into the classroom to provide services. Sometimes referred to as "push-in" or "collaborative" intervention, the therapist may actually team-teach a particular lesson with the classroom teacher or provide assistance to the child at his or her desk during a lesson by the teacher. When classroom teachers share instructional time with SLPs in the classroom, useful techniques that may prove to be beneficial to other children in the classroom (as well as the child with a cochlear implant) can be demonstrated and practiced. Of course, common planning time is essential to make collaboration worthwhile; however, the payoff for this investment may be well worth the difficulty in scheduling time for this activity within the school day. Even when the SLP assists the child individually (or within a small group that includes peers from the classroom), there is a chance that the teacher will be able to observe and overhear some of the exchanges between the SLP and the child with an implant. This may be sufficient to begin a dialogue between the two professionals on the adoption of particular strategies that may enhance a child's performance in the classroom.

TEACHERS OF CHILDREN WHO ARE DEAF OR HARD OF HEARING

In a manner similar to the school-based SLP, teachers of children who are deaf or hard of hearing (TOD) may find themselves in placements that span a continuum. These range from small instruction classrooms for children with hearing loss to mainstream settings where, as itinerant teachers, they provide services to children within a district but at many different locations. Teachers in small instruction classrooms generally have well-defined roles for working with children with implants. In addition to planning and implementing instruction for language and content, teachers are expected to provide opportunities for listening and talking during the school day to foster the development of spoken language. Attention to the development of clear and intelligible speech through the encouragement of carryover of skills practiced with the SLP may also be considered the task of a teacher in a small instruction classroom. Whether these classrooms are part of a school for deaf children or housed within a larger regional program, there are often clearly defined policies and procedures for working with implanted children. Teachers in more isolated, single class settings may find less administrative and supervisory guidance when it comes to designing programs for children with implants. Often, they are supervised by a special education professional who does not have direct experience with deafness. When teachers of deaf children with implants are in simultaneous communication (SC) programs or programs for deaf children that have traditionally been more oriented to manual communication, the challenge to create an environment that encourages audition and values spoken language may leave teachers feeling somewhat isolated from their peers. It is important for these teachers to seek the same kind of support recommended for the novice SLP: find other teachers who have successfully negotiated this new territory and profit from their experiences. Often, the mere validation of the difficulty of the task is sufficient to provide the motivation to persevere. The added benefit of sharing particular strategies and techniques will make the effort to network with teachers experienced in providing services to children with implants in SC settings worth the investment of time to locate them. Once again the reader is referred to Appendix A.

Perhaps one of the most challenging positions for working with children with implants is that of the itinerant teacher of deaf children. When children with implants reach the mainstream, their need for assistance and support varies widely. Even the most skilled implant users will require accommodations, and it is often the responsibility of the TOD to monitor the effectiveness of such accommodations. Children with implants who have made sufficient progress in small instruction classrooms to warrant mainstream placement will face new challenges there. The TOD may be called on to provide direct assistance to the child for a number of hours per day or per week. Sometimes this assistance takes the form of preteaching; at other times instruction may be reinforcing or remedial. The "degree of difficulty" of any district's curriculum may influence the level of service provided to a child and the level of mastery that can be expected. Decisions to provide instruction on a breadth of topics will reduce the child's opportunity to learn any one topic in depth. Sometimes helping a child learn how to explore one area of interest fully will be the wiser path to follow, but will result in less material covered overall. Like the SLP, the TOD may find a need to provide services to the child in the classroom and carve out time to consult with the classroom teacher for the purpose of information exchange. This affords the classroom teacher the opportunity to specify the areas in which the child needs specific assistance; the TOD can then impart a strategy or technique that might enable the child to be a more active participant during lessons. Of particular importance is heightening the classroom teacher's appreciation of the complexities of the vocabulary and grammar of English as it relates to content instruction. Idiosyncratic gaps in word knowledge and unfamiliarity with certain syntactic structures of English may preclude an otherwise capable child of demonstrating comprehension of classroom discussion or text. Difficulty in answering test questions may occur as the result of misunderstanding the language of the question and not a lack of content knowledge. As a specialist in the language needs of children with hearing loss, the TOD can call attention to the instances of complex grammar and challenging vocabulary in lessons and textbooks that may cause additional difficulty for the child with an implant in a mainstream classroom.

EDUCATIONAL AUDIOLOGISTS

School-based audiologists are generally individuals who have specialized in pediatric audiology and have made a commitment to understanding the impact of hearing loss on learning in schools. Educational audiologists (EAs) can be found in schools for the deaf or regional programs and assume the responsibility for ongoing assessment and monitoring of the proper functioning of equipment used by children with hearing loss. Some schools specializing in working with children with cochlear implants are now providing mapping services for their students. For the most part, children still return to implant centers for their mapping. Some cochlear implant centers may send personnel into the schools to map children and may be assisted by the district EA. There are certain advantages to providing mapping on site and within the school day. The most obvious is the efficiency with which mapping can be performed along with the value of input from the various school personnel involved with the child with an implant. As larger numbers of children with implants enter district schools the role of the EA may expand.

Educational audiologists are also responsible for managing the use of personal FM systems with cochlear implant devices. This creates certain challenges for which the EAs have the most knowledge and skill from their years of experience with FMs and hearing aids. Managing the acoustic environment to ensure that it is advantageous for a child with an implant is also part of their role. For additional information about the use of assistive devices with a cochlear implant, the reader is directed to chapter 11.

Educational audiologists are knowledgeable about technology, understand auditory skills development in children, and are aware of the academic demands of the classroom. In some cases, EAs may, in fact, be responsible for direct service delivery relative to developing listening skills. More often, this professional (in schools and programs fortunate enough to have one) may provide some of the mentoring to SLPs and TODs alluded to earlier. As an example, the state of Colorado has a model program for CI mentors in regions across the state that is directed by an educational audiologist. In this program, teachers and SLPs in rural or remote areas of the state have access to an expert in cochlear implant habilitation that is geographically accessible to them. The reader is directed to www.cde.state.co.us/cdesped/SD-Hearing.asp for more information on the Colorado Cochlear Implant Mentor Program.

AUDITORY VERBAL THERAPISTS

There is a growing trend for school districts to engage the services of a certified Auditory Verbal Therapist (AVT) for children with cochlear implants. Based on the premise that concentrated focus on auditory development will yield the greatest gains, auditory verbal therapy is one approach to developing listening skills and spoken language skills in implant recipients. Although it is more likely that AVTs will provide private practice therapy outside the school setting, the movement to bring these professionals into the schools may assist in team building, which is often compromised when service delivery occurs outside the school setting.

CLASSROOM TEACHERS

The classroom teacher in a general education setting is a vital member of a child's habilitative team. It is in this professional's care that large portions of the child's school day is spent. The general education teacher may have little, if any, information and/or direct experience with hearing loss and cochlear implants. However, this teacher brings a wealth of content knowledge and classroom management skills for the purpose of planning and implementing motivating lessons. To create an auditory learning environment in the classroom that allows a child with an implant to be successful there, the classroom teacher will likely need guidance with regard to encouraging the development of auditory skills. It may be that a teacher will enthusiastically embrace the notion of playing listening games that review content. The growing trend for listening and speaking to be addressed in statewide standards and the assessment instruments that measure whether or not they have been met may make this recommendation more readily acceptable to the classroom teacher. If listening skill development is considered appropriate for all children, not just the child with a cochlear implant, the mainstream teacher may be more willing to allocate instructional time for this purpose. The novelty of a listening screen in the classroom for focused auditory play may be just the "hook" that keeps children engaged in this new instructional activity.

When classroom teachers' awareness of the complexity of language that is found in classroom and content texts is heightened, they will be better able to monitor the child's ability to follow and comprehend instruction. Keeping the TOD and SLP apprised of classroom themes or content units will allow these speech and hearing professionals to incorporate authentic classroom materials in their intervention. It is vitally important that the teacher monitor performance and share that information with the other members of the habilitative team so that supports may be added as deemed necessary.

In preparation for working with a child with a hearing loss in the mainstream, the classroom teacher will generally receive information about teaching this population. A number of resources exist for this purpose including Mangiari's (1993) *A Child with a Hearing Loss in Your Classroom? Don't Panic!* and Otto and Kozak's (1998) *Questions Teachers Ask* (both available through AG Bell). However, we would like to include some global tips here for the instructional personnel in schools to consider.

SUGGESTIONS FOR ENHANCING A CHILD'S PARTICIPATION IN REGULAR EDUCATION SETTINGS

- Establish a genuine and personal relationship with the child with an implant. Be sure to engage the child and go beyond the smile.

- Don't be afraid of the child with a cochlear implant or his/her equipment. Determine what your role will be in management of the device.

- Understand and use additional classroom amplification systems.

- Consider a buddy system for all children in the classroom so as not to single out the child with the implant. Each child in the class may have a buddy that can be a partner in the classroom or would be available for contact after school about homework or other school issues. Make sure the child with the cochlear implant is assigned a responsible buddy.

- Establish high, but realistic, expectations for the child with a cochlear implant. Make modifications to initial expectations as warranted by performance.

- Make sure that the directions that are given to the class are clear. Consider instituting a routine that calls for one child to restate directions to gauge their clarity.

- Use visual materials to support content whenever possible. Use of the board to support or enhance verbal instruction will benefit all children in the classroom, but especially the child with an implant.

- Be careful in the development of authentic assessment materials. Do not include complex language that obscures the evaluation of content knowledge.

- Develop and use a consistent verbal attention-getting phrase that is linguistically appropriate for the child's age. Share that with the TOD or SLP so they can work on a child's recognition of that attention-getting device.

- Be tolerant/aware of the communication habits of the parents of children who have previously been in special education placements. They are used to direct and easy access to all school personnel. Establish a protocol at the start of the school year that works for everyone involved.

- Establish routines and follow them consistently so that the child can become accustomed to recurring patterns in scheduling and procedures. Be sure to be explicit about changes made in daily activities.

When a child's successful participation in a general education classroom is supported by an additional service provider such as an educational interpreter, a transliterator, or a note-taker, care must be taken to include these individuals in discussions regarding the implementation of the habilitative plan. Classroom instruction will proceed much more efficiently when parameters for roles and responsibilities of student support personnel have been clearly defined. Regular meetings of the entire habilitation team will ensure good communication and a cooperative effort put forth by all individuals involved.

SPECIAL INSTRUCTIONS FOR THE "SPECIALS"

In addition to the classroom teacher, a number of instructional personnel will see the child on a regular basis. It is important for these teachers to be aware of the tips outlined above. Subject-matter-specific instructions are included here.

THE MUSIC/CHORUS TEACHER

Many children with cochlear implants enjoy music education activities successfully and some become quite accomplished with instrumental or vocal music. The important role of melody in speech production of a child with a cochlear implant can be supported through music education that includes attention to vocal quality, vocal variation, and phrasing.

The music teacher who has a child with an implant in class will want to ensure that the device is functioning properly. If the child is old enough, it may be sufficient to just quickly verify that the child has good function with the device that day. Keep in mind that it may be difficult for the child to understand directions over the musical activity be it singing or band practice. It may be helpful to establish certain phrases that can be used consistently to communicate direction (e.g., "Strings, be ready for your entrance"). Vocal music may contain words and grammatical structures that are unfamiliar to the child. Enlist the support of the itinerant TOD or SLP in setting up clear guidelines for the child to ensure understanding of the logistics of the music class as well as practicing proper pronunciation for those in choral music.

THE ART TEACHER

Be aware that a child in an art room will often need to split attention between the model of the product and the process of its creation. Directions that are presented while materials are being distributed may be difficult for the child with an implant to follow because of the competing activity. On the other hand, the largely creative aspect of art allows a child to participate on a par with his or her peers as the relative language load of the task is minimized. Furthermore, there is often greater opportunity for one-on-one teacher-student interaction in art class as the teacher circulates about the art room and the children are working on their projects. The art teacher should take advantage of these opportunities to engage the child in conversation about particular aspects of the child's work. Children with artistic tendencies should be confident in their exploration of the many aspects of art and celebrate their talents and accomplishments.

THE PHYSICAL EDUCATION TEACHER

General physical education classes incorporate gross motor activities that are well within the capabilities of the implanted child. However, it is important to remember that the external device should be secured during these activities to prevent damage. This is easily accomplished through the use of a sweatband to hold down the behind-the-ear processor. For children using body processors, additional tethering equipment may be needed. Children with cochlear implants are able to participate in the varied aspects of the physical education curriculum; implanted children are no different from hearing children with regard to the use of protective gear.

Physical education classes and school sports often allow students with strengths in bodily/kinesthetic intelligence (Gardner, 1983) the opportunity to excel at something in a world in which verbal/linguistic intelligence has high value. Many successful experiences in general education for children with hearing loss have begun with prowess on the court or out in the field. Physical skill begets acceptance and, for the very skilled, even admiration despite the difference in hearing status. Even though students with cochlear implants have greater opportunities to have successful engagements with their hearing peers in the classroom, status may be enhanced when students are athletically inclined. To nurture the positive outcomes associated with physical skill, the PE teacher will want to ensure that a child's physical accomplishments are matched by skillful play and knowledge of scoring procedures. This means that rules and plays need to be understood by the student using an implant. Complex and detailed instructions for playing team sports should be made explicit to the implant recipient. There is nothing more embarrassing for a player than making an error not from lack of skill but from lack of rule knowledge in the heat of competition.

Furthermore, the acoustic environment of most school gymnasiums presents particular challenges for a child using implant technology. The absolute size of the facility and the many hard surfaces found in gyms make it a highly reverberant listening environment. The background noise associated with physical activities, whether it be a bouncing ball or cheering crowd, will make it more difficult for a child with an implant to follow directions called out from the sidelines during play. For this reason, it may be helpful to develop some particular hand symbols or gestures to cue plays.

Among the additional instructional professionals with whom the child may have contact are the media specialist or librarian and the computer teacher (in those school programs that have remained committed to the concept of a "computer class"). It would be prudent to include these professionals in any discussion of accommodations for the child with the cochlear implant. Even though their absolute contact time may be limited, issues related to seating arrangements, precautions, communication tips, and general expectations may be addressed.

OTHER SCHOOL PERSONNEL

It would be an oversight not to mention other members of the school community who are also a part of the child's life away from home. From our vantage point, two of the most influential individuals in schools have yet to be named: the school secretary and the building custodian. When these individuals know the student with an implant by name, two powerful allies for the child are added to his or her "corner." Opportunities for the child with an implant to interact with these power brokers may serve to enhance a relationship that can provide support and assistance outside the instructional team.

Among the other adults with whom a child may come in contact on the way to school and in the lunchroom are the bus drivers and cafeteria workers. When these individuals with daily (and crucial) interaction with the child are "in the loop," the greater is the likelihood that communication with the child with the implant will be successful.

SUMMARY

Although it may "take a village" to *raise* a child, it "takes a school community" to *educate* one—especially a child with a cochlear implant. Community members who work cooperatively and not competitively and respect all the players, regardless of their roles, will be more likely to create an educational environment that will assist a child with an implant in reaching his or her fullest potential with the device. At the very least, all instructional and noninstructional school personnel, especially those in mainstream settings, should have basic knowledge about the cochlear implant device and be encouraged to establish a personal relationship with the child with an implant. Fundamental communication tips will be helpful to all who see the child during the course of the school and particular instructional strategies for those "special" teachers will ensure that everyone is an active player on the child's habilitative team.

Chapter 5

THE MAPPING PROCESS AND BEYOND

Central to the habilitative process of children with cochlear implants is proper adjustment of the device to ensure that the best signal is delivered to the auditory nerve. Like traditional hearing aids, the amount of sound conveyed to the ear must be in proportion to the degree of hearing loss and consider the comfort of the recipient. Hearing aid fitting procedures have always used the concept of comfortable listening level to provide a signal that is loud enough yet pleasing to the listener. These basic characteristics of sound perception hold true for fitting a cochlear implant as well. The difference lies in the method by which sound is delivered to the ear. Traditional hearing aids use a direct acoustic signal whereas the cochlear implant converts the acoustic signal into an electrical one. The goal for sound delivery, however, is the same. Sound should be sufficiently loud but comfortable for the user. If it is too loud, it will be unpleasant and create a negative response. If the sound is too soft, then it will be imperceptible and fail to provide an adequate signal to the recipient. Thus, *mapping* a cochlear implant utilizes the basic theories of hearing aid fitting with the new delivery system being the electrode instead of the earmold.

MAPPING

The procedure known as mapping is the method used to adjust the implant so that sound can be heard by the user. It takes place over time as the child's perceptions with the implant change. The time of the initial activation, or switch-on of the device, may vary from center to center but generally occurs 2 to 4 weeks after surgery. The purpose of this activation is to optimize the speech signal through electrical stimulation of the cochlea. This process begins by accessing the internal hardware that was implanted through the external hardware that the child will wear on a daily basis. The internal and external components are linked through a transmitter that is worn on the head and held in place by a magnet. Selection of the appropriate magnetic strength is important so that there is enough attraction to hold the components in place without creating too much pressure to compress the skin in that area. Too much magnetic attraction can cause irritation of the area under the magnet, creating a reddish appearance on the skin. For the school professional monitoring the child, any severe redness should be reported to the parent and implant facility immediately.

It is often helpful for school personnel to observe a mapping on site or review one of the many videotapes that are available from the manufacturers. This experience provides visual familiarity with the process so that the school-based professional does not view mapping as a function performed in isolation of therapy. By observing active mapping, the SLP, teacher, or audiologist can learn to work cooperatively with the implant facility and communicate information about the auditory/speech behaviors that can assist in the process. Because certain parameters will be adjusted during the mapping process, the school-based professional will require information about these adjustments from the implant facility to better understand progress (or lack of progress) during therapy.

Mapping the implant is based on the stimulation of residual neural elements in the cochlea and requires the assessment of either psychophysical or objective measures from the implant recipient. These measures assist the programming audiologist in setting the threshold and comfort levels for the individual implant system. These two parameters are important to set in a cochlear implant as they determine the softest and loudest level of sound that will be heard. The levels that determine threshold and comfort ensure that sound delivered to the electrode array is comfortably loud but not too loud for the listener.

Functionally, to set the levels, the programming audiologist uses hardware and software specific to the type of implant system being adjusted. In other words, a Nucleus implant cannot be mapped using Clarion equipment. Each system requires a computer, an interface box, and special software for this purpose. The interface box or "pod" is connected to the computer via a cable. The speech processor is connected to the interface so that the programming audiologist can access the implanted electrodes via the external transmitter (see Figure 5–1).

Once connected the audiologist will systematically activate each electrode in the array and determine the amount of current required to provide a comfortably loud sound. The implanted electrodes correspond to frequencies in the same manner the normal cochlea does. Low-frequency electrodes are located at the apex, and high-frequency electrodes are located at the base. Each of these electrodes will deliver information depending on the input signal. However, the level of electrical current that each electrode requires

Figure 5–1. Mapping Equipment (Courtesy of Cochlear Americas)

before it can respond will be determined by the perception of the user. To set the level of electrical current, the audiologist will identify certain parameters. In some cases, the threshold (T-level) and comfort level (C- or M-level) will be assessed for each electrode in the array. In other cases, the audiologist may set the comfort level and the computer will automatically determine the threshold level based on a predetermined mathematical formula. Regardless of the specific device, the completed map will have each electrode in the cochlea set to activate at a particular level and stop responding once sound reaches a comfortably loud level.

Threshold and comfort levels can be assessed using either traditional behavioral methods or more objective methods. Traditional techniques utilize methods that are usually employed when finding acoustic thresholds in children. These can be obtained through conditioned play audiometry in which the child listens for a sound being sent to a particular electrode and then performs an activity (e.g., placing a block in a bucket) once it is heard. Older children might raise their hand when they hear the sound. For the very sophisticated listener, the audiologist might ask the implant recipient to count the number of "beeps" being delivered to the electrode. (*Note:* Some generations of Clarion devices do not require the assessment of threshold levels.) As children gain experience with their implants, T-levels will change somewhat over time. However, large changes in T-levels are not seen after long-term experience with the implant.

More recently, as larger numbers of children receiving cochlear implants are infants and toddlers, a more objective method of assessing threshold and comfort levels has been developed. Techniques known as neural response telemetry (NRT) or neural response imaging (NRI) as found in the Nucleus and Clarion devices, respectively, utilize the responses of the auditory nerve that are measured through dedicated software. These responses can be obtained while the child is still in surgery (and under anesthesia) or after implantation while the child is connected to the computer for mapping. In either circumstance, obtaining an NRT or NRI does not require the child to perform any time-locked task. Using this procedure the child sits (watching a video or engaged in an activity) as the computer automatically accesses this information. The end result, when using either objective measures or behavioral measures, is that every map generated will consist of electrical levels for each electrode in the array that will begin stimulating at the lowest level (T) and cease stimulating at the highest level (C or M). The difference between these two levels is known as the *dynamic range*.

The dynamic range represents the point from which sound is allowed into the implant to the point where sound no longer will be available. This range is important because it permits the user to access sound at low levels, have it grow to a certain loudness level, and then limit further loudness growth. When implant recipients have narrow dynamic ranges, sound enters the auditory system at a particular level, grows slightly, and then halts very quickly. This makes it difficult for the implant recipient to use incoming speech to make basic discriminations and, in some cases, may even limit detection. It is not unusual, however, for implant recipients to have narrow dynamic ranges during the very early stages of implantation. These ranges will widen over time as children gain experience with their implants. In cases of congenitally deaf teenagers, narrow dynamic ranges may take longer to widen and may not widen substantially over time. Overall performance may be affected and the therapeutic approaches that are being implemented may require change.

Besides T- and C/-M-levels, the mapping process also includes the adjustment of numerous other parameters. These will vary depending on the device and the generation of the implant in use. Adjustments will be made by the programming audiologist based on information provided by the parents, the recipient (when possible), the therapist, and the teacher. This information exchange is discussed in greater detail later in this chapter. At the completion of a mapping session, several different "programs" are developed. These programs are essentially different maps that are stored in the speech processor in a program slot that can be accessed by the user, parent, or school professional. Programs are maps that differ according to some parameter that the programming audiologist identified as possibly contributing to better auditory perception. To determine the effectiveness of any one program, information from the parents, SLP, teacher, or educational audiologist can help the programming audiologist at the next mapping appointment.

Because the map is being adjusted over time, a schedule of mapping must occur. This schedule depends on the age and ability of the child and the individual implant center monitoring the child's performance. Generally, there are more frequent mappings initially; as the age and the duration of implant use increases, mapping decreases and, in some cases, may only occur once a year. When school professionals communicate with implant teams on a regular basis, it assists in better recipient care and management and avoids suboptimal mapping.

Suboptimal mapping can occur when a child is mapped too infrequently, too frequently, or by an audiologist who lacks experience in mapping. When children are mapped infrequently, the amount of power being delivered to the implant may not be sufficient for auditory perception to develop. If one equates this to hearing aid fitting, it would be akin to fitting a low-powered hearing aid in a child with a profound hearing loss. There is simply not enough sound getting into the cochlea to stimulate the auditory nerve. Similarly, if a child is switched-on one month after surgery and does not return to the implant center for a year, that child will have very limited auditory access. Bear in mind the earlier discussion regarding changes in dynamic range that occur over time, which contribute to the way sound is received by the electrode and grows to acceptable loudness levels. A child's auditory system may require more sound to hear but, if not remapped, sound will not be accessible.

At the other extreme from too infrequent mapping is mapping that occurs too often. Children must have experience with a map to learn to listen to the sounds around them. At times, parents and therapists may not identify behavior changes that occur immediately postmapping and will make an erroneous assumption that the child requires a map change. Too many map changes within a short period may, at times, create confusion in recipients as signals change just as they are learning to identify them. There is no single schedule of mapping that is recommended. A rule of thumb, which again will vary from center to center, is that children should receive their initial switch-on, and be remapped at 1 month, 3 months, 6 months, and 1 year. After 1 year, depending on the age and ability of the child, mapping may be done every 6 months or yearly. School-based professionals should check with the parent and the implant center to ascertain the schedule so that they can be proactive in the process.

Finally, suboptimal mapping can occur as a result of the experience (actually, the lack of experience) of the programming audiologist. Again, like hearing aids, the more familiarity the audiologist has with the procedure and the equipment, the better the overall fitting. As more of the cochlear implant systems begin to use automated types of procedures such as NRT or NRI, better cochlear implant mapping can occur, thereby minimizing the effects of experience on outcomes.

Ultimately, mapping should provide the implant recipients with sufficient sound that will enable them to learn to listen and develop auditory and spoken language skills. Unfortunately, there are children who will be constrained by physiologic issues that will affect the ability to map and thereby limit performance. As noted earlier, the foundation of mapping is built on the premise that there are remaining neural elements in the cochlea that can be stimulated. Unfortunately, there are implant recipients who may have anatomic constraints (such as a malformed cochlea) or are deaf from birth and have been deaf for a longer period of time (as in the case of the congenitally deaf adolescent) who may present more challenging mapping circumstances. These children may demonstrate narrow dynamic ranges that do not substantially increase over time or may have interference from stimulation of the facial nerve along with stimulation of the auditory nerve. These physiologic constraints do not necessarily mean that the implant will not be successful; a different orientation to therapy may be required to maximize the sound that is available to the child.

Additionally, even the best cochlear implant will not be able to override the effects that occur in the central auditory processing system. As many SLPs who work with children with auditory processing disorders (APD) know, the presence of normal hearing does not guarantee that a child is able to comprehend the signal that is sent to the brain. For the deaf child who receives a cochlear implant, issues of central processing cannot be overlooked in accounting for reduced performance. Clearly, children with cognitive or learning difficulties will have limited ability to contribute to the mapping process. As the technique of more objective measures improves, some, but not all, of the obstacles, may be overcome. Mapping simply cannot compensate for problems that occur once the sound leaves the cochlea.

COLLABORATING IN THE MAPPING PROCESS

Once mapping has occurred, it is helpful for the SLP working with a child with an implant to obtain some basic information from the implant center to ensure that maps are being properly used. Recall, that at each mapping session, more than one map will be generated and placed in a program slot to be used at certain times. It is helpful for school professionals to be aware of the schedule for changing programs so that performance can be assessed for a given map. In addition to the schedule of program changes, the settings for the speech processor should be provided to those monitoring implant performance and use. Again, like hearing aids, the cochlear implant speech processor will have certain controls that are at the disposal of the user. Most often these include the parameters of volume and sensitivity. Volume in a cochlear implant behaves in a manner similar to that of a hearing aid. Increasing the volume on a hearing aid will increase the loudness; increasing the volume on a cochlear implant will also increase loudness. However, in cochlear implants, a second parameter, known as sensitivity, can be adjusted as well. Sensitivity sets the level of responsiveness of the microphone relative to the proximity of the speaker. With a low-set sensitivity, the speaker would be required to be very close to the microphone of the speech processor. With sensitivity set higher, the speaker can be farther away. It is important for school-based professionals and parents to know the exact settings for the speech processor to ensure that the maximal acoustic signal can be accessed. This type of information should be provided after every mapping session.

SLPs working with children with implants must obtain baseline performance measures to serve as a standard for determining the appropriateness of an individual map. At the beginning of the mapping process, reports may include general observations of auditory responsiveness; later reports may take the form of more objective measures as the child progresses. Daily session logs, which document a child's performance with an individual map, can assist in making judgments about the positive or negative aspects of a particular program. (A sample of a log is offered in Appendix B.) However, to make these judgments, the SLP must understand the general performance trends that children with implants demonstrate. These were reviewed as part of the zone in chapter 2.

The goal of session logs or objective measures is to provide feedback to the programming audiologist to assist in the mapping. This collaborative approach will contribute to the mapping process and ultimately support the goal of better outcomes for the child. Progress regarding specific auditory and speech performance in the therapeutic and natural environment can supply valuable information to the audiologist performing the mapping. Additionally, changes noted in the child's speech intelligibility and the consistency of the child's responses over time can trigger a reaction in the programming audiologist to adjust certain parameters in the map. The key to good mapping is to work in tandem with the school-based team so that any concerns they have regarding the child's performance can be addressed.

To provide more precise information to the programming audiologist, it is sometimes helpful for the therapist to analyze the overall error patterns that a child is demonstrating. Although specific phoneme perception/production cannot be adjusted with individual electrodes, certain patterns of electrode adjustment can lead to better perception. For example, consonantal errors are corrected more often by manipulating high-frequency information whereas vowel errors are addressed by adjustments in the lower frequencies. It is always important, however, to remember that children who use cochlear implants require consistent auditory- and language-based therapy to learn the sounds. Mapping itself can only provide the signal to the cochlea. It is up to the implant recipient to learn how to use the signal to learn spoken language. Unfortunately, in some cases, even the best mapping cannot override other deficits that may be present in the child. As individual children gain experience with their implants, they will progress at different rates and achieve different outcomes.

Recall that the zone of cochlear implant performance takes into account aspects of device management that contribute to success for the individual recipient. Device management includes factors such as wear time, duration of implant use, proper functioning of the implant, and the appropriate adjustment of the device. To monitor a child's progress and modify therapeutic goals, the school professional must have working knowledge of how these factors interact with habilitation, and ultimately performance. Collaboration among the teachers, SLPs, and audiologists can assist the child, family, and implant team in providing the best route to successful implant use.

WEAR TIME AND DURATION OF IMPLANT USE

Children who use their implants all waking hours of every day will learn to integrate the signals to perceive spoken language. Studies indicate that children will perform better as they continue to wear their implants over time (Miyamoto et al., 1994). Conversely, children who use their cochlear implants in a limited manner will not make the same gains as those who consistently use their devices. Unfortunately, lack of substantive progress may eventually lead to nonuse.

Parents and school professionals can work together to ensure maximal wear time for each recipient. Children who selectively limit implant use can fall into two basic age groups: young toddlers and adolescents. To implement strategies for dealing with each age group, a commitment on the part of the parents, school personnel, and, in the case of the adolescents, the recipients themselves, must be made.

Generally, children who have issues with wear time at very young ages often present with behavior challenges in other areas. These are children who may be the first- born (or only child) in their families with parents who are struggling to learn the art of behavior management. In many cases, it is a battle of wits in which the parent is often the loser. Because these mothers and fathers are new to parenthood, they do not have a clear enough definition of what is acceptable behavior regardless of hearing status. To effectively deal with their child's conduct, the adoption of a behavioral management program is often recommended. Adherence to such a program often leads to an acceptable outcome. Wear programs that couple the child's use of the device with appropriate ramifications or reinforcement work best. For example, a child may not be allowed to leave the house until he or she wears the implant. Parents need to be prepared to follow through on this condition to create the link between wearing the device and the consequences of noncompliance. Although the burden of implementing a wear program falls on the parent, it is the guidance of the early interventionist or preschool professional that can assist them through the process. Often, the support of school personnel will assure the parents that they are not hurting the child but rather teaching a valuable lesson in appropriate behavior. Once a management program is implemented, results can be seen in a very short period of time.

Unfortunately, this is not always the case with the adolescent recipient. Here, the child has more "free will" and will often exercise it to demonstrate his or her independence. In these circumstances, behavioral management may be a formal contract that is agreed on by all parties. Contracts will often limit usage to a particular time or portion of the day in order to control some aspect of the teen's exposure to auditory stimuli. Theoretically, in limiting use, the ultimate goal is to increase use. This may not be effective unless the adolescent obtains some internal or external gratification from the amount of time the implant is being worn. Behavioral contracts remain an option in cases in which children selectively stop wearing their implant. Parents and school professionals can negotiate these contracts (and sometimes the therapy that occurs in conjunction with them) to encourage the teenager into daily and more long-term use. Increasing wear time in a slow, systematic manner prevents the implant recipient from feeling overwhelmed. Success in the use of behavioral contracts with this age group is highly variable.

School professionals who have limited or negative experiences with the implant may interpret these students' lack of commitment to the cochlear implant as additional evidence to reinforce an unfavorable impression of the device. Without a positive approach to therapy by the professional, the adolescent may focus more on what cannot be heard instead of what can be heard. Habilitation should incorporate strategies that represent beginning auditory skills (detection, pattern recognition, and closed set identification) to ensure success. It may also be useful to emphasize speech reading to enhance communication ability. Regardless of the therapeutic strategy selected, successful experiences with auditory information from the implant will foster its continued use.

PROPER FUNCTIONING OF THE DEVICE

Contributing to a cochlear implant's consistent use is its proper functioning. The cochlear implant system is composed of both internal and external components that require regular maintenance. The internal portion of the device must be monitored to ensure stability over time. It is important to assess the integrity of the electrodes and the electronics of the internal receiver. This task can be performed by the implant center on a regular basis and should be part of the routine management of the device. School professionals, as a rule, do not have access to the software or hardware required to perform this task at the present time. It is conceivable that, as implants become more prevalent, the role of the educational audiologist may be more active in the assumption of this responsibility. In the meantime, school personnel should have a baseline of performance for each child so that deviation from it might signal a need for more intensive monitoring. This deviation may include a fluctuation in auditory performance within and between therapy sessions, the report by the child of signals that are intermittent, or the occurrence of sudden negative sensations. The possibility of a compromised internal device must not be overlooked. In such cases, it is important for the speech and hearing professional to be aware of the proper procedure for referral to the implant center to assess the integrity of the internal components. More often than not, however, it is more likely that the problem is located in the external components of the cochlear implant system.

The external hardware must be adequately maintained by the parents, professionals and, when appropriate, the child. For school-based personnel, knowledge of the operation of the device and troubleshooting techniques is essential. Each manufacturer provides information in these areas that can be accessed via video, online, and in print form. The teacher, speech-language pathologist, and/or audiologist should know how to perform daily listening and visual checks of the device. Listening checks might include the detection or identification of the Ling six sounds (ah, ee, oo, sh, s, m). In addition, observing the condition of the external implant components to ensure they are not damaged will contribute to the good daily use that is required of every implant recipient to make progress. Each manufacturer provides device-checking systems that are easy to use. These might include microphone monitors that allow school-based personnel to listen to the quality of sound that is being delivered from the microphone or general system assessors that provide information about the overall functioning of the device. System analyzers can quickly identify if the implant components are operational. These devices do not necessarily provide information about where the problem might be located in the system, but offer a rapid method of determining general function. Communication with the cochlear implant facility is necessary so that school-based personnel have an understanding of the monitoring method used to assess implant viability. Clearly, any concerns the school might have about the function of the device should be communicated as soon as possible to both the parent and implant facility.

BEYOND MAPPING

Although not directly related to the mapping process, there are a number of issues of which the school-based professional must be aware. These take the form of day-to-day precautionary measures that will vary depending on the age of the child. Knowledge of issues concerning the role that electrostatic discharge plays along with constraints regarding after-school activities (that are still the responsibility of the school) are required by speech and hearing professionals.

Cochlear implants are susceptible to static electricity that, in most cases, has very minor effects. Static electricity is the buildup of electrical energy that occurs naturally in the environment. There are some circumstances in which there is a greater possibility of its occurrence. Electrostatic discharge (ESD) occurs when an individual is in contact with synthetic materials or equipment that have a buildup of static electricity. The result of ESD in the general population is the sensation of a small "shock" when the individual touches something or someone after the exposure. In most cases of exposure to ESD by the child with a cochlear implant, there is little effect other than the same uncomfortable feeling that everyone experiences. In a small number of cases, the child's map on his or her speech processor may become "corrupted." Corrupted maps usually do not require any additional return to the center as the processors are manufactured so that when ESD occurs, the program will automatically change to the next available one. If there is a large amount of ESD, then all programs may be affected. In this unusual case, the child would have to return to the center for a remapping. In a very small percentage of cases, there may be damage to the internal components of the system. For this reason, precautions should be taken to ensure that ESD is managed carefully by the schools. Each manufacturer provides a guide to ESD that is accessible online or in print.

In addition to precautions for ESD, children who actively participate in sports should ensure that they abide by any of the rulings concerning the use of helmets. There are certain sports, even with helmets, that hold higher risk for the cochlear implant recipient and participation in these activities should be discussed with the implant facility, parent, and child. Children with cochlear implants successfully participate in a variety of sports activities without harm or injury to their device. For this reason, the school-based professional should not overstate concern relative to either extra-curricular activities or ESD.

SUMMARY

Like hearing aids, the cochlear implant system must be properly fit to ensure maximal auditory input. The fitting process, known as mapping, is performed by an audiologist experienced with the device. Mapping can be facilitated when information concerning the child's performance with the implant is provided to the program-ming audiologist. Most often, this is the responsibility of school-based professionals who monitor the child academically and therapeutically. The more collaboration there is between the school and implant facility, the more likely it will be for the child to obtain the best map for his or her cochlear implant system. School personnel with knowledge about mapping will be able to con-tribute to the process as opposed to being a spectator to it. In addi-tion to mapping, speech and hearing professionals may be called on to assist in monitoring device wear time and maintenance.

Chapter 6

DEVELOPING AUDITORY SKILLS

Thinking Outside the "Box"

The development of listening skills for the purpose of learning spoken language in children who are deaf has a long, albeit contentious, history. From the roots of deaf education in Europe to today's satellite program for oral deaf education, encouraging children with hearing loss to sharpen their auditory acuity as a means to learn to talk has been advocated by many (Calvert & Silverman, 1975; Goldstein, 1939; Pollack, 1964). Although each of the methodologies designed to emphasize listening for children with hearing loss has yielded success stories, the same approaches have resulted in limited achievement by others. Constrained by hearing aids that could not provide the auditory access sufficient for spoken language learning for children with profound hearing loss, a generation of young deaf children found alternative ways to learn to talk. However, the availability of implant technology with its potential to provide auditory input to even the most profoundly deaf youngster, demands a reconsideration of the possibility of spoken language development for all children with this level of hearing loss.

If this is the case, school professionals who are serious about the charge of teaching deaf children to talk, need to have a particular knowledge base and set of skills to facilitate the development of auditory proficiency for the purpose of learning spoken language. It is likely that children using cochlear implants will require more than just auditory access for language learning. Conscious and purposeful spoken language input with high expectations and opportunities for spoken language output will set the stage for language development. But where should the teacher or speech and hearing professional begin? Because parents are seeking implants for their infants as well as their teenagers, it is virtually impossible to delineate a single program for developing auditory skills. Despite this fact, we can begin with a discussion of auditory hierarchy as a backdrop for successful listening that will lead to spoken language development.

Perhaps the most widely accepted hierarchy of auditory skill development was proposed by Norm Erber (1982) in his seminal work, *Auditory Training*. Erber's experiences at a school for deaf children in Australia led to the creation of a statement of auditory skills from a developmental perspective. In an earlier publication (Chute & Nevins, 2002), we presented a reconceptualization of Erber's auditory skills hierarchy that provides a habilitative framework for looking at auditory skills. The similarities and differences between the two hierarchies are presented in Table 6–1.

Both these hierarchies begin with the most basic of all auditory skills: the **detection** of sound. According to Ling (1976), the detection of speech occurs in the frequency region of 250 Hz at an intensity level of approximately 25 dB HL. Detection is necessary

Table 6–1. Two Hierarchies of Auditory Skill Development

Erber (1982)	Chute and Nevins (2002)
Detection	Detection
Discrimination	Pattern Perception
Identification	Segmental Identification
Comprehension	Comprehension

but not sufficient for processing spoken language and deriving meaning from it. We are of the general belief that detection of sound is an immediate outcome for all but very few individuals who receive a cochlear implant. What varies is the child's ability to indicate with a conscious and intentional response that sound has been heard. The younger the child, the more we rely on objective measures of detection such as physiologic responses rather than subjective measures such as behavioral observations.

Erber's second stage of auditory skill development is **discrimination**; in a true discrimination task, the listener determines whether two presented stimuli are either the "same" or "different." By his own admission, Erber suggests that discrimination is a task generally reserved for remediation that is initiated in response to an error made by the child on an identification task. In the "habilitative" hierarchy suggested by Chute and Nevins (2002), we label the second level of auditory skill development, **pattern perception**. At this level of skill development, the child makes a selection from a small, closed set of words (or phrases) that have different patterns or syllable numbers to indicate that something more than simple detection has taken place. Pattern perception can also be observed at the sentence level (contrasting sentences that vary in length or phrasing) and at the level of continuous discourse (a set of directions versus a story read aloud).

The auditory skill that Erber titled **identification** encompasses a broad range of response tasks that indicate that a listener can provide a label for what has been heard. Erber (1982) differentiates between specific identification and categorical identification. Specific identification calls for the child to "describe the stimulus exactly" (p. 41) while categorical identification allows the child to identify the class of speech stimuli without naming it particularly. Categorical identification, according to Erber, may include labeling a sentence long or short or specifying the place where a pause occurs in a sentence. We prefer to differentiate between the *suprasegmental* cues from which pattern perception is derived and the *segmental* cues upon which our version of identification is based. We qualify this level as **segmental identification**, suggesting that, at this level, something more than cues available from patterns are considered in a listening task. In segmental identification, patterns remain constant and the listener must access vowel or consonant information to recognize what has been heard.

Perhaps an example would be helpful at this point. Children working at an auditory skill level of pattern perception should be able to choose from a closed set of words in an auditory-only condition. By its very definition, a closed set is one in which the child is provided with all possible choices. The child is forced to select one of the stimuli, which may be chosen purely by chance. We generally recommend the presentation of listening tasks in thematic or content-based sets. Thus, during a lesson on animals that live in the zoo, the following closed set (using manipulatives, pictures, or printed words as choices) might be suitable:

Single syllable	Bisyllabic	Polysyllabic
seal	monkey	elephant

Although a child may not be able to distinguish any of the particular sounds within these words, pattern perception will allow the child to select the correct word based on the number of "beats" heard. If the child hears only a single beat, then the choice would be *seal* (two beats, *monkey*, and three beats, *elephant*). Now, if the stimulus presented is *monkey* and the child incorrectly chooses *seal*, the clinician or teacher may take a page from Erber's book and create a new, more simplified listening task requiring a discrimination judgment of same versus different. The child is asked to listen to two stimuli "monkey/seal" or "monkey/monkey" and determine if they are the same or different.

A pattern perception task would be easy for a child presenting with skills at the segmental identification level for the "degree of difficulty" is not commensurate with the child's current skill level. For a child demonstrating segmental identification, any one of following closed sets might be appropriate:

Single-syllable words in closed set

ape	owl	seal

Two-syllable words in closed set

tiger	monkey	zebra

Three-syllable words in closed set

polar bear	elephant	gorilla

Purists might say that, in the third example, "polar bear" is not appropriate to include because it is not a polysyllabic word like the others in the set. We believe that the coarticulation effects of this animal name dictate that it is perceived as a single polysyllabic word rather than as a two-word phrase. Thus, it is a perfectly acceptable token in this polysyllabic set.

Suppose that, in the second example, the word *giraffe* had also been included in the set. This word has an unaccented-accented syllable combination that is different from the other accented-unaccented syllable pattern. Some would argue that the difference between *lion* and *giraffe* can be ascertained through pattern perception alone. Although this may be true for children with sophisticated listening levels, experience suggests that some segmental (vowel) identification would be necessary to complete this task, especially as set size increases.

Identification is a skill that can also be demonstrated in open-set listening tasks in which there are no examples or choices available to the child. Open-set segmental identification is a skill more sophisticated than closed-set identification. The child is challenged to scan all the items available in auditory memory to "locate" the correct response. Between closed and open sets are bridge sets, which allow for the naming of a category or topic to limit the endless number of choices that are a part of open-set tasks.

The final and most complex level of auditory skill development is **auditory comprehension.** At this stage, the listener does not label what has been heard, rather he or she acts in response to what has been said to show that it has been understood. Responding appropriately to questions demonstrates auditory comprehension, in addition to other content tasks that are elaborated on later in this chapter.

There is an inherent danger in utilizing a hierarchy of skill development to guide habilitation. It lies in the temptation to start at the very beginning and follow a linear path along the hierarchy without considering the complexity of language used to develop successive skills. One cannot consider auditory skills without considering the linguistic make-up of the stimulus that comprises the auditory input. When a toddler gets her jacket in response to dad's direction, "It's time to go," she is demonstrating, by actions that she has understood the auditory message. The skill of auditory comprehension is also demonstrated by the child in middle school who correctly answers the teacher's (auditory-only) inquiry, "What is the difference between communism and capitalism?"

For the preschooler, pattern perception at the word level may include tokens such as "school" and "hospital" (in a discussion of places in our community). For the older child, the same auditory skill may be practiced in the context of a discussion of citizenship, where tokens such as "vote" and "election" may be contrasted. Clearly, there is a language effect to the development of auditory skills such that a child should be challenged across skill levels with varying linguistic inputs. This ensures that a step-by-step building block approach does not limit the performance of a child capable of higher level auditory skills with simple and familiar language.

Unfortunately, many published auditory skills curricula, have inadvertently perpetuated the tendency of speech and hearing professionals to follow a bottom-up approach to listening. The utility of the skills checklist that accompanies many of these curricula guarantees their continued usage, especially when the checklist serves the dual purpose of tracking individual progress and developing IEP goals. However, limitations in the use of an auditory skills curriculum include the decontextualization of materials and their general inability to target multiple auditory skills in the context of a single activity.

FROM THEORY TO PRACTICE

Recall that the task of developing auditory skills is made more complex by the fact that children of all ages are receiving cochlear implants. We would like to suggest that children who are implanted at early ages need to have a top-down approach to listening. By this we mean that fluent and connected spoken language should be used as the linguistic input. In using normal conversation (with the vocal elements of child-directed speech), the rhythm and melody of spoken language is available to the child to serve as the fertile soil from which later language learning occurs. Thus, there is some utility in addressing the development of auditory skills based on age at implantation. Our discussion will focus, then, on four major groups: infants and toddlers, preschoolers, school-aged children, and teenagers.

EARLY IMPLANTATION: INFANTS AND TODDLERS

The continuing widespread adoption of Universal Newborn Hearing Screening, coupled with Food and Drug Administration (FDA) sanction for implantation as early as one year of age for profoundly deaf infants, has changed the face of Early Intervention (EI) services for children with hearing loss. The ability to identify hearing loss before a newborn leaves the hospital creates an opportunity for early, early intervention. When parents access EI services soon after the hearing loss is discovered, research has indicated more positive outcomes for language learning (Mayne et al., 2000a; Mayne et al., 2000b, Moeller, 1998). When quality early intervention services are complemented by auditory access, the potential for spoken language acquisition commensurate with a child's hearing age-mates grows enormously (Kirk et al., 2002). Early identification and the fitting of amplification in a timely fashion set the stage for the development of auditory abilities and the spoken language that follows in a more natural manner. This is in marked contrast to a building-block approach whereby discrete auditory skills are practiced, and language structure and function are intentionally taught, not simply facilitated.

It is not our intent to suggest that spoken language input is then capricious; general principles of language development serve as the foundation for interactions between parents and caregivers and child. It may be helpful to review some of these principles to ensure that language input for an infant before and after implantation follows guidelines of best practice.

Spoken Language Input Should be Purposeful, Abundant, and Functional

Making language *purposeful* suggests that opportunities for inducing the rules of language are provided through participation in natural, conversational exchanges. The important role that rhythm and intonation play in communicating intent must not be overlooked at this early stage. To communicate the suprasegmental aspects of spoken language, it follows that connected discourse, rather than single words, be a sizable part of the language model to which the child is exposed. Incorporating principles of child-directed speech may also contribute to the systematic development of language. Features of child-directed speech include the use of pitch that is somewhat raised, the production of an interesting intonation contour, and a somewhat slowed rate of speech. The concept of the inflected utterance, which utilizes consonant vowel clusters, can contribute considerably during this period. In fact, these nonlinguistic elements of language are among the first a child attends to auditorily and the implanted infant demonstrates early after implantation.

With regard to building language content, the simultaneous processing of an experience and the spoken language that is a part of that experience is a benefit afforded by cochlear implant technology. This, in turn, provides opportunity for the children to learn labels for objects in their environment as well as to process the action words of everyday activities in which they are participants. Putting labels, descriptors, and action words together to form grammatically complete and correct utterances is also part of the spoken language-learning task. It is commonly accepted that children induce the syntactic rules of language by participating in real conversations (Kretschmer & Kretschmer, 1978); creating communication exchanges that encourage turn-taking for language input as well as for language output should be highly valued.

If one could conclude then, that purposeful input relates to the *quality* of the spoken language that is directed to the child, providing *abundant* language implies a need to attend to the *quantity* of that input. As school-based professionals in the field of speech and hearing, we are well aware of the need to bathe a child in language, providing multiple opportunities for language throughout the day. Parents of children with language delays are often advised to "narrate the child's world." This activity requires that parents describe everyday events as they occur in real time. This concept, although evident to language development specialists, is sometimes foreign to parents of the children who need it most. Parents of children with hearing loss have a tendency to produce directive language or to limit overall language input (Gallaway, 1998) as they believe the child is unable to hear it. If we accept the notion that parents are indeed the first teachers, it would behoove us to spend time in desensitizing parents to any discomfort in providing ample spoken language input.

Finally, if spoken language is to be *functional* for the child, we must ensure that a good part of the language repertoire that is being developed will allow the child to get needs and wants met. Important early function words such as "more," "up," and (unfortunately) "no" will prove to be powerful elements in a child's early vocabulary. Once a child has access to words such as these, parents must hold the child accountable for using them. Although it is sometimes easier for parents to "just do it" themselves, they should refrain from anticipating the child's requests and wait for the appearance of a communication attempt to signal the child's needs or wants. Learning to wait can be painstaking for today's busy parent, but the payoff in functional language development is most certainly worth it.

Interactions Based on Age-Appropriate Cognitive/Motor/Play Activities Should Be the Basis of Exchanges with the Child

The temptation to "do" an activity for the practice of a particular auditory skill or language structure should not override what is considered to be developmentally appropriate given a particular child's age and ability. Making interactions auditory in natural and developmentally appropriate play can be accomplished quite easily through positioning. Whether or not a child is placed in a high chair for better auditory access is likely a matter of personal philosophy and professional beliefs. Regardless, we acknowledge that babies do spend times in high chairs and there is no doubt that a compliant child in a high chair may be more focused on the activity at hand (especially if it involves food!). But children should only be placed in high chairs when the activity is appropriate for that setting. It is more natural for the child to spend time out of the high chair than in one and, therefore, a more appropriate environment for interaction should be explored. As the child ages, activities may be supplemented with listening "games" that emphasize auditory input, but these are to be used judiciously. A child's own learning style will dictate how subsequent exchanges are presented.

Create a Good Auditory and Visual Environment for Spoken Language Learning

In traveling about the country meeting professionals who provide home-based EI services, we hear again and again that creating a good acoustic environment for the development of listening skills is one of the first important "lessons" presented to parents of children with hearing loss. The electronics age that has brought so many conveniences of life has also ushered in a cacophony of background noise in which competing signals from Dolby sound-equipped televisions, computers games, and sound effects generated by battery-operated toys fill the home. The need for a quiet environment is frequently overlooked, and it is the EI professional who must often make the first attempt at heightening the parents' awareness to the level of background noise that exists at home (to which they have likely become habituated over time). It is equally important for the child to have an adequate visual environment; sufficient lighting and limited visual distraction will contribute to the child's attention to the task at hand.

Establish Routines in the Home for Language Learning

One of the more compelling accounts of the language-learning process in children suggests that systematic development of language is accomplished through participation in routine events with mature language users (Nelson, 1986). Although the role of the speech and hearing professional is important at this stage, the parent assumes the primary responsibility in providing the language interaction. It is through participation in the daily routines of the household that the child begins to explore and learn. Briefly stated, it is only when a child is familiar with an "event" such that he or she is aware of the sequence of action and the "actors," that there is sufficient mental space to focus on the language of the event. With repeated participation in familiar routines, the child learns the language associated with them. The parent, then, introduces new language into the routine and additional learning is facilitated. With today's busy lifestyle and the mosaic of our multicultural society, the notion of a "routine" may seem somewhat archaic. Perhaps if we can conceptualize these events as "recurring" even if they are not routine (happening at the same time every day), we can capitalize on the notion that repeated events such as eating, dressing, and entering and exiting the house may all be considered appropriate for systematic language input. Once the "script" of the recurring event is established, new vocabulary and structures can be introduced in the context of the now-familiar activity. Thus, parents set the stage for future communication development as the child transitions from home to school.

PRESCHOOLERS

There are two distinct groups of preschoolers who are cochlear implant recipients. The first are the youngsters with a history of implant use, learning speech and spoken language with the assistance of implant technology from the age of 12 to 24 months. These children will often present with near-normal language, impressive speech intelligibility, and social skills commensurate with their age and demeanor (a shy or reserved child with a cochlear implant will likely still be shy and reserved). For these children, continued vocabulary and language accrual driven by concepts and content development that is age-appropriate should maximize the auditory advantage provided by the implant. Listening games that sharpen auditory skills, introduce noise and/or distance, and encourage the development of the auditory-speech feedback loop may be utilized. Care should be taken to keep expectations for this group high, yet the teacher/therapist should be vigilant to ensure that steady development across all domains is occurring.

The second groups includes children who receive their implants during the preschool years. Generally speaking, this places them in a somewhat longer duration of deafness category, especially if these are congenitally deaf or deafened within the first year of life. There could be any number of reasons that children in this subset of preschoolers do not receive an implant as soon as it was chronologically possible. These include limited or no information about the technology of implantation from early interventionists, recent arrival in the United States, or reluctance on the part of the parents to make the final decision about implantation, to name a few. Regardless, the fact that these children present as 3- to 5-year-olds, without having had the auditory access for early spoken language learning, makes the task somewhat more challenging. We would recommend that all children have the "opportunity" to process connected spoken language; those that show the potential for learning to talk in a manner more similar to the infant toddler group (albeit at a later age) should be encouraged to take a more naturalistic route to language learning. Aggressive auditory management at this stage is necessary to determine each child's potential to benefit from an intervention strategy that parallels normal language development. Other children in this age group, for a variety of reasons, may require somewhat of a more structured approach to the development of listening skills, especially if they are on the older end of the continuum. For these children, particularly, planned listening games to heighten attention to auditory input can help to "jump-start" the auditory system; early success should be ensured by creating motivating activities that are within the child's conceptual, linguistic, and auditory ability. Previous experience with listening with hearing aids can improve the early outcomes of implant use. For this second group, the key is to continue to develop concepts and language while priming the auditory pump.

Listening Games and Activities Appropriate for Preschoolers

Virtually any activity that is planned for a preschooler can be made into an auditory one with some minor adaptations. In fact, we would advocate the "overlaying" of auditory skills on established activities rather than turning to an auditory skills curriculum for listening practice. The former is highly contextualized, allows for targeting multiple skill levels within a single activity, and, by its very nature, uses familiar vocabulary and language. Utilizing classroom content allows for the dual outcomes of concept review and auditory skill development. Prepackaged (or boxed) auditory curricula present activities one skill at a time. They are decontextualized in that they do not follow classroom themes and, while attempts have been made to use common vocabulary and language, it may be that some of the "kit" vocabulary is not in the lexicon of any particular child. This is especially true when children come from culturally and linguistically diverse backgrounds.

The selection of any classroom theme, then, should provide a vehicle to develop auditory skills while reinforcing content. As an example, within a larger unit on animals, a subunit includes a discussion of animal habitats. Within this subunit, the principal learning objectives include naming various habitats and matching animals to their appropriate environment. For this introductory concept of habitats, we will focus our attention on three places animals live: land, water, and trees.

Among the animals that we may include in this discussion of habitats are:

Land dwellers: deer, skunks, rabbits, chipmunks, coyotes

Water dwellers: whales, crabs, starfish, dolphins, sea horses, octopus

Tree dwellers: owls, squirrels, monkeys, woodpeckers

If one takes a close look at the animals that are identified in the unit, we can see that another way they can be categorized is in lists based on syllable number. Thus, whales, crabs, deer, skunks, and owls all belong to the single-syllable category; rabbit, chipmunks, starfish, dolphins, squirrels, and monkeys can all be grouped together in a two-syllable list. Coyotes, octopus, and woodpeckers make up a polysyllabic list. These lists can now be used to practice auditory skills in tasks that also reinforce the concepts and the vocabulary introduced in the units.

As stated earlier, words can be used to practice auditory skills of pattern perception and segmental identification and, with the right stimulus, auditory comprehension. If a child presents with a developing skill of pattern perception, the teacher or therapist can work *across* lists to form closed-set listening tasks. This level of activity may be more appropriate for the child who received an implant while attending preschool as opposed to the child who received the implant as an infant. The dialogue for this basic listening activity might include the following:

"We are going to listen to some of the animal names that we have been learning about. Maybe I'll say owl or maybe I'll say octopus." The target is presented in an auditory-only condition (after an auditory plus visual practice as necessary) and the child indicates what was heard. To take this listening activity a step further into the domain of content review, the teacher or therapist might ask the child to then take the animal and place it in the proper habitat . . . if "owl" is the auditory stimulus the child chooses the owl (picture, toy manipulative) and then places the owl in a tree (picture or model of a tree). Should another child in the classroom have segmental identification skills (as in the child with experience with an implant prior to entering preschool), the task remains the same, but the choices that are available come from *within* a syllabic list. The directions for this segmental identification activity may be, "Listen for the name of the animal that I say. Here are the names to listen for: squirrel, monkey, dolphin, starfish, rabbit, chipmunk." The child who is given this task cannot rely on patterns but must hear some of the vowel and/or consonant sounds to complete it successfully. Once again, after the correct token is chosen, the child can be further instructed to reinforce the content by placing the identified picture in the correct habitat. This two-step process requires the child to, first listen for the name of the animal and then, select the picture from a closed set. Once chosen the child is then directed to place it in the proper habitat. To make this task one that challenges a child with auditory comprehension abilities, the teacher or therapist might give the following direction: "I'll name one of the animals that we have been talking about and you tell me where the animal lives." The teacher says, "woodpecker" and the child say "tree." In this one-step process, the child draws from his vocabulary base and demonstrates understanding by making a novel response that is not simply a repetition of the original stimulus. All three of these examples can be generalized across content areas including social studies, math, and reading.

To create opportunities for the practice of listening skills with more linguistically complex materials, key concepts from a content unit or the main ideas of a story that is read can be utilized. These can be written in a summary paragraph that serves as the sentence-level language input for auditory development. Such a main idea paragraph on animal habitats has been designed with both content review and auditory purposefulness in mind.

Where Animals Live

Animals live in many different places.

Some animals live on land.

Deer, rabbits, and chipmunks live in fields and woods.

Some animals live in water.

Crabs, dolphins, and starfish live in the ocean.

Some animals live in trees.

Owls, squirrels, and monkeys make their home in trees.

All animals find a place to live.

Analysis of the sentences that make up this paragraph should uncover that they have both varied and similar patterns. The first three sentences in the summary all have different lengths and/or patterns, yet within the paragraph are two sets of sentences that can be used as tasks for segmental identification. It should be obvious that greater auditory skill is required to differentiate between "Some animals live on land" and "Some animals live in trees" than is required to tell the difference between "Animals live in many places" and "Crabs, starfish, and octopus live in the ocean." To challenge a child with auditory comprehension skills with this material, questions can be posed: "Does a monkey live in the ocean?" or "Where does a deer live?" Sometimes, a true/false judgment can be made: "True or false: An animal that lives in a tree is a rabbit." This procedure, too, can be generalized to other content and stories. Thus, with a single-concept vocabulary list and the paragraph that accompanies it, a number of auditory skills can be practiced, thereby ensuring that the needs of children at varying skill levels will be met.

SCHOOL-AGED CHILDREN

Children who reach elementary school as veteran implant users who have been able to maximize the potential of the device, will often be in mainstream classes demonstrating age-appropriate language and academic skills. They continue to need careful monitoring to ensure that as the academic demands of the curriculum grow, they have the support needed to maintain placement. The challenge with children in this age group comes when implant experience begins after five years of age especially when there has been limited auditory input and limited spoken language development during that time.

When a child receives a cochlear implant in a time period beyond the toddler years, it is important to give the child the opportunity to develop the auditory skills that will enable subsequent learning through the auditory channel. Generally speaking, this requires a combination top-down and bottom-up approach to listening experience. Connected discourse will provide the child with access to the rhythm and melody of spoken language. Recall the earlier mention of the inflected utterance; incorporating words that can be voiced with different intonation patterns will allow the child to capture auditory benefit from the implant soon after initial switch-on. Think of some of the ways in which children might use intonation in this age group: "No way!" "Awesome!" "Sweet!" can all be used as commentary in particular situations. Establishing a context for using this language creates a fun way to practice both speech perception and speech production as the child attempts to produce these patterns as well.

The demands of the elementary curriculum as well as pressures from "No Child Left Behind" Act make instruction time a precious commodity in the school day. Compartmentalized auditory skill practice is not as functional as is the infusion of auditory learning opportunities throughout the school day. Capitalizing on classroom content as the vehicle for practicing listening skills makes intuitive sense for the busy classroom teacher. Further, the degree to which the speech-language pathologist can assist in this endeavor by integrating classroom material into individual speech, language, and auditory sessions may also contribute to the achievement of educational as well as speech and auditory objectives. That being said, we return to the protocol for theme-based listening activities introduced earlier and ramp it up to meet the curricular challenges of the elementary grades.

Let us assume that the social studies topic under discussion is "Our Nation's Capital." In the same manner as described for the preschool group, we may look at the content vocabulary of this lesson. If the category is "places of interest in Washington, DC," then the following words might be a part of the unit: *monuments, memorials, museums, zoo* as general terms and particular places might include *The White House, The Jefferson Memorial, The Air and Space Museum*. If the category is "people of Washington, DC," then the words *president, senators, justices,* and *FBI* might be taught. "Special events of our nation's capital" might also be addressed in this unit, including: *the Cherry Blossom Festival* and *Fourth of July fireworks at the Mall*. All of the information presented during this rich unit may provide the opportunity for listening practice when an auditory perspective is overlaid on the instructional content.

Looking at the content from an auditory perspective, it immediately becomes apparent that there are a large number of polysyllabic words in this unit. For children with pattern perception ability, tasks that require the recognition of landmarks based on patterns may be initiated. For example, then, a child may be asked to choose the one that was heard when the choices are: the White House versus the Jefferson Memorial or the Capitol versus the FBI Building. Children with segmental identification ability will need different and larger closed sets. Students who do not rely on patterns can often have more tokens in a set; a closed set for children with segmental ability might include the words monument, museum, capital, and the White House. All the vocabulary from the Washington, DC unit can be categorized by syllable number as well as by event, place or people.

In a manner similar to the discussion of animal habitats, a summary paragraph detailing some of the key points of the unit may also be created for listening practice (and content review). One such iteration of a summary paragraph is suggested below.

Our Nation's Capital

The capital of the United States is Washington, DC.

Visitors from all over the world come to Washington to visit its landmarks.

Some people climb to the top of the Washington Monument while others walk along the Vietnam Memorial Wall.

Many tourists enjoy visiting the various museums in Washington.

If you are interested in flying, the Air and Space Museum is the place for you.

If you are interested in the past, the Museum of American History is the place for you.

There are many outdoor activities to enjoy in this historic city.

April is the time for cherry blossoms in Washington.

July is the time for fireworks in Washington.

Whenever you visit our nation's capital there will be lots of things to see and do.

Although it is preferable to begin with a unit that is already being taught in the classroom, there are other sources of fact-filled summaries available through teacher stores or publishers such as the Evan-Moor Corporation. Generally available as reading and writing tools, grade-level materials for grades 1 through 3 or 4 through 6 may serve as the jumping-off point for producing more concise summaries on a host of topics ranging from owls to clouds to geology and more. For the speech-language pathologist who may need assistance in generating content-driven tasks, these teacher resources may be quite an asset to lesson development.

TEENAGERS

The adolescent implant recipient requires special attention in the development of listening tasks that will be motivating and lead to early success. It is critically important to catch the teen's attention and interest in participating in listening tasks as a means to developing auditory skills. Experience has shown that youngsters who receive cochlear implants after the age of 12 generally will perform best if there has been a history of hearing aid use. Often, this subset of teens experiences a sudden decrement of hearing as they reach adolescence and are lost without the auditory input to which they have been accustomed. Adapting to the new sound that is delivered through the implant will take some time and a commitment to building new auditory representations to replace those previously delivered via hearing aids. Because this age group presents with special considerations, content-driven protocols are often abandoned for more interesting material. The procedures remain the same, but now topics related to music, sports, fashion, cars, instant messaging, and drivers education replace science or social studies themes.

Still another group of teenagers, those with less orientation to listening throughout their lives, is also receiving implants. These include the subset of teens who are congenitally deaf and have worn hearing aids with very little benefit. This group is at risk for nonuse of the device if an acceptable level of performance with the implant (which may be a variable level for different teens) is not experienced. Listening to and categorizing music according to rhythm and beat may be one way to lure the teenager into continued wear time. Downloading (inoffensive) lyrics and "singing along" with the performers is another way to tap auditory, speech, and voice abilities. For all groups of teens, we encourage the use of speech tracking, a procedure first introduced by DeFillipo and Scott in 1978.

Speech tracking is an activity in which a word-for-word repetition of the speaker's input is required by the listener. A reading selection, chosen because of its high interest and motivation for the teenager, provides the connected discourse that serves as the tracking material. The object of speech tracking is for the listener to increase the rate of recognizing the speaker's output (a function of words per minute) over time. The rather simplistic procedure calls for the speaker to read from the text (in manageable phrases) and accept only a verbatim response from the listener. Several strategies may be implemented to facilitate this task, most notably the use of gestures or hand signals to help represent the words in question. For example, the reader may indicate the number of syllables in a target word using a motion that "taps the beat" of the word as it is being said. Envision the word "automobile" being presented along with a hand motion that counts the four beats of the word. Of course, some materials are better suited to speech tracking than others. Passages with many unfamiliar words, or many proper names will be more difficult to track than more general information. When the material is chosen by the teen listener, the odds for successful participation in the tracking task increase. However, speech tracking is material-sensitive, so it is best to use consistent sources to obtain performance changes over time. With continued practice, it is anticipated that the rate of tracking will increase. Visual plotting of progress may be sufficient reinforcement for a teen to persevere in the development of listening skills.

SUMMARY

Age at implantation, the extent of the auditory oral language base, and a child's predisposition to processing auditory input once access is available will all factor into the development of an appropriate habilitation plan. It is preferable to use connected discourse in natural and routine settings to accomplish the development of listening skills. However, systematic attention to the development of particular listening skills will be required by (and be advantageous to) many implant users. Although auditory curriculum for the purpose of building skills are available, the best "bang for the instructional buck" may come from a protocol in which listening is infused into the content themes already a part of the academic demands of the day. This requires that the teacher or speech-language pathologist view content not only from a cognitive perspective but from an auditory perspective as well. Once a professional acquires the vision to see listening opportunities in everything that happens in the classroom or therapy room, the rest is easy!

Chapter 7

CLEAR SPEECH: THE POSSIBLE DREAM

One need only to listen to profoundly deaf children talk today to know that there has been a dramatic improvement in recent years in speech development for children with this degree of hearing loss. Decades of archival data support the following generalization: the greater the hearing loss the less intelligible is the speech of deaf children (Carney, 1986; Hudgins & Numbers,1942; Markides, 1970). In a 1987 attempt to create a "Spoken Language Predictor," Geers and Moog developed categories of speech perception as a means of predicting later spoken language capacity. They determined that children who were capable of better speech perception were more likely to develop understandable speech. In recent years, the cochlear implant has provided a tool for ameliorating the effects of profound hearing loss on speech production. Deaf children now have the potential for clear oral resonance in lieu of nasality, accurate vowel production instead of neutralization of vowels, prosodic elements instead of monotonic speech, and more precise articulation as opposed to the omissions, substitutions, and distortions characteristic of deaf speech in the past. Despite the unprecedented auditory access provided by the cochlear implant, children still benefit from intervention that facilitates the development of speech. Best practice paradigms suggest that meaningful and natural interactions that develop *spoken language* replace isolated sound development and/or speech drill and practice activities. Focusing on spoken language allows the professional to address both speech *and* language as they interact and become the vehicle of the child's expressive language capabilities.

SPEECH AND LANGUAGE

It has always been important to separate what a child *knows* from what a child *says*. What a child knows is generally referred to as receptive language, which corresponds to all the child's knowledge of the world that is coded into meaningful representations. Because it is true that receptive language develops in advance of expressive language, one cannot infer a child's total language ability from expressive speech output alone. This is particularly the case when children use sign language and have nonspeech representations for what they know about the world. With this in mind, the thrust of this discussion is to charge the speech and hearing professional to help a child with a cochlear implant form a direct pathway from total language knowledge, however it is represented in the brain, to spoken language output.

SPEECH DEVELOPMENT

Most children have the capacity to produce speech that has certain human characteristics because of the anatomy and physiology of the human vocal tract. Once the lungs provide sufficient air to produce sound, the breath stream travels across the vocal folds, into the pharynx, and through the mouth to shape most of the sounds of auditory/oral languages. In some cases, the sound is sent through the nasal rather than oral cavity resulting in productions that have different resonance than do oral sounds. Regardless, movement of the tongue, teeth, and lips will factor into the final outcome of speech production. For the most part, a child with a hearing loss, be it mild or profound, has the physical ability to produce the sounds of any particular oral language. Arriving at the point where complex strings of speech are intelligible to the naïve listener depends on the availability of a peripheral hearing mechanism that processes incoming speech as well as the quantity and quality of the speech input to which the child is exposed.

Although infants will produce attention-getting sounds early on, it is not until about 8 months of age that they will generally begin to produce speechlike output in babbling. The journey toward attempting the complexities of mature speech production will require another two to three years. Continued study of the process of speech development in infants has led to some interesting new perspectives on the role of physical maturity in speech production. Davis and MacNeilage (1995) explored babbling and the emergence of the first words. Their work has led to a reconceptualization of the role of physical patterns in early spoken language and speech development. These researchers identified common patterns created by the basic opening and closing of the mouth and other jaw movements. These patterns also appear to be present in the early development of French, Swedish, and Japanese infants. Patterns include *bilabial consonant + central vowel* (mama), *alveolar consonant + front vowel* (dada), and *velar consonant + back vowel* (gogo). In a follow-up study of an infant with hearing loss, McCaffrey et al. (1999) observed a young child who received a cochlear implant at 25 months of age. Prior to implantation, the child's speech production was characterized by a phonetic repertoire made up largely of nasals, labial stop consonants, and mid-central vowels, a finding she reported as consistent with speech production data of toddlers with profound hearing loss. After implantation, McCaffrey and her colleagues described speech production characterized by a decrease in the number of nasal sounds produced with a simultaneous increase in other consonant types, most notably the alveolars. With regard to vowel productions, the young implant recipient produced a greater number of vowels with the appearance of diphthongs also noted. Some of the same motor patterns found in the speech of hearing youngsters as identified by Davis and MacNeilage (1995) were also found in the postimplantation speech production of the subject of McCaffrey's study: there was a tendency for labial consonants to be followed by central vowels and for alveolar sounds to be followed by front vowels. One might infer, then, that there is some need for the availability of sufficient auditory accessibility to trigger or reinforce this motor tendency in early speech development. Whether this is true or not, the recognition of the role of basic physiology of the speech production mechanism in early speech development cannot be overlooked. More investigation into the acquisition of speech by our youngest implant recipients should yield further direction for the practicing speech and hearing professional guiding the development of spoken language in children with implants.

MODELS OF SPEECH DEVELOPMENT FOR CHILDREN WITH HEARING LOSS

Perhaps the best-known professional associated with the development of speech skills in children with severe-to-profound deafness is Daniel Ling. His classic text, *Speech and the Hearing Impaired Child: Theory and Practices* (1976) served as the definitive authority for many teachers and speech and hearing professionals interested in the assessment and the development of speech in children with significant hearing loss. Ling's recommendation for repeated practice to achieve automaticity of a phoneme or combination of phonemes parallels the current-day practice supporting "auditory bombardment" or focused auditory input (Bowen & Cupples, 1998; Hodson & Paden, 1991) offered as a means to assist a child in developing intelligible speech. Ling's comprehensive developmental hierarchy became the most widely used reference for the order of acquisition of speech sounds for the profoundly deaf child. Keep in mind, however, that his text was published in 1976 (an incredible 30 years ago). Written from the experience of working with the child who used hearing aids, Ling's hierarchy can no longer be considered applicable to today's child with a cochlear implant. Now speech and hearing professionals are encouraged to look to the literature on the sequence of phoneme development as observed in hearing youngsters. Auditory access through the cochlear implant makes these resources a more valuable referent than Ling's hierarchy; the speech and hearing professional may consult any one of a number of developmental hierarchies available for this purpose.

Shriberg (1993) has offered one such inventory of sound development that may be of interest to professionals working with children with implants. He classified the phonemes into three major categories, thereby proposing the division of the 24 consonantal sounds of English into "The Early 8," "The Middle 8," and "The Late 8." Consonant sounds were assigned to each of these broad categories and include: The Early 8—m, b, y (as in yes) (IPA—International Phonetic Alphabet—will not be used), r, w, d, p, and h. Middle 8 phonemes include: t, k, g, ng, f, v, ch, and j (as in jump); Late 8 phonemes include; sh, th (voiceless), th (voiced), s, z, l, r, and zh (as in treasure). Using Shriberg's classification as an organizational frame, Lof (2004) reviewed five sets of norms to plot the average age of developmental mastery (the point at which 90% of the children in the sample produced the sound accurately) for the phonemes in each of Shriberg's groups. Lof found that most of the developmental mastery of phonemes in the Early 8 clustered around 3.0 years of age. The sound "y" heard in "yes," showed the greatest variance in development; one study cited its appearance at 2.6 years of age, another did not report developmental mastery until 5.6 years of age. Almost counterintuitively for speech and hearing professionals experienced in working with children with hearing loss, the phoneme "p" showed the greatest discrepancy in mastery. Earliest development of "p" occurred at 2.6 years with the latest report of its occurrence at 6.6 years of age!

In an analysis of developmental mastery for the "Middle 8" phonemes, Lof found a much wider age range for the sounds in this stage with: k, g, t, and f clustering in the 3.0- to 4.0-year range. The phonemes v, ch, and j (as in jelly) clustered in the 5.6- to 7.0-year range across the five studies surveyed. (Only three studies reported developmental mastery for "ng"; one at 2.0, one at 3.0, and one at 6.0 years.) When looking at the "Late 8" sounds, Lof noted that most of the developmental mastery occurred between 5.6 and 8.0 years, although some studies reported mastery of the "s" and "sh" before age 5. In his discussion, Lof called into question the notion of a fixed, universal orderly development of speech sounds and further postulated that children with disordered speech production may not follow the same developmental sequence of typically developing children. Finally, he urged a rethinking of the notion that some (early-developing) sounds are prerequisite to learning (later-developing) other sounds.

It may be that following such a general outline as proposed by Shriberg would be most useful in designing speech intervention for children who use cochlear implants. Interestingly, anecdotal reports have suggested that children with implants have early curiosity for some of the higher frequency phonemes that are audible with their new auditory access to sound. When this interest is manifested as a true production attempt, the speech and hearing professional would be wise to consider providing assistance in developing its precision regardless of which of the "8" categories the phoneme can be found.

FACILITATING THE DEVELOPMENT OF SPEECH/SPOKEN LANGUAGE IN THE YOUNG CHILD

It is rather difficult to arbitrarily separate out speech development from spoken language development when describing the task before the young child learning language. For the purpose of discussion, let us use the term "speech" to refer to the motor act of producing sounds to communicate meaning. We stipulate the point that, in the absence of a spoken language token, a child may still have a receptive language representation of a particular action or object. In fact, children who use a manual language may have a number of expressive signs; it is the intent of this chapter, however, to offer guidelines for the development of spoken representations of inner language through a focus on the development of speech skills.

Foundations of Speech

Imagine that you are on an airplane. Through your peripheral hearing you determine that two of your fellow passengers are engaged in a conversation in an otherwise quiet cabin. You can't help but pay attention to the conversation; but upon more careful listening you realize that they are not speaking English. You do not recognize any of the words, but you have a sense that they are speaking an Asian-Pacific language, perhaps Japanese. How is it that you have come to this conclusion when you do not know any Japanese words?

The rhythm and intonation of our spoken languages provide clues to their identity. In fact, some languages rely so heavily on pitch and intonation contours that meaning is changed immensely just by changing pitch. In spoken English, pitch change can signal, among other things, that a question has been posed. A rising intonation pattern lets the listener know that you are asking a question even if your facial expression is not visible. Individuals who have command of spoken English use rhythm and intonation contours that assist them in communicating meaning.

Almost coincidentally, one of the earliest outcomes of cochlear implantation appears to be the ability to perceive and produce variations in rhythm and intonation contours or suprasegmental aspects of spoken language. These features of speech, in fact, can be observed even before the development of a sophisticated language system. In a study of toddlers and young children receiving cochlear implants, Chute and Bollard (1999, personal communication) used an instrument specifically designed to capture the young, pre- or perilinguistic child's ability to imitate intonation contours using an instrument called the Suprasegmental Recognition and Production Test (SRAPT). Designed as a model-imitation task, children as young as 18 months of age were able to demonstrate the perception of suprasegmental aspects of speech through their productive response to the examiner's prompt. Using consonants and vowels in isolation and in combination, the examiner modeled, for example, a falling stress stimulus as in "uh-oh" meaning, "oh dear" or a peak-stress-fall stimulus as in "ooooo" (I like that). Soon after implantation, children who received cochlear implants were able to produce these and other "inflected utterances," a skill they did not have prior to receiving an implant. This research suggests, then, that some of the very features of spoken language that contribute to its general structure may be available to even our youngest implant recipients. Implications for the early interventionist, teacher of children with hearing loss, and speech-language pathologist are clear: before dwelling on precision of production look to the rhythm and melody of the language.

Inherent in the production of good rhythm and intonation patterns is the availability of a "good" voice and clarity of vowels. As alluded to earlier in this chapter, profound hearing loss has had historical implications for the development of a voice quality that is typically within the range of what the human vocal tract will produce. The ability to hear the human voice, replicate it (with only minimal variability as dictated by the individuality of a vocal tract), and monitor it was unavailable to persons with profound deafness even with the most powerful hearing aids. This resulted in alternative methods of producing speech that was "managed" by an insufficient monitoring system. Consequently, characteristics of deaf speech were identified with terms such as: "breathy, hypernasal, hyponasal, harsh, and strident." The absence of intonational contours was frequently noted as were timing and intensity abnormalities.

As if this were not enough to render deaf speech difficult to understand, the production of vowels with precise boundaries so as to make them distinguishable from one another was made impossible by the frequency limitations of hearing aids. When an individual did not get second formant (high-frequency) information to assist in auditorily shaping the production of a distinct vowel, the result was the overproduction of an undifferentiated neutral vowel (uh) in many contexts. Despite hours of therapy and the implementation of visual, tactile, and/or kinesthetic strategies to aid in vowel production, clear speech was not a reasonable goal for many profoundly deaf children. Even deaf individuals who worked hard at consonant articulation precision had difficulty with overall intelligibility because of the one-two combination of substandard vowel production and atypical rhythm and intonation patterns.

Early auditory access to the characteristics of the human voice as it functions in natural, communicative exchanges should be sufficient for many children to enable them to replicate what is heard and monitor their own attempts at "matching" what they say with what they hear. Even though a child will likely receive an implant after the babbling milestone has passed, professionals who embrace the concept of "listening age" (commonly accepted as a recalculation of age beginning with the time of auditory access) may expect that a child will experience this and other developmental stages at an age adjusted for the time at which the implant was activated. For example, a 24-month-old child who received an implant at age 18 months has a listening age of 6 months. This youngster, despite his chronologic age, may be set to do some developmental babbling very shortly as there has been a period of auditory input, which may serve to trigger this productive expression.

Another outward sign of the power of auditory access comes in the "jargoning phase." This is a time when articulation precision has not yet been developed and the child produces speech that is not intelligible but uses adult intonation patterns in a delightful yet perplexing string of utterances. Children with implants have been observed to demonstrate "jargoning" ability within their own idiosyncratic time frame. The appearance of jargon signals that the child is on a developmental path that should lead to the ultimate production of clear speech with minimal focused intervention on the production of particular phonemes. However, it should be noted that any child may demonstrate a need for speech production assistances that is not necessarily an outcome of hearing loss. The speech-language pathologist will want to monitor and inventory the acquisition of speech sounds, using some of the developmental norms suggested earlier as a yardstick for referral.

When a child who is somewhat older (between the ages of 3–5, for example) receives an implant, the temptation is great to jump into consonant work to give shape to the emerging vocabulary. Speech and hearing professionals who understand the importance of a solid foundation for speech production will again begin with voicing, vowels, rhythm, and intonation if these important elements are absent at the time of implantation. Children who are older may be ready to participate in formal testing. Traditional tools for assessing and evaluating speech may be administered to these youngsters in order to objectively assess the child's skills and abilities and contextualize them by considering both chronologic and listening age.

Articulation and Intelligibility

When assessing the speech production of children with cochlear implants, it is necessary to evaluate both articulation and overall intelligibility. Historically, any one of a number of articulation tests have been administered to deaf children to assess a child's ability to produce consonants of English in various positions within a word (i.e., initial, medial, and final). These instruments most often call for a child to name a picture; the child's response is reviewed by the examiner (in most cases, a speech-language pathologist) and the quality of the production of the target is noted. Assessments designed for hearing children primarily evaluate the production of consonants but, in general, do not consider the production of vowels.

Teachers of deaf children and speech-language pathologists may be more accustomed to compiling inventories of speech sounds. Using a model-imitation task, which may or may not be supported by print prompts, both vowel and consonant productions are evaluated. But, for children with hearing loss, the ability to produce the individual phonemes of English does not tell the whole story with regard to evaluation of speech production skills. The many additional aspects of producing clear speech are not addressed in standard tests of articulation or phoneme inventories. Features of spoken language production that contribute to intelligibility include: voice quality, rhythm, intonation patterns, and rate of speech. A number of instruments to assist intelligibility evaluation, many of which rely on reading ability, are available for the objective measure of the understandability of speech. Other assessment tools "predict" intelligibility through the measurement of particular vowel and voiced/voiceless consonant contrasts. Regardless of which formal tool is selected to evaluate the speech production skill of children with cochlear implants, regular video-recording of the production of connected speech is recommended as a means to chronicle changes in speech intelligibility over time.

PROVIDING SPEECH SERVICES

The speech-language pathologist is considered to be the lead professional in providing speech intervention in schools today. Although a number of schools for deaf children continue to utilize a "teacher as speech teacher model," the responsibility for assessment and development of an intervention plan usually falls to the SLP. More often than not, SLPs work with children with implants individually for intensive and focused practice on the integrated development of auditory, speech, and spoken language skills. Just how much time is to be devoted to this individualized intervention is one of the questions most frequently asked when considering the development of an IEP to meet the needs of a child with a cochlear implant. Best practice principles suggest that a child who is a new implant recipient receive more services earlier on in the process in an effort to "jump start" listening skill and spoken language development. The crucial relationship between listening and speaking cannot be overstated. Thus, time devoted to building auditory proficiency serves the dual function of developing speech production ability. Children who are longer term, successful users of the implant and demonstrate the ability to be auditory learners may need less attention to speech development, although continued support for vocabulary and content learning may be asked of the speech and hearing professional.

An intervention plan for children who receive a cochlear implant may include both developmental techniques and corrective strategies as dictated by the presenting level of the child's speech at the time of habilitation. On one end of the continuum is the child who simply requires a clear spoken language model from which he or she can induce the rules of pronunciation and follow, for the most part, normal developmental milestones for speech production. On the other end of the continuum may be a late-implanted, congenitally deaf teenager with speech that is largely unintelligible due to the absence of underlying breath support and a harsh vocal quality, as well as poor vowel production and a limited consonant repertoire. What is a reasonable goal for this student? Should the interventionist attempt to systematically develop sounds, both vowels and consonants, and begin a building block approach to speech production? In a recent program sponsored by the State Department of Education in Wisconsin, Quinn (2005) reported a protocol for intervention that might be appropriate for a recipient fitting a profile such as described above. For users presenting with largely unintelligible speech, Quinn suggested that the student identify words, phrases, and sentences that would be useful in the negotiation of daily interactions. A student's speech therapy plan would then provide ample opportunity to produce these key linguistic elements; with each production, the interventionist would evaluate overall clarity and provide specific feedback on "making it clearer." Sometimes this might require that the student raise volume; sometimes the student may need to put final sounds on key words; sometimes the student may need to address the rate of speaking. Idiosyncratic error patterns preclude the prescription of a specified plan. Quinn also warned that, in working with such a student, there is no guarantee that subsequent productions of a practiced phrase would not include new errors. After months of therapy, improvements in speech production on preselected key words and phrases may be noted but it is not likely that there will be a measurable difference in overall intelligibility. However, real differences in functional communication "success" may foster a sense of progress because speech, albeit controlled and limited, is being understood. Speech-language pathologists who develop intervention plans that begin with good assessment and identification of the highest priority need of the child will be more likely to make *measurable* progress, even if progress is slow.

The Speech Team

It would be short-sighted to assume that individualized speech intervention for a set period of time daily or weekly would be sufficient to promote real and meaningful changes in speech production in more naturalistic settings. To facilitate the generalization of speech (and spoken language and listening) skills into the classroom or home environment, carefully planned carryover strategies may need to be implemented. One way to encourage generalization is to heighten the awareness of the parents and classroom teacher to a child's "personal best" as demonstrated in the structured setting. This can be accomplished in a number of ways, the least intrusive of which might be written communication regarding acquired and targeted skills. However, there is nothing more powerful than an actual demonstration of acquired skills. Teachers have positively commented on a child's unanticipated performance after hearing a student's "personal best" production of a particular phoneme, word, or other speech skill. Knowledge of the level of personal best will enable the teacher (or parent) to set higher standards for speech production in the classroom (or home) environment.

The rather recent phenomenon of "push-in" or collaborative service delivery for any professional providing related services presents an ideal opportunity to assist in helping the classroom teacher become more familiar with a child's particular skills and abilities. Push-in services are characterized by individualized, goal-based intervention that takes place within the classroom, not the therapy room. As the field of speech-language pathology moves toward greater acceptance of "push-in" speech services (in contrast to more traditional "pull-out" services) a dual benefit may, in fact, be observed. First, because the child with an implant has an opportunity to use acquired speech skills in the classroom, the direct relationship between pull-out activities and meaningful use of these skills outside the therapy room can be demonstrated. Second, when an SLP provides services in the classroom, the teacher can oversee and overhear the strategies and techniques that elicit best production (Garber & Nevins, 2005). When these same classroom teachers "raise the bar" for spoken language output in the classroom, and have strategies or prompts to assist the child in producing clearer speech, there is greater likelihood that intelligible speech will be an effective communication tool that has value beyond the therapy setting.

SUMMARY

For many years the oral/manual debate was fueled by poor outcomes in speech production of children with the greatest hearing loss. Today, cochlear implant technology overrides the need for this controversy. Functionally intelligible speech is a possible goal for many implant recipients; for the youngest children receiving implants, the developmental path toward clear speech is straightforward. Using guidelines established by the larger field of developmental phonology, and relying on the auditory capacity of implant technology, education and speech and hearing professionals should expect that, under the right conditions, children can develop intelligible speech. A more corrective and rehabilitative approach may be required by children who are implanted at later ages. However, underlying developmental principles for intelligible speech production still apply and should not be ignored. All professionals on the child's habilitative team should assume responsibility for encouraging the child's best speech production at all times; the speech-language pathologist is encouraged to share particular strategies and techniques that will assist educational professionals in meeting this goal.

Chapter 8

AUDITORY ACCESS AND LITERACY DEVELOPMENT

In the two decades of cochlear implant use in children, research has systematically focused on the various outcomes associated with implantation. From speech perception to reading achievement, advantages to children using this technology have been investigated and quantified. Benefit from implantation on measures of speech perception and speech production were clearly apparent early on for many youngsters with profound hearing loss, especially those with a short duration of deafness. After identifying the positive effects of implantation in listening and speaking, it was natural for the speech and hearing community to look for advantages in language development as a function of implant use. Deficits associated with the English language development of youngsters with profound hearing loss using hearing aids have been well documented. It was anticipated that auditory access from the cochlear implant would assist in the language learning process of these children. Indeed, the early use of the cochlear implant during the language learning years has resulted in linguistic gains on both receptive and expressive measures of language as higher levels of syntactic complexity have been reached earlier by implant recipients. As each new frontier explored yielded advantages to implant users over profoundly deaf hearing-aid users, the educational community was poised to see whether or not there could be a link between cochlear implantation and improved reading performance. Although there have always been individual children with hearing loss capable of reading at levels commensurate with their hearing age-mates (among them, deaf children of deaf parents), the larger majority of deaf children have achieved reading comprehension levels at a national average of fourth grade.

The good news is that for many children with severe-to-profound hearing loss, the gains provided by the cochlear implant have given them a greater chance to achieve reading comprehension ability more similar to their hearing age-mates. How is it possible that an auditory device results in improved reading comprehension? A closer look at the development of reading skills sets the stage for exploring the relationship between the cochlear implant and reading comprehension development.

PREREQUISITES FOR READING SKILLS DEVELOPMENT

According to reading specialists, a number of skills are necessary for children to develop in advance of reading instruction. These include sufficient cognitive development to support reading, experiential knowledge with a wide range of developing schema, substantial vocabulary, linguistic competence in English, and the ability to infer meaning. It would be naïve to suggest that any discussion of reading could begin without stating the obvious—the ability to derive meaning from print requires a cognitive system that will support the decoding of arbitrary written symbols to form words that can be retrieved from the mental lexicon. For the most part, this is a native ability, although the richness or lack of a good environment for learning may influence cognitive development. It is sufficient to say that, unless a child has normal range cognitive function, reading achievement will be limited as a result of this constraint (and not hearing loss).

A second factor that contributes to reading success is background knowledge, that is, the amount and organization of prior knowledge a student has stored in memory to assist in reading with comprehension. Children reading stories that present familiar themes (such as caring for pets or making new friends) will have real personal experience to help them understand what they read. On the other hand, reading stories that have little basis for connecting to their own lives (as in an urban student reading about chores on a farm) makes it more critical for readers to build meaning from the text without the benefit of prior knowledge regarding what is being read. The greater the store of this knowledge and the better organized it is for retrieval, the more likely the reader will be to interact successfully with the text to derive meaning. This storage and retrieval system is often referred to as the child's schema (Rumelhart, 1982). Children with reduced or underdeveloped schemata are at risk for reading with only limited comprehension.

The relationship between vocabulary and reading comprehension has been investigated for decades. While there is no evidence to suggest a *causal* relationship between the two (i.e., reading with comprehension is a result of a good vocabulary), there is most definitely a *correlation* between vocabulary and reading comprehension. It has been observed that "good readers" have "good vocabularies" (and vice versa). Stanovich (1986) labeled this phenomenon the "Matthew Effect" citing that, with regard to vocabulary and reading, the "rich get richer" and (unfortunately) the "poor get poorer." Stanovich would maintain that most vocabulary learning is the result of avid reading and the encountering of less common words in print. It makes sense, however, that children who can easily decode familiar words during early reading experiences will be more likely to develop the positive feedback loop that encourages continued reading and vocabulary accrual. Coming to the reading task with a well-developed spoken language vocabulary will set the stage for the first important task of reading: learning to read known words. The first tier of vocabulary in early reading tasks should present the emerging reader with little challenge. However, students who begin the reading task with a vocabulary gap (showing a spoken vocabulary that is limited in breadth and depth as compared to their age-mates) are at risk for increasing the size of that gap as the demands of the curriculum grow over time. This will evoke the "Matthew Effect" (in this case, the negative, the poor get poorer) and may result in a child's spending decreased time in reading to avoid frustration.

Considering the fact that listening and talking are opposite sides of the reading and writing coin, it seems only natural that linguistic competence is necessary for reading with comprehension. In fact, many of the tasks that are presented to young readers to gauge comprehension require a spoken language response. A new emphasis on story retelling as an assessment of "getting the main idea" requires the ability to develop a cohesive narrative that focuses on key points and not minor details. Thus, the ability to produce a response that includes a number of related ideas is necessary.

Furthermore, young readers rely on an auditory representation of their oral language to determine if what they have read "sounds right." For example, a child who reads, "Sally heard Jimmy call out to *her*" will likely read the pronoun correctly (and not misread it as "here") because it sounds the way English should sound. Knowledge of the syntactic rules of English, though still implicit at the very young ages, assists in decoding text successfully. Children with an age-appropriate syntax system, should demonstrate the ability to limit word choices based on their knowledge of grammar. Attention to the tense system of English will also assist the reader in predicting what words might come next. "After Bobby paid for his new sneakers, he wore them home." In this sentence the use of the past tense verb in the independent clause, "wore" is signaled by the use of the verb "paid" in the dependent, introductory clause.

In addition, reading phrase units is reliant upon a larger understanding of how spoken language sounds. The appropriate use of voice and pausing in reading with comprehension is also reflective of linguistic understanding. Consider the way in which you might "chunk" the reading of the following sentence, mindful of the use of the relative clause: "It was the man who saw the thief, that the police wanted to question."

The ability to make inferences is a necessary skill in order to read with comprehension. Fountas and Pinnell (2001) state that inferring involves "going beyond the literal meaning of a text to derive what is not there but is implied." Contemplate, however, that this same skill may be developed (before text is involved) by discussing pictures or talking about characters in movies. This and other strategies for expanding meaning may be developed in spoken language activities so that they will be available for use in the later years when applied to reading tasks.

How will a cochlear implant assist a child in developing prerequisite skills for reading? It appears that children with implants have an advantage in developing the background knowledge and experiential schema that have been shown to contribute to reading success. Consider the young deaf child with a cochlear implant who has the opportunity to simultaneously process an event or experience and the language and vocabulary of that event because of the auditory access provided by the device. This is in stark contrast to the opportunities historically afforded a deaf child with hearing aids; deaf children using traditional amplification often had to "practice" language before participating in a particular activity. Parents and teachers would laboriously prepare the child for what was about to occur, anticipating what might happen, and then arrange for the experience to take place. Once the actual event was over, it was once again time for extensive linguistic elaboration on the shared experience. The cochlear implant allows for the efficient dual processing of language *and* events such that less time is required in preparation and follow-up. This enables a child with an implant to have more quality experiences, along with the simultaneous exposure to the language that serves to organize them. The more efficient the learning, the greater are the number of opportunities for expansion of experiences. Here, too, the rich get richer.

Study of the receptive and expressive vocabulary of youngsters who use cochlear implants has yielded impressive gains when compared with severe-to-profoundly deaf children using hearing aids (Schopmeyer et al., 1997) This advantage in the development of the lexicon in both breadth and depth is generally attributed to the superior auditory access provided by the implant, which allows for incidental learning of vocabulary. The ability to "overhear" new words, and the context in which they are used, allows the child with the cochlear implant to add to the vocabulary stockpile available as the reading process is begun.

The same phenomenon at work in learning vocabulary applies to the development of spoken language. Deaf children who use cochlear implants have an advantage over their peers with profound hearing loss who have used hearing aids to learn spoken language. Overhearing mature language experts allows these language novices to build auditory representations of adult syntactic forms. This mirrors the universal manner in which children acquire linguistic competence. Research supports advanced development of syntax in children with cochlear implants when compared to their profoundly deaf peers using hearing aids (Robbins et al., 1994).

The domino effect of positive outcomes attributed to the use of the cochlear implant in speech perception, speech production, vocabulary learning, and syntax development has set the stage for youngsters to learn from their world experiences and develop the thinking skills that will catapult them into emerging literacy. A discussion of strategies to foster the acquisition of reading skills in children who use cochlear implants appears later in this chapter.

PARENTS AS PARTNERS ON THE LITERACY TEAM

Recall the earlier acknowledgement of the relationship of spoken language skills to reading ability. With that in mind, any and all efforts to develop language and vocabulary can essentially be seen as making a contribution to reading development. Both professional and popular literature on child-rearing emphasized the important role that parents play in providing language input. In addition, capitalizing on the literacy artifacts and events that take place in the home allows parents to help their children learn to read. Calling attention to the functional use of reading and writing in daily activities is one way that parents can prepare their child for later success in reading. Creating a literacy-rich environment that includes opportunities for shared book experiences will also help children learn how to talk about books. Parents can encourage their children to make connections with text and assist them in developing some higher order thinking skills such as predicting and evaluating as they interact around books. In preparation for code breaking, parents can play word games and rhyming games that draw attention to sounds and symbols. Auditory access provided by the cochlear implant makes activities such as these appropriate for children in advance of formal reading lessons.

LEARNING TO READ

Recently phonics instruction has enjoyed a resurgence among literacy experts. After years of a whole language approach in which experiences contributed more to reading than decoding, a back to basics movement ushered in the return of phonics as a code-breaking methodology. Fortunately, for profoundly deaf students using cochlear implants, learning sound–symbol relationships is made easier due to the improved acoustic representation provided by the device. Consonants are made more audible by the enhanced high-frequency information delivered by the implant, thus contributing to their correct identification. As children with implants are entering the mainstream at earlier ages, many will be learning to read in classrooms with their hearing peers and have the auditory access that allows them to benefit from phonic instruction.

Best practice in phonics teaching calls for direct, systematic, and intensive instruction in which graphophonemic relationships are developed (Adams, 1990). Consonants are generally taught before vowels, as there are fewer variations in the sounds that are represented by a particular symbol. For example, the symbol /d/ represents its associated sound, as in the word "dirty" with greater consistency than does the symbol /a/ which sometimes represents the sound which occurs in the word "cap" and sometimes in the word "cape."

The professional responsible for reading instruction first introduces consonant sounds in initial positions. Once a number of sounds have been presented, children are challenged to categorize words according to initial consonants. Vowel symbols are then introduced. Consonants in the final position receive additional instruction and, after a number of consonant and vowels are established, instruction moves to blending sounds into regular CVC words. Teachers are encouraged to present reading selections that apply newly learned relationships in easily decoded material. Over time, the ability to recognize all regular sound-symbol relationships as well as exceptions to the rules contributes to the fluent reading of connected and meaningful text.

Another approach to beginning reading instruction has its roots in practices that have long been a part of education of deaf children: the language experience approach. With elements of whole language, language experiences can be considered a top-down approach in that emphasis is on the reader and his or her background knowledge rather than the text itself. Many children with hearing loss have successfully learned to read using language experience stories written expressly for them by the classroom teacher. Capitalizing on shared experiences, the teacher and students write a paragraph summarizing an activity, lesson, or field trip. There is high predictability in the text for the emerging reader because students have knowledge of the sequence of events of the activity, the "characters" of the experience, and their actions. Subsequent rereadings of the language experience encourage the transfer of predictable words to sight vocabulary and print.

The use of basal readers as an all-inclusive code-breaking and reading comprehension program has both its supporters and detractors. Historically, basal readers presented an incrementally more challenging text for the emerging through the independent reader that spanned a child's elementary school years. Those who support the use of basals, praise its systematic development of reading skills and its wealth of associated materials (teacher guides, student workbooks, and assessments). Those who are uneasy about the use of basal readers in the classroom are concerned about defining a reading curriculum with a basal reading program and question the authenticity of the reading experience promoted by basal texts.

Regardless, there continues to be teacher support for the use of basal texts in classrooms across the country including those in which children with hearing loss are taught. Significant changes in appearance and content of basals over the years have contributed to their longstanding acceptance. Today, teachers who view the basal reader as one tool for reading instruction, and use it selectively based on the needs of the readers in his or her classroom, may find that the conscious decision to use or adapt basal materials makes for more focused and effective instruction.

READING TO LEARN

Once sufficient code-breaking has taken place, there is an observable shift in the complexity of the vocabulary and syntax of text that students are asked to read. In addition, the maturity of themes that children consider in their reading grows. In the most progressive classrooms, the majority of a child's school day is spent in authentic reading and writing activities that may include guided, as well as independent, reading and writing. There may be vocabulary development for new words in Language Arts, word study or analysis for understanding spelling and pluralization, and content reading in science and social studies. These activities represent Chall's (1979) "critical third stage of reading"; unfortunately, this is the point at which a plateau in reading ability has been observed by researchers studying the reading achievement of deaf children (Allen, 1986; Marschark & Harris, 1996). In a discussion of the literacy milestones reached by deaf children with cochlear implants, Spencer et al. (2003) stated that "level three skills are crucial, because once mastered, a child is then capable of learning and analyzing information from multiple viewpoints. If a child has difficulty acquiring stage three reading skills, this affects a host of academic areas, including writing" (p. 238). In their sample of 16 pediatric implant users, age-matched to 16 hearing children, Spencer and her colleagues found that the 9- and 10-year-olds that they studied had all attained Chall's critical stage of reading, level 3. Furthermore, Spencer and her colleagues found a strong correlation between language performance and reading performance. Thus, one might hypothesize that the documented language gains attributed to the use of the cochlear implant led to commensurate gains in reading skills.

The reader is advised, however, to temper expectations for near-average reading achievement for all children who receive cochlear implants. It is likely that reading ability varies in the population of implant users in the same manner as in the general population; general performance with cochlear implants varies as well. Thus, it is prudent to be cautious in interpreting the results of Spencer's study. In fact, in one of the more recent studies of reading achievement of deaf children using cochlear implants, Geers et al. (2005) found that, on average, a group of twenty-six, 15- to 16-year-old students with implants achieved reading comprehension grade equivalent scores of 7.7; 52% of those subjects scored within the normal range of reading as measured on the Peabody Individual Achievement Test. All the students in the Geers study received implants before age 5, with the majority of students receiving implants after age 3. These students had been tested at ages 8 to 9; in that study of 181 children, (62%) were found to be scoring within the normal range of reading comprehension. Based on the longitudinal data reported in 2005 study, Geers et al. concluded that the early use of the cochlear implant facilitated language and literacy development. Good readers in high school exhibited good language, phonologic decoding, and speech perception in elementary school. However, all children who scored within the average range at age 8 or 9 did not demonstrate age-appropriate reading levels at age 15 to 16. Some students struggled with reading after grade 4 and were unable to meet the demands of reading as the curriculum advanced.

BEST PRACTICE FOR LITERACY DEVELOPMENT IN CHILDREN WITH COCHLEAR IMPLANTS

There is nothing to suggest that special strategies or practices need to be implemented for the development of reading comprehension in deaf children with cochlear implants beyond those considered to be best practice for all children. However, there are a number of particular areas in which a child with an implant should be monitored and supported for maximal development. These include those that are traditionally at risk: vocabulary development, complex syntax, figurative language, and the development of metacognitive strategies for reading with comprehension.

VOCABULARY BUILDING

Beyond the initial task of the emerging reader to learn to decode known words, the lifelong reader will need to successfully engage in vocabulary accrual activities in order to add to the lexicon. By 4th grade, a child is expected to recognize, in print, 3,000 of the words that are in the mental lexicon at age 6 (Chall, 1983). Following that accomplishment, the task of vocabulary learning includes learning new meaning for known words ("operate" for "run"), learning new words that represent known concepts ("image" for "picture"), and learning new words that stand for new concepts ("unfathomable," "disintegrate") (Gunning, 1996). In fact, it has been suggested that young readers must learn an average of eight new words each day to keep pace with the lexical demands of texts they read. Any child, especially a child with a cochlear implant, is at risk for having idiosyncratic gaps in the mental lexicon. Indeed, although children with implants have been shown to have better receptive and expressive vocabularies than their profoundly deaf peers using hearing aids, an interesting observation can be made about the challenges that remain in the area of vocabulary accrual.

On more than one occasion, it has been noted that, although children with implants have a number of lexical items in a particular category, they will often be unfamiliar with the superordinate term that labels the grouping. For example, the child may know "ring," "bracelet," and "necklace" but be unable to supply the term "jewelry" to refer to the class. This may suggest the need for vocabulary networking and semantic mapping as instructional strategies particularly appropriate for children with implants.

Whether vocabulary is learned incidentally or intentionally, there are a number of factors that will contribute to its growth. The successful learning of vocabulary for a child with an implant is dependent on opportunity, a good acoustic environment, and the availability of a mature language user to help map the new word into a child's existing lexicon. The first factor, opportunity, addresses the importance of rich experiences to provide the impetus for new vocabulary learning. A child who is reticent to explore the world and who has few experiences beyond home and school may have limited prospects for acquiring new words in novel, yet meaningful, circumstances. The second factor, a good acoustic environment, speaks directly to the need for a vocabulary learning experience that is free from background or ambient noise. Given the fact that incidental learning is possible with the cochlear implant, the ability to overhear someone's use of new words presumes an auditory environment which does not compete with the novel lexical items. Consider how difficult it is to process familiar words in a background of noise; it is virtually impossible to understand unfamiliar words in anything but the best acoustic environment. Finally, the third factor, the presence of a language expert to facilitate learning new words, is extremely important, particularly in situations in which the meanings of novel words cannot be determined by context (either auditory or print). The availability of a source that can help the student "map" the new word into the lexicon by relating it to the student's existing store of knowledge can mean the difference between learning a new word or having it fall by the wayside.

Some reading specialists would argue that the challenge of building vocabulary is so huge that no amount of instruction will make a dent in the task. The recommendation by others to provide *intentional* instruction in vocabulary learning has appeal for students who are unsuccessful in acquiring new words from reading literary texts. Explicit instruction in learning how to learn new vocabulary should "enhance the speed, quantity and quality of vocabulary development" (Fountas & Pinnel, 2001). Any number of resources will assist the speech and hearing professional in locating direct instruction strategies for teaching vocabulary, most notably Johnson's (2001) *Vocabulary in the Elementary and Middle School.*

COMPLEX SYNTAX

As early as second grade, sentences that appear in reading texts become increasingly more complex. Sometimes this complexity takes the form of sentences that contain both dependent and independent clauses, while at other times, it may be because of the use of relative clauses. From a third-grade basal reader comes the following sentence: *They understood what their father had meant when he said that sooner or later they would find a treasure in the earth.* In still other circumstances, the tense system of English presents particular challenges to the reader. Consider the following sentence from the same third-grade basal reader: *We would never have been able to get out of the valley if the water had caught us.*

For students who are challenged to read authentic literature in the form of trade books, the likelihood of encountering complex syntax grows logarithmically. Dialogue may also become more colloquial, which may be difficult for some readers to appreciate. In Beverly Cleary's *Dear Mr. Henshaw* (1984), Leigh Botts, the main character, has this to say about writing: *"It wasn't so bad when it wasn't for a book report or a report on some country in South America or anything where I had to look things up in the library."* Teachers and speech-language pathologists who are aware of these difficult grammatic structures may want to spend an extra moment in ascertaining that the author's intent is not obscured for the child with a cochlear implant by the complexity of the syntax.

An additional aspect of our language that has always proved troublesome to young readers with hearing loss is the use of figurative or nonliteral language in texts. Reading and assigning meaning to nonliteral language contributes to comprehending text. It is true that implant recipients have greater opportunities to hear and process idiomatic language in meaningful conversational contexts. They should be able to bring a greater store of nonliteral language and their real meanings to the reading task. The unfortunate fact about this linguistic phenomenon is that almost every instance of figurative language requires it own interpretation. Knowing that "dropping someone off" means to bring that person to a particular place on the way to another destination will not assist the reader in understanding that referring to something that is a "drop in the bucket" means it is a small amount. Calling attention to the not-so-obvious use of nonliteral language found in reading selections may simply be "a drop in the bucket" but doing so may serve to reinforce the concept that sometimes words don't quite mean what they say.

MONITORING READING COMPREHENSION

Mature readers develop comprehension-monitoring strategies that will assist them in reading with meaning. The idea of thinking about reading, often referred to as metacognition (literally, thinking about thinking) is hypothesized as allowing the reader to process text in a deeper way. Expert readers know that reading is supposed to make sense and, when faced with problems that arise during reading, they implement strategies to assist in returning to smooth and fluent reading. The difference between an experienced and inexperienced reader is the availability and selection of particular strategies that will allow this reading recovery. The speech and hearing professional is once again referred to more comprehensive discussion of metacognition in Fountas and Pinnel's (2001) *Guiding Readers and Writers*.

CHALLENGES TO THE READING PROCESS

The premise of this chapter has been that the child with the cochlear implant is obtaining maximal benefit and is functioning auditorily and linguistically at age-appropriate levels. As implant performance will vary depending on a number of factors that have already been presented in the "zone," teachers of children who are not reaching reading benchmarks will require a different instructional approach. In these cases, the school-based professional is directed to resources expressly designed for teaching deaf children in more traditional methodologies appropriate for their auditory status.

For example, when phonic-based approaches do not appear to be working, the school-based professional may take a more experiential approach to instruction whereby reading vocabulary is learned in stories about shared activities. Vocabulary learned through experienced stories can then be used to create novel stories for decoding and comprehension without the benefit of direct experience. It is important for the speech-language pathologist, classroom teacher, and reading specialist (if available) to work collaboratively in this or other alternative approaches to provide a consistent format for breaking the code.

SUMMARY

Auditory access provided by the cochlear implant presents the young recipient with the opportunity to develop some of the skills prerequisite to reading instruction: vocabulary, command of the syntax of English, and a well-developed storage system for cataloging world experiences. Implant technology will also support today's emphasis on phonics instruction as the preferred path for breaking the code of reading during early literacy instruction. More children with implants are reading at higher levels of achievement than previously seen when using hearing aid technology. Although this cannot be perfectly predicted by performance in the elementary years, data suggest that children who demonstrate good reading ability at age 8 to 9 will be more likely to continue with these abilities in upper grades. Despite the advantages seen by large numbers of deaf children using cochlear implants in reading achievement, it must be remembered that the cochlear implant will not overcome reading deficits beyond those directly associated with peripheral hearing loss. The incidence of reading disability will likely be seen in the population of implant users in the same proportion as it is seen in the population of hearing children. Children with cochlear implants will continue to need support to capitalize on the auditory advantage of the cochlear implant with regard to reading comprehension.

Chapter 9

SUPPORTING COMMUNICATION WITH SIGN

By the early 1970s, the options for educating deaf children had evolved into two distinct camps—one that espoused an auditory-oral approach while another embraced the use of sign language. The limitation on hearing aid technology often was the driving force behind placing children in one of these two tracks. As parents grappled with decisions to keep their children oral, the use of "total communication" (a term often used to include any use of sign language with any use of speech) as a hybrid option emerged. In the early days of cochlear implantation, the number of children using total communication far exceeded the number of children enrolled in auditory-oral programs. Interestingly, that trend seems to have reversed itself as children as young as 12 months of age are receiving implants. Specifically, young children receiving implants (before the age of two), often become successful spoken language learners as a result of the early auditory access provided by the implant. However, there are still a sizable number of children who use sign language and receive cochlear implants. Some young children can be considered "short-term" sign communicators in that they use sign to accrue language visually prior to auditory access. Once they receive the implant, focus on spoken language input and output through the auditory channel begins in earnest. "Long-term" sign communicators may include children for whom the parents have made a conscious choice to include sign language as part of a comprehensive communication plan. For these children, the use of the cochlear implant is largely seen as another tool for overall language learning. The child's own responsiveness to spoken language input, or "auditory inclination," will dictate the degree to which listening and speaking will become a part of the communication repertoire. Both short-term and long-term groups have been observed to make progress with the cochlear implant (Geers et al., 2000; Robbins et al., 1999). Providing habilitative support for these two distinct groups is the challenge facing school-based professionals today.

SHORT-TERM SIGN COMMUNICATORS

Acknowledgment of the role that sign language plays in language development for deaf babies of deaf parents has resulted in a movement by general society to utilize this methodology to communicate early with their infants. The impetus to teach hearing children to sign is based on the research in language acquisition of deaf children of deaf parents using American Sign Language (ASL) at home. Because the manual "articulators" develop before the oral musculature required for speech production, the first expressive word in sign generally appears before the first spoken word in hearing children (Wilbur, 1987).

Encouraged by the larger acceptance of sign, some hearing parents are choosing to teach their deaf infants sign language as they age toward the FDA-approved 12-month mark for implantation. One must keep in mind that, in the context of hearing parents using sign, it is likely that single-word communication is used to develop a few key concepts and signs (open, more, milk, hurt, etc.). This building block approach to language development is one that is not generally proposed for language learning. As suggested elsewhere in this text, fluent and connected language (whether the language be sign or spoken) provides access to the rhythm of language (whether auditory or represented visually) on which subsequent language builds. Consider that deaf parents are signing fluently to their children and their experience in language learning parallels the experience of hearing parents communicating fluently with their hearing children. Hearing parents are learning certain signs to use with their children and are most likely not modeling sign *language* but sign *vocabulary.*

Children who have used sign communication for longer periods of time and get a cochlear implant pose a particular challenge to the speech and hearing professionals with whom they work. As the child continues to use sign for communication and academic purposes, the professional who is accustomed to the immediate visual feedback possible in sign may rely on this modality and not provide enough auditory or spoken language support. This results in two dilemmas. The first presents itself when early interventionists, teachers, and speech-language pathologists are asked to set aside their familiar modality of communication, (i.e., sign) to implement spoken language strategies that will challenge the child's auditory and speech output. The second dilemma emerges from the first, as the speech and hearing professional must infer comprehension of the spoken language input as opposed to seeing it. Early auditory development models suggest that there is a natural lag between spoken language input and expressive language output. When children are in the period of auditory absorption, there is little indication that they have indeed heard what was presented. This uncertainty causes many professionals to be reluctant to de-emphasize sign input for fear of losing precious time in cognitive and social development in a language that has already been established. This cycle of uncertainty contributes to reduced auditory input, resulting in reduced spoken output. Experience suggests, however, that it is possible for short-term sign communicators to make a full transition to oral communication after a period of implant use that includes aggressive auditory habilitation. It is during this period that the child is primed to respond to the "auditory inclination" that is now possible. This is only accomplished if the interventionist buys into the effectiveness of *spoken* language input leading to overall learning and *spoken* language output. Until and unless this becomes the belief system of the professionals providing services, the child will not receive the support that is necessary to maximize the potential of the implant and make the transition to oral language.

Professionals often ask, "Can't I sign at all to the child with an implant?" Although it is difficult to present a definitive answer to the question without knowing a particular child in a particular situation, it may be helpful to recall the paradigms that are used when learning any second language. For example, popular language learning tools create conversations or dialogues that accompany real life, routine situations. Repetition of these routine situations is the key to successful learning of language and vocabulary. The more exposure to the language, the more it will accrue. This occurs whether the language is developing from English to Spanish, Spanish to English, or sign to English. Thus, we would suggest that in a "total communication" classroom there should be certain periods of the day designated as spoken language times. These may include activities or events that are recurring in the child's daily schedule, such as welcome circle or snack. In these familiar activities, the child can anticipate the language exchange that is about to occur and rely on that memory of the event and its language to assist in learning the appropriate spoken language script.

For the child that seems to make good use of the implant, a professional may gradually build to the point at which new instruction is presented orally only. Consider that it is not necessary for the child to systematically replace all acquired signs with their spoken language counterparts. Rather, new labels for new concepts can be provided using spoken language. In this way, the language learned prior to implantation when visual access was the preferred route to learning is distinct from the language learned after implantation when auditory access was possible. The speech and hearing professional will want to monitor this learning carefully, keep good records of indicators that the child is indeed processing spoken language, and return to known signs, when necessary, to avoid communication frustration. For example, a teacher can *accept* signs from a child in response to a question, but not *use* signs for instruction. When a child uses a sign response the teacher can provide the spoken word and prompt the child to imitate the model. In so doing, transfer of acquired signs to spoken language occurs naturally.

LONG-TERM SIGN COMMUNICATORS

There are a sizable number of cochlear implant recipients who present with sign communication that has "high value on the communication currency market" (Robbins, 2002). These are students for whom a sign system has developed sufficiently to allow it to serve as an efficient tool for communication and academic content learning. These same children, however, may not have the communication skills to engage nonsigners in conversational exchanges. It may be that parents seek implantation for their successfully signing children for the purpose of widening the "circles of intelligibility" to which they have access (Calvert & Silverman, 1986). (The concept of "circles of intelligibility" graphically represents the increasing numbers of individuals with whom a deaf speaker can communicate effectively.) The habilitative team is presented with a quandary when long-term signers receive cochlear implants: to sign or not to sign. Ironically, a child's linguistic abilities through sign, can be used as a foundation for initial auditory work. Concepts and language can be presented in sign first. Once established, the sign can be removed to build auditory skills thereby providing the implant recipient with a familiar model prior to replacing it with the newer auditory model. This ensures early success with listening activities. Furthermore, auditory success enhances the auditory feedback loop which drives the percepts that support production of speech. At this point in time, responses are highly predictable thereby creating the perfect opportunity for the use of speech.

When long-term sign communicators are being educated in schools for the deaf or regional programs for deaf children an obvious dilemma presents itself: How can the teacher provide auditory input to one child when the other children in the classroom rely on sign? Where will the teacher find time to encourage listening skills (and how does one do that anyway?) When long-term sign communicators are being educated in mainstream classrooms with sign interpreters, the challenge to develop auditory skills presents different questions. How can the child follow rapidly paced classroom instruction auditorily if listening skills are just emerging? What is the role of the sign language interpreter in this circumstance? Who takes the lead in providing systematic development of auditory skills and in which venue is this accomplished? An attempt to answer these questions follows as it relates a discussion of small-instruction classrooms for deaf children using sign and mainstream education supported by educational interpreters.

SMALL-INSTRUCTION CLASSROOMS

The term "small-instruction classroom" is used here to replace the more commonly used "self-contained classroom." It is a representation of the learning needs of the children in these classrooms and/or the placement choices made by the parents of, in this case, sign communicators. Within small-instruction classrooms that are designated as Total Communication (TC) or Simultaneous Communication (SC) there is a continuum of actual communication practices that must be scrutinized to determine whether or not they will effectively support the auditory needs of a signing child who receives a cochlear implant. In fact, many schools for deaf children are struggling with the very issue of the relative *instructional* role of audition in classrooms previously designated as SC classrooms. A number of premises have emerged from our experience in working with schools and programs for deaf children that may have utility for discussion here.

Premises for Children Who Sign and Use a Cochlear Implant

1. Parents choose implantation in order to add spoken language to their child's communication repertoire.

2. There is a period of time immediately after implantation in which aggressive auditory management must be instituted to jump-start auditory skill development and determine a child's own auditory inclination.

3. Acquisition of benchmark auditory and speech behaviors is made possible by their direct facilitation.

4. Children's auditory potential and communication needs should drive the creation of instructional groups rather than attempt to fill classrooms that have certain communication designations.

5. There is no signing in an auditory/oral classroom.

6. Auditory input is not auditory instruction

7. School-based professionals need knowledge and skills for implementing best practices in auditory instruction

8. There are benefits that schools and programs for deaf children can provide to children who use implants outside of auditory skill development.

A closer look at each of the premises is warranted to understand the issues facing school professionals working with children who sign and use cochlear implants.

Premise 1: Parents choose implantation in order to add spoken language to their child's communication repertoire.

Experience with hundred of parents of deaf children, the majority of whom are hearing themselves, has led us to conclude that the parents' decision to get an implant for their child is weighted by two important beliefs. The first is that they are choosing the best technology available to them to ameliorate the effects of severe-to-profound hearing loss on their child's subsequent speech, language, and literacy development. All parents are driven by a desire to make good choices for their child; parents who choose implantation never do so without the conviction that they are providing a positive option for their child's future. The second belief is that the cochlear implant will provide direct access to sound, that will, in turn, prompt better listening and *speaking*. Parents are aware that the implant is an auditory device, but more often than not, they are more interested in the spoken language outcomes made possible by the cochlear implant. That being said, it is important that schools utilizing sign communication for instruction develop programs for children with implants that build in an aggressive spoken language component to their listening agenda to effectively meet parents' expectations for performance outcomes after implantation.

Premise 2: There is a period of time immediately after implantation in which aggressive auditory management must be instituted to jump-start auditory skill development and determine a child's own auditory inclination.

Research has indicated that for children who are using sign language "noticeable changes in communication should be seen after three months of implant use" (Robbins, 2002). We would suggest "aggressive auditory management" that must be reviewed every 6 to 9 months be recommended for all new implant recipients regardless of age at implantation. Preimplant assessments will serve as the baseline for determining the starting point of auditory skill and spoken language acquisition. Results from both formal and informal assessments will drive the subsequent planning and/or placement decisions after an introductory period. For children who do not demonstrate the appropriate benchmarks, a review of factors related to implant use and habilitation should be undertaken. Children who demonstrate measurable progress in both perception and production of spoken language (recall that production will always lag behind perception) will continue in a program of aggressive auditory management.

To ensure that the focus on auditory skill development is given proper emphasis, a brief expectation shift with regard to the development of new content for middle-aged and older implant recipients may need to be made. Value should be given to time spent to developing auditory skills as well as learning new academic content. Keep in mind that the general principle of using familiar material to develop new skills is equally applicable in the development of listening behaviors. This may result in less content being covered but the new skills acquired may assist in later academic learning.

Premise 3: Acquisition of benchmark auditory and speech behaviors is made possible by their direct facilitation.

There are a number of checklists and curricula that will provide direction for the systematic development of listening and spoken language skills (McClatchie & Therres, 2003; Wilkes, 1999). Often, expectations for time periods by which particular behaviors will occur relative to time of implantation will also be provided. However, the older the child and the more experience he/she has with a visual language system, the more likely that direct practice of the very behaviors that are being targeted will need to be provided. Rest assured, this is not the same as "teaching to the test." In the case of the development of auditory and spoken language skills, the presentation of activities that identify specific skills as outcomes have a greater likelihood of developing those skills as opposed to activities that provide unfocused "auditory input." Benchmark behaviors will likely not occur in children using sign language unless a child is given both instruction in and opportunity to practice a particular skill.

Premise 4: Children's auditory potential and communication needs should drive the creation of instructional groups rather than attempt to fill classrooms that have certain communication designations.

As schools and programs for deaf children attempt to provide instruction for children with cochlear implants within their walls, the temptation to allow labels rather than children's needs to drive programming is present. Creating auditory/oral classrooms with implantation being the sole criterion for placement regardless of presenting skill level, creates distrust on the part of the teachers and speech-language pathologists who have worked with them. Teachers who believe that implantation has created a return to lockstep auditory/oral instruction for all children who receive the device are troubled by any child's potential to become another "oral failure" reminiscent of some of their past experiences. Rather than conceptualizing the accommodation of children with implants as classes to be filled, introducing the concept of a continuum of auditory instruction in all classrooms may yield greater acceptance by all staff members. This may be represented by the graphic in Figure 9–1, in which auditory/oral-only instruction is represented by the far left circle (no signs are utilized) and on the far right, the circle represents a classroom in which there is no spoken language used (as in an ASL-only classroom).

Premise 5: There is no signing in an auditory/oral classroom.

On one end of the continuum of auditory instruction for children who sign is auditory/oral instruction. In this instructional setting visual input is reserved to mean speech reading assistance to the auditory signal and no formal signs are used. Natural gestures may continue to be utilized to supplement auditory/oral information. Print, as a visual representation of spoken language, may be used as well. Children with sufficient skills to benefit from auditory/oral instruction will likely be grouped based on auditory ability and cognitive/academic functioning.

Premise 6: Auditory input is not auditory instruction.

Because SC classrooms, by definition, provide speech with sign, there is the danger of acceptance of this arrangement to be sufficient for the development of auditory and speech skills. Even when there is talking and signing at the same time, the nature of the input should be considered. In order to provide a genuine spoken language model, grammatically complete and correct English must be the foundation of the SC classroom for children with implants.

Auditory/Sign Instruction Continuum

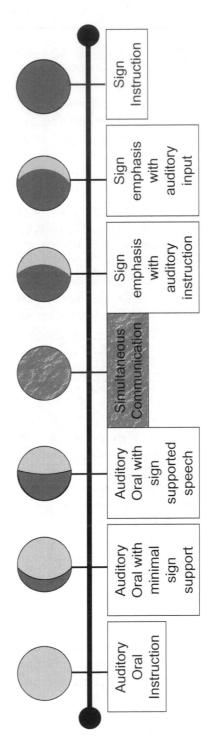

Figure 9–1. Auditory/Sign Instruction Continuum

The rhythm and melody of spoken English that is readily accessible to children with implants will be absent in classrooms in which teachers say only the words they sign. However, when given the opportunity to process a familiar visual signal or attend to an auditory signal that carries less meaning, children with implants who are experienced sign communicators will likely take the path of least resistance and follow instruction visually. This results in a classroom in which there is auditory *input* but not auditory *instruction* (see Figure 9–1). Purposeful instruction that requires auditory attention *and* processing as well as expects spoken language output will better move the child along in the acquisition of the skills targeted by implantation. Several questions were posed earlier in this chapter. Recall that teachers often ask for guidance with respect to providing auditory input to one child when other children in the classroom rely on sign. The individualization of instruction that is demanded by the child's IEP makes it necessary to provide opportunities to challenge one child's skill and ability regardless of the needs of other children. In others words, if *everyone's* needs are always met, then *no one's* needs are ever met. For example, the teacher can pose a question individually to a child with an implant in an auditory-only modality at some point in the teacher-learner exchanges. Additionally, the teacher is directed to find time to encourage listening skills throughout the course of the school day. This can be done during content review times or routine activities when language is predictable. It is only when a child receives opportunities to listen to and produce spoken language only that auditory instruction is taking place.

Premise 7: School-based professionals need knowledge and skills for implementing best practices in auditory instruction.

Cochlear implants represent a relatively new technology when considered in light of the content of teacher preparation programs, and graduate programs in speech-language pathology and audiology. While a number of studies have identified some change in university curricula with regard to implantation (Chute, 2003; Harrington & Powers, 2004), there are numerous individuals charged with providing services to children with implants who have limited knowledge of the technology and what it can and cannot do. Furthermore, strategies and techniques for facilitating the development of audition and spoken language were omitted from many teacher education programs as the emphasis on sign and Deaf Culture issues replaced dwindling interest in speech production by deaf children in all but a very few programs. Thus, there is a cadre of school-based professionals who, through the vagaries of the university training protocols, are ill-prepared to assume the responsibilities facing them when it comes to children with implants. Until recently, teachers and school-based professionals have attempted to acquire new knowledge and develop new skills through attendance at local, regional, state, and/or national conferences. However, there is a movement by State Departments of Education and school and district administration to take responsibility for seeking out and providing guidelines for service delivery and professional development opportunities for school-based professionals. This development, as well as the commitment to educational outreach now provided by some implant manufacturers, is promising.

Premise 8: There are benefits that schools and programs for deaf children can provide to children who use implants unrelated to auditory skill development.

Schools for deaf children continue to explore their ability to provide an environment in which the development of each child's potential with a cochlear implant can be realized. If these institutions can do so, they may be able to provide a place in which deaf children with and without implants have an opportunity to gather and share experiences with others as they explore their individualities of deaf life. They will have access to continued development of sign skills, availability of deaf role models, and an environment in which the development of self-esteem and an identity within the Deaf Community is fully valued. Parents may find these features of a comprehensive educational program attractive for their deaf children with implants and choose education in these settings as being "the best of both worlds."

The identification of the underlying premises that drive instruction in classrooms that use sign language contextualizes the discussion that applies to teachers of deaf children in service delivery.

The issues facing speech and hearing professionals in mainstream education require special consideration.

Mainstream Education for the Child Who Signs

It is not only the deaf child using spoken language who has enjoyed the benefits of mainstream education. So too have children using sign with age-appropriate or near age-appropriate language, reading, and content skills been afforded placement in the general education classroom. Their success in this environment owes a great deal to the educational interpreter. In many instances, this is a single individual that is engaged for a particular child (or children) and who "follows" the child from class to class, from year to year. The responsibilities accorded the educational interpreter are many; when a single interpreter follows a single child over the course of a number of years a strong bond often develops between the two. Sometimes this bond is a healthy one and it grows and changes as the child matures; the child develops more independence and moves through the educational system. At other times, the relationship that develops is one of enabling and dependence that scripts itself into certain behaviors and expectations on the part of the interpreter and the student. Add a cochlear implant to either scenario and suddenly there is confusion and uncertainty as to the role of the educational interpreter for the child with a cochlear implant.

The field of educational interpreting has grown to a viable professional discipline within the larger domain of sign language interpreters. Principles and procedures for providing support to deaf children in school settings vary from those applied to work with deaf adults in other settings. As a recognized subspecialty, guidelines and codes of ethics have been prepared by both the professional organization of interpreters, the Registry of Interpreters for the Deaf (RID), and State Departments of Education. Unfortunately, little has been written by recognized experts in the field of educational interpreting about the role of the interpreter for a child who receives a cochlear implant. Seals (2000) has offered one of the only reported treatises on the role of the educational interpreter for children with cochlear implants, although a number of professionals in the implant community have attempted to provide some guidelines for this important member of a child's education team.

THE EDUCATIONAL INTERPRETER

Fundamental to the process of counting on the educational interpreter in the child's habilitative team is including this professional in information dissemination and discussions regarding the changes in the child's Individualized Educational Plan (IEP) as a result of implantation. Experience suggests that interpreters have residual misunderstanding about the technology of the implant that stem from the early, vehement objections of the Deaf Community to implantation in children. Thus, providing information to the educational interpreter about the acoustic access made possible by the implant may provide the rationale for some of the recommendations suggested by the habilitative team. There is some anecdotal evidence to support a number of general observations about emerging auditory skills that can be made about a child with a cochlear implant in a mainstream classroom with an educational interpreter. These observations should be shared with educational interpreters who are assigned to work with children with implants both in the immediate and longer-term postimplantation period.

Because the educational interpreter is often focused on a single child, this professional has the unique opportunity to gauge a child's emerging responses to sound. In the same way that parents are cautioned against testing a child, so too should the educational interpreter refrain from asking the child, "Did you hear that?" Rather, the educational interpreter is encouraged to alert the child to sounds that have occurred or are about to occur (e.g., "I just heard some loud voices in the hallway"). Once the child demonstrates sound detection on his/her own, the educational interpreter may want to label the sound for the child so as to help establish an entry in the child's personal "environmental sound dictionary" (Chute & Nevins, 2002).

Reports from mainstream classrooms indicate that after implant activation there is a gradual and subtle shift in attention that occurs as a child's ability to process sound grows. Initially, the child continues to focus solely on the educational interpreter for all classroom communication. Then, as the child explores the new auditory access, quick glances at the teacher are often observed. With building confidence, the child with an implant may be observed to divide time between attention to the interpreter and the teacher more equally (this may be dependent on the familiarity of the material). It is at this point that many interpreters become uncomfortable because the child isn't "paying attention" when, in fact, it is only that the child has shifted the focus of his or her attention. Educational interpreters will want to continue to provide interpretation and may need to be prepared for an absolute shift in the amount of time that a child with an implant watches and listens to the classroom teacher and makes use of the interpreter's services. We would maintain that a shift in the child's habitual attention does not necessarily signal the need to terminate interpreter services. It simply suggests that the child is making some personal decisions about the way in which these available services will be utilized.

In a similar vein, interpreters should be sensitive to and encourage a child's emerging spoken language skills. Rather than automatically voice for the child with an implant, the educational interpreter may wish to provide the child the opportunity to use developing speech skills. This calls for judiciousness on the part of the educational interpreter; communication frustration should be avoided but not at the expense of abundant opportunities to use developing spoken language skills.

An important component of the changing relationship between an educational interpreter and a child with the cochlear implant deals not simply with audition but also with the child's developing maturity. If building communication independence is an identified goal of implantation, the educational interpreter must constantly review practices to determine if they are supportive of this end result. Candid discussions with the student regarding personal communication responsibility in situations in which this is an appropriate expectation will remove ambiguity about roles in particular settings. Once a student, the classroom teacher, and the educational interpreter have opened the lines of communication, the greater the likelihood that advances in both audition and independence will occur.

In an effort to expand English language skills during content learning, the educational interpreter may need to reconsider standard practices that may actually hinder development of English vocabulary and structure. Under principles for interpreting with conceptually accurate signs, the interpreter may sign "person in charge" for "head." In so doing, the student with an implant may fail to learn this multiple meaning for the word "head" as it was auditorily presented by the teacher but not presented by the interpreter.

Similarly, content-specific vocabulary such as "overpopulation" needs to be acknowledged with more than a sign simplification to "too many people." These real-life examples are from classrooms in which responsible educational interpreters are utilizing conceptually accurate sign. Practices such as these may assist immediate comprehension of the subject matter but fail to build more sophisticated English language vocabulary as found in science and social studies content. Increasing the breadth and depth of English vocabulary is a goal for a student with a cochlear implant. When that student also receives services from an educational interpreter, accommodations such as fingerspelling a multiple meaning word or complex lexical item may need to be incorporated. Procedures and protocols for interpretation for an individual child should be decided upon by the entire educational team and reviewed periodically to assess their effectiveness in assisting the student in comprehending classroom instruction.

SUMMARY

Children who sign have benefitted from cochlear implantation such that many of them, after a period of initial sign use, transition to auditory/oral communication. Still other children continue to use sign along with their implants in educational contexts in which opportunities to listen to and produce spoken language are plentiful. A signing child's own "auditory inclination" may be observed in the immediate postimplantation period. This will drive the development of an IEP that specifies the amount of auditory instruction provided along a continuum of spoken language opportunity within a school or program for the deaf. Other children with implants who sign will be in mainstream settings and will utilize the services of an educational interpreter. This professional should be considered an important member of the educational team and, as such, participate in the planning of policies and procedures that will encourage a child's optimal use of the cochlear implant in the classroom.

Chapter 10

SPECIAL POPULATIONS WITH COCHLEAR IMPLANTS

As more children receive cochlear implants, the diversity normally observed in the larger group of children with hearing loss has filtered through to the implant population. In the early days, implantation was reserved for children who had very profound hearing loss, no other disabilities, and were generally from families where English was the only spoken language. Additionally, children receiving cochlear implants came from families of hearing individuals who very often had access to resources to support them after implantation. As knowledge about implantation has become more mainstream, pediatricians, physicians, schools, and the general media now provide level-one information about this technology on a regular basis. Most recently, the latest IDEA legislation (2005) includes clear language that places cochlear implantation in the list of options for which parents of deaf children would be counseled. The impact of the changes in this law is yet to be realized but, by virtue of the fact that more parents will be informed earlier about implants, the number of potential recipients should grow. Although there is still more work to be done in "getting the word out," the growing diversity of families who have begun to access implantation has contributed to an increasing list of those that can be classified as being part of "special populations." As these are newly evolving groups, data on performance of special populations are scant at best and virtually nonexistent in most cases. Nonetheless, they represent a growing trend that requires the attention of professionals in the academic and medical fields.

For purposes of this chapter, children in the "special population" category include children for whom there is a spoken language in the home other than English, children from lower socioeconomic groups, deaf children of deaf families, children with abnormal cochleas, children with auditory neuropathy, and children with disabilities. The challenges for members in these groups require intervention from school-based professionals that is distinctly different from the more traditional cochlear implant recipient.

CHILDREN WHOSE HOME LANGUAGE IS OTHER THAN ENGLISH

The United States has always been known as a country in which immigrants from all over the world have found their home. There has been no change in this trend as the United States has evolved into a leader of nations around the world. The diversity of cultures, languages, and religions continues to explode as population growth across the country increases. Statistics on children born abroad and living in the United States indicate that 2.5% of children fall into this category (U.S. Census Bureau, 2000). More importantly, the Bureau estimated that approximately 16%, or 8.8 million children in classrooms in the United States speak a second language. It is disturbing to note that 5% of these children are having difficulty learning English as a second language. It is equally distressing to consider the ramifications of these numbers as one considers deaf children with cochlear implants when their home language is not English.

Nationally, Spanish represents the fastest growing language in the United States today. This is not to presume, however, that it is the only language which the classroom professional must address. Languages such as Urdu, Hindi, Korean, Mandarin, Cantonese, and Arabic have also been on the rise as whole groups of cultures move to different portions of the United States to set down their roots.

In fact, because there are so many Spanish-speaking individuals in the United States, there is more likely a chance of identifying professionals in the school system who have knowledge and skills in this language more than any of the other languages. In spite of this fact, the issues facing school personnel appear daunting at times when providing services to these children.

The concerns before teachers, speech-language clinicians, and audiologists for this growing group can be divided into four categories: communication with the family, communication with the child, advocacy, and therapeutic intervention. Each of these areas can have a significant impact on performance. Recall that the zone delineates those factors that contribute to successful implant use. Entry point into the zone and progress through it will affect ultimate benefit with the implant. School professionals who lack an appreciation for the effects that the language of the home plays in implantation may view the implant as being unsuccessful. In fact, in the few studies performed in children with English as a second language, children with implants have demonstrated good outcomes, albeit at a slower rate (Guiberson, 2005; Waltzman et al., 2003). Certainly, these trends must be kept in mind as the school-based professional interacts with these children and their families.

COMMUNICATION WITH THE FAMILY

It is not unusual for family members who do not speak English to avoid school functions including teacher conferences. This may be due to embarrassment on the part of the parent but is often mistaken as lack of concern for the child in school. School-based professionals must make every effort to provide a comfortable, nonthreatening environment for non-English-speaking parents so that they can engage in as many aspects as possible of the child's school life. It is sometimes possible to identify someone in the school who speaks the same language so that an open exchange can take place. Although bringing a friend or family member can assist with translation, this is not the preferred way of communicating as information may be filtered before it is shared with the parent, which may potentially lead to miscommunication. Clearly, the best approach is to engage the services of a professional interpreter to ensure accuracy. Scheduling translation services will make certain that all parties needed for an interaction have been duly informed.

For non-English-speaking parents who may be contemplating implantation for their child, counseling by school professionals will ensure that parents understand the commitment to the process. Again, the importance of having a unbiased interpreter present to translate the information is crucial. When speaking with parents who have some command of English, it is important to limit the use of jargon and offer statements that are rephrased and repeated often. This is not to insinuate that the family should only be given simplistic information, but instead, the school professional should ensure as much understanding as possible by offering the information several times in a variety of formats. Colloquialisms and euphemisms should be avoided at all cost. When talking with parents with limited English skills, the school professional should acknowledge the importance of privacy so that parents may speak freely.

Culture differences must be carefully considered so the professional remains nonjudgmental. Eye contact, facial expressions, concepts of cleanliness, theories of disease, managing of time, status designations based on age, sex, class, and occupation will differ substantially as one digresses from North American culture. Eye contact in many cultures is avoided and can be considered disrespectful to both the speaker and the listener. Facial expressions may vary from those that are expressionless to those that may appear mismatched with the message being delivered. The very presence of silence in a conversation may lead the school-based professional to think that the parent either did not understand what was being said or was not interested. Cleanliness and hygiene may not be within the same societal norms; school-based personnel should be careful not to draw erroneous conclusions about a family's concerns about their child. Theories of disease will also vary substantially. Many cultures view the medical profession with great skepticism and may rely instead on clergy or family elders. This distrust becomes particularly challenging when counseling parents about implants in order to begin the evaluation process. Professionals may feel frustrated that the parent does not immediately follow through with the suggestion to seek an evaluation for their child. Similarly, certain cultures may manage their time differently when it comes to addressing the "medical needs" of their child. Likewise, in many cultures there are certain designations based on age, sex, class, and occupation. Information delivered by a female may not be as acceptable as that delivered by a male; as noted previously, some families may be more accepting of information from clergy than from medical personnel.

Without a doubt, it is important for the school-based professional to be cognizant of cultural differences when communicating with parents whose knowledge of English is limited or nonexistent. However, it is important for parents to realize they must begin to accrue competence in English to continue to keep pace with their child's academic needs and provide assistance with homework and projects. To be most effective, building a trusting relationship over time with genuine concern will work to everyone's advantage.

COMMUNICATION WITH THE CHILD

It is important to assess a child's language competence in English and identify the major language facilitators at home with children whose first language is not English. For children in the early intervention period, professionals should encourage the use of the home language by the parents as they assume the role of the child's first language teachers. For the toddler, who is also spending time at school, the issues may be quite different. Some of the child's day will be spent listening to and producing the home language while other portions of the day will be spent in English. For the older child, issues of refining speech and/or grammar in English are of extreme importance and school personnel should be sensitive to the individual needs and temperament of the child. Acknowledgment of the home language becomes especially relevant if there is another child in the class who also has a similar non-English language. These children may "converse" in their home language while in school or may use vocabulary that switches between both languages. If, by some chance, the teacher or therapist has knowledge of the home language, it can be helpful to use that language to ensure that the child has understood the task at hand. This also demonstrates to children that the school professional values them and their home language.

For the child with a cochlear implant, language-based lessons that use classroom content work best in reinforcing classroom discourse as well as assist in teaching linguistic concepts. For the young implant recipient, classroom routines that are repetitive and are highly contextual will aid the child in developing language in a natural manner. A multisensory approach that allows the child to access language input in a visual and auditory modality works best. However, school professionals must remember that eye contact may have cultural ramifications and that the lack of it may not signal anything more than a cultural difference. Other characteristics of culture may present themselves in the use of certain intonational contours (or lack of them). Recognizing the challenge of harnessing the affective quality of speech in either of the child's languages may require some additional techniques that are integrated in a systematic fashion.

There are a number of strategies that school personnel should be cognizant of when working with children for whom English is not their primary language. The rate of speech should be slightly slower but not elongated so that the natural flow is not compromised. Repetition of other children's answers or questions is also helpful as well as ensuring that the child has some additional time to process what has been said. Teachers and therapists should also be aware of the fact that children who may have proficiency in everyday spoken English may not easily transfer this ability to the academic demands of the classroom (Cummins, 1984). The important issue for school personnel is to allow the development of both languages and not try to suppress the native language in the development of English. Cummins notes that there is more success when the two languages are allowed to mature, and when the home language and culture are not "devalued" by the school.

Finally, the use of computers and Web sites that provide exercises for English as a second language has grown substantially through the years and may facilitate some of the process of learning. However, the overuse of this technology can be a disadvantage especially if left unmonitored by professionals. Parents should participate in homework activities and feel free to talk at home in their native language, so that they are engaged in the process of learning with their child. Interestingly, for children implanted early, the development of spoken language skills in both languages occurs in a manner similar to the hearing child. There may be a slight delay in the emergence of one or both languages but these appear to reach parity over time.

ADVOCACY AND THERAPEUTIC INTERVENTION

Parents whose native language is not English often fall victim to a system that is challenging even for those who speak English. At times, non-English-speaking families of deaf children are the last to learn of the potential of the cochlear implant. At other times, counseling these parents about the implant is minimal and they often leave with the impression that implantation is an instant cure. Families of children who are investigating a cochlear implant should be in communication with other families of the same cultural background. This will provide them with a much needed support base that will help them through the process. Many of the manufacturers have information about cochlear implants in a variety of languages. This information is accessible to professionals to assist them in communicating with the families.

Promoting advocacy and intervention strategies works best when communication with the parent and, when appropriate, the child, is done in an organized and controlled manner with plenty of time for questions and discussion. Families should be a part of the intervention and not feel as if they are outside the therapeutic program. All too often the child's therapy is performed at school and there is little communication with the family about the content of the lessons that are being presented. If the therapist and the teacher do not have any skill in the home language then it is important to identify someone who can act as the intermediary on a regular basis. Engaging the family in the process is always the most successful route when children receive cochlear implants— whether they are native English speakers or not.

CHILDREN FROM LOWER SOCIOECONOMIC HOUSEHOLDS

Although cochlear implant surgery is supported by most insurance providers and state and federal authorities, the necessary follow-up may receive only limited funding or none at all. The mere placement of a cochlear implant in a child does not guarantee success with the device. As noted previously in the discussion of the zone, outcomes are related to a complex set of factors that contribute to success with an implant. Surprisingly, nowhere in the list of factors is the socioeconomic status of the family. This is an emerging area of research that has just begun to be identified by implant facilities (Svirsky & Holt, 2005). The question is not so much one of absolute dollars that a child's family may have, but more one of the degree of access that a certain socioeconomic milieu may provide. Clearly, some families have the financial means to access additional therapy whereas others cannot; however, financial independence does not ensure success although it may contribute to it.

Certain issues place families who are supported through public assistance programs at a distinct disadvantage. For example, children who have equipment break-downs generally wait longer for replacement components as paperwork required in these cases is cumbersome. Children from lower-income families may not be able to purchase batteries when needed and may experience delays in waiting for the correct governmental agency to approve the request. Finally, and most often, these families do not have the same advocacy skills that other parents may have because of limited support structures in their community-at-large.

Recently, Svirsky & Holt (2005) reviewed a subgroup of young children with cochlear implants and found that those from lower socioeconomic families tended to do poorer on tests of speech perception. Likewise, Stern et al. (2005) found that White and Asian children had higher proportionate rates of cochlear implantation than Black and Hispanic children. These authors also noted that implanted children were more likely to live in areas with higher median incomes. Geers (2003) examined the speech production performance of 181 children with cochlear implants and reported contributing factors as nonverbal intelligence and educational programs emphasizing oral-aural communication, suggesting that these may be related to socioeconomic status as well.

Implications for school personnel are far-reaching for this group. Families from lower economic strata should receive the same kind of information that other families receive about cochlear implants. Professionals should not prejudge families based on income. All parents of deaf children should receive information about cochlear implants. Those with fewer resources require that additional professionals be involved in assisting them through the process. Social workers, psychologists, and local community groups should be accessed to help these parents. This support must be maintained after implantation to ensure that the child is able to maximize implant use. For children on public assistance, issues of broken equipment and methods to ensure a seamless procedure for replacing it should be in place from the beginning. All too often these issues are not addressed until there is a circumstance that requires attention. It is only then that the school or implant facility will investigate how to manage the bureaucracy that must be negotiated for follow-through. This usually results in wasted time while the child endures a period of no sound, thereby interrupting any progress being made. When procedures for equipment replacement are developed at the time of implantation, school professionals will be able to provide children with better services in an uninterrupted manner.

In addition, families from poorer households may not have access to the same general technologies (such as home computers, DVD players) as other children. This should not prevent the therapist from using resources of the school or community-at-large to assist these families. More work may be required by the school professional, but it will assist economically disadvantaged children in making the most of the device.

DEAF CHILDREN OF DEAF FAMILIES

Historically, the response of the Deaf community to cochlear implantation has been contentious. Implant technology was introduced during a period of emerging political and cultural change in the Deaf world, which was partly responsible for its lack of acceptance. As the Deaf President Now (DPN) movement was occurring in the late 1980s, Deaf culture had finally captured the attention of the nation and gained strong political support across the country. Occurring almost simultaneously with this movement was the FDA approval of cochlear implants in children. Skepticism of this technology from the Deaf community was high as there had been numerous other "advances" in the past that were unsuccessful and sometimes bordered on quackery. As a result, the 1990 position paper from the National Association of the Deaf (NAD) vehemently opposed implantation in children. As positive outcomes with implants became more publicized and the consistency of responses of individuals with implants appeared in research around the world, the Deaf community revised its position. In 2000, the new NAD position statement recognized cochlear implants as an option in a "whole child" approach to treating deaf children.

Although the number of implants was growing rapidly in the population of deaf children born to hearing parents, the number of deaf children of deaf parents (as well as congenitally deaf adults) accessing this technology remained extremely small. In 1995, in a paper published by Chute et al. the first report of a deaf child from a deaf family reached the field.

Since that time there has been a growth, albeit a slow one, in this population. In 2000, the documentary entitled *Sound and Fury* was nominated for an Academy Award and received attention across the country as the media learned of its content. In the film, two families are chronicled as they each try to decide if their child should be implanted. One family is a deaf family with all deaf children. The other family is a hearing family with one deaf twin. The hearing family, however, has deafness in their background. The discussion of Deaf culture and what families want for their individual children is charted throughout the production. The final decisions went along traditional lines with the deaf family rejecting the implant for their child and the hearing family forging ahead with implantation. Interestingly, however, the Deaf family decided to implant their child several years later. This trend of deaf children from deaf families receiving implants represents a very special population of implant users.

The needs of children from deaf families center on the use of spoken language in the home and the quantity and quality of language access for the child. In deaf households where parents wear hearing aids and use oral language for communication, the amount of exposure to sound may be limited. Despite exposure to spoken language, the child will have a less than adequate speech model from which to develop perceptive and productive skills. Depending on the presence of extended family members with hearing in the household, the outcomes with this group may appear to be poorer than children of hearing parents implanted at similar ages and durations of deafness.

In returning to the discussion of the child followed in the documentary *Sound and Fury*, the deaf family moved into the same household as the hearing paternal grandparents so that there would be a continuous spoken language model that could be accessed daily. This case is unusual and may not reflect the other instances in which deaf children of deaf parents receive cochlear implants. The challenges facing school professionals working with these children are enormous and require resources beyond the scope of those that are generally provided for children with implants from hearing families.

For families who communicate only through ASL, the child's exposure to spoken language will be restricted to his or her attendance at school (provided the school uses spoken language for instruction!). With minimal exposure to auditory input, this group is at high risk for nonuse or limited benefit. When deaf families select a cochlear implant for their deaf child, it is important to gain an understanding of their expectations for making that decision. If the child receives an implant and remains in an ASL school environment, support for that child will, in many cases, be limited. School personnel may not be accommodating of implantation and may not provide substantive support from the outset. This situation will clearly result in nonuse as there will be little reason to wear an auditory device when there is no auditory stimulation.

On the other hand, for the child who is enrolled in a classroom that uses a form of simultaneous communication, school professionals need to foster listening throughout the school day. Often parents of children who use simultaneous communication wear hearing aids to access sound in a limited manner. When the child returns home, these parents can call attention to environmental sounds around the house to encourage listening. Extended family members and community members can also provide spoken language stimulation when the child is not in school. It is important for the school-based professional to have an appreciation for the slower progress that will be observed in this group and to make continued efforts to bring consistent sound to the child. This new generation of implant users remains a small group for whom a great deal of study is still required.

CHILDREN WITH ABNORMAL COCHLEAE

Although the majority of deaf children are born with normal anatomy of the inner ear, there is a small percentage whose anatomic construction is compromised. The normal cochlea has 2½ turns and consists of both bone and membrane. The tiny hairs inside the cochlea are more than 20,000 in number and are situated in a very distinct pattern. The high frequencies (pitches) are at the base of the cochlea while the low frequencies (pitches) are at the apex or top. Most children born deaf have the normal anatomy of 2½ turns but have diminished capacity relative to the number of hair cells that are present. Approximately 20% of individuals with congenital sensorineural hearing loss have identifiable abnormalities of the inner ear (Jensen, 1969). In these cases, the cochlear structure is abnormal and can consist of fewer than 2½ turns or no turns at all (this is known as a common cavity). These malformations are known in the otologic literature by a variety of names but are often clustered together under the category of "Mondini" deformity. The extent of the deformity can often have a deleterious effect on the implant's ability to function. Therefore, children who have any type of inner ear malformation may perform differently from their deaf peers with normal anatomy.

The ramifications of cochlear malformations may be exhibited in the effectiveness of the map. Because of the malformation, children with Mondini deformities may have very narrow dynamic ranges (see mapping issues in chapter 5) and/or facial nerve stimulation on some or all of the electrodes. When the facial nerve stimulation occurs on some of the electrodes, the programming audiologist can delete these during the mapping process. When facial nerve stimulation occurs across the entire array, the output of the implant must be reduced to a level below which facial nerve stimulation occurs. This may result in poorer performance due to less than optimal stimulation.

The speech and hearing professional working with a child with a Mondini deformity requires information from the implant center to tailor therapy for the child. If the child has electrodes that have been deleted from the map, it is important for the SLP or teacher to look for extraneous eye or facial movement that may suddenly occur. If the child has a map that has been reduced because of facial stimulation across the entire array, then the SLP may need to focus therapy more on using the device for limited sound awareness and as an aid to speech reading. Children with reduced input levels may not have sufficient auditory access to conversational speech to learn spoken language. Clearly, it is important for school-based personnel to have a reporting mechanism at their disposal to inform the parent and cochlear implant center of any negative responses they may observe.

CHILDREN WITH AUDITORY NEUROPATHY

It is only in the past 5 years that children with auditory neuropathy have gained notoriety as professionals have become aware of the presence of this particular disorder. Auditory neuropathy has now more correctly been labeled auditory dys-synchrony, because it represents a lack of synchronous activity in the auditory nerve. In these cases, the cochlea may only have a mild or moderate hearing loss, but the signal is not carried from the cochlea to the brain via the central pathways. The electrical stimulation from a cochlear implant may, in many circumstances, synchronize the activity in the nerve and permit the child to experience auditory sensations. In the most severe cases (which are probably those that can be labeled a true neuropathy), the implant is unable to override the central processing problems that exist thereby resulting in poor outcomes. Numerous studies (Berlin et al., 2001; Peterson et al., 2003) have followed children with known auditory dys-synchrony, with varying results. Again, this may be directly related to the extent of the dys-synchrony which remains difficult to assess with present test methods.

The speech and hearing professional should be aware of this diagnosis in children who receive cochlear implants. Habilitation strategies most often incorporate more than just an auditory approach. Berlin et al. (2003) have reported the successful use of cued speech with this population. (Cued speech is a system that uses hand signals to remove the ambiguity of those sounds that look similar on the lips. It acts as an aid to speech reading.) Whether it is cued speech or speech reading or sign-supported English, those children with auditory dys-synchrony have more success when there is an additional modality to support their listening skills. In some cases of severe dys-synchrony, benefit from the implant may be restricted; regardless, the SLP should approach therapy by accessing the auditory system as an adjunct to the visual system.

CHILDREN WITH DISABILITIES

Often when thinking of the "special population" of cochlear implant users, the first category that comes to mind is children with disabilities. As just discussed, children in the "special population" group can include those in a variety of other categories. However, children with disabilities represent a distinctly different grouping from the others already mentioned. Even when referencing children with disabilities, the classification can be further delineated into two distinct groups, those with cognitive handicaps and those with noncognitive handicaps. In the early days of implantation, children with additional disabilities were often denied implants as there was not enough documented evidence about implant performance to warrant placing the device in a child with other issues. The fear was that children who had other disabilities might reject the implant as a foreign signal and that behavior might worsen. As the results with implantation played out in a positive manner, more and more implant centers began to "dabble" in placing these devices in children with handicaps. More often than not, the first group to receive the implant was children who were classified as having "noncognitive" handicaps.

Children with "noncognitive" handicaps include those individuals who may be deaf and also display a disability in areas that are not related to processes of perception, memory, and reasoning. These might include children who have low muscle tone, mild cerebral palsy, or severely reduced visual fields and still maintain normal IQ functioning. These are in direct opposition to children who demonstrate marked decrements in cognition and include children with low IQs, pervasive developmental delays, or autism. The decision to implant children in either of these categories requires more in-depth evaluations and precise counseling of parents.

NONCOGNITIVE HANDICAPS

Children who are deaf and also present with low muscle tone at birth often require the additional services of both the occupational therapist and physical therapist to ensure that all aspects of the child's functioning are treated. The effects of low muscle tone are frequently observed in the areas of delayed speech production and speech perception. It is not unusual for children with low muscle tone to exhibit oral-motor difficulties, which can continue into the postimplant habilitation period. It is important for parents and professionals working with children with a diagnosis of low muscle tone that they are at higher risk for retinitis pigmentosa (a disorder that leads to blindness later on). For this reason, these children, in particular, should be carefully monitored by an ophthalmologist.

The cochlear implant has been shown to be an effective treatment for children with reduced vision not just for hearing but for ambulation as well. Children who are deaf/blind and have received a cochlear implant have developed good auditory skills commensurate with their age and duration of deafness. An added bonus to hearing has been a positive change in their ability to move about in a less cumbersome manner. Children have also demonstrated an increased ability to ambulate more effectively on uneven terrain or that which is unfamiliar to them (Chute & Nevins, 1995). This additional benefit allows the child to access more speaking and listening opportunities.

It is important to remember that, even if a child is not blind, the incidence of visual problems, such as myopia, is not uncommon in this population. In a study of deaf children, it was found that 38% also required visual accommodations to correct their myopia (Leguire et al., 1992). It is especially important for school professionals to pay attention to the child's ability to see in class and to report any concerns to the parents as soon as possible. Teachers should be cognizant of children's ability to see peripherally as well as directly in front of them, as the loss of peripheral vision may signal some additional concerns.

In addition to children who have poor visual acuity or low muscle tone, the group of children with mild forms of cerebral palsy have also demonstrated promising results with a cochlear implant. These children tend to have normal IQs and may exhibit mild muscle weakness in the arm or leg. Children in this category respond in a manner that is consistent with those with similar ages and durations of deafness, although a slight delay in initial progress may be noted. It is not unusual to observe performance changes after 12 to 18 months of implant use as compared to 6 months in the general population of implant users. Fortunately, once the auditory system "clicks in" progress follows similar patterns of performance.

COGNITIVE HANDICAPS

Children with cognitive handicaps have been slow to receive implants and remain a group that requires individualized decision-making. When there are marked cognitive issues with a child, the addition of an auditory signal may, in some cases, produce a negative response as the child is unable to assimilate the new sound. Experience has shown that children in this classification perform better when implanted earlier. In fact, in the larger studies that have monitored children with these severe levels of handicap, those that have been implanted later have produced the poorest results (Bertram et al., 2000). Although there are always exceptions, experienced implant facilities will approach implantation of this group with great caution. That being said, if a child has severe autism or multiple disabilities and is implanted early, data suggest that these children will wear their implants and utilize them to relate better within their environment. These children will not receive sufficient auditory benefit to learn to communicate orally and will require additional supports. However, they may be more behaviorally manageable when using their implants. Older children with severe cognitive disabilities have very poor outcomes and parents should be guided away from the cochlear implant as a form of treatment. Often parents will request an implant for "safety reasons" so that the child can hear environmental sounds. Although this is a well-meaning intent, for children with severe cognitive deficits the meaning of an environmental sound often eludes them, thereby making the implant useless with respect to this issue.

The speech and hearing professional must understand, however, that this group is very slow to demonstrate even the simplest abilities. It may require 24 to 36 months of continued use with the cochlear implant to observe detection and later pattern perception. The use of a multimodality approach will work best with this group so that the child can begin to couple the sounds from his or her implant to the sign or object being presented. Slow progress is something that the parent must be prepared for, and supported through, by the school-based professional. For professionals who may be skeptical of implantation, the lack of progress of this group may reinforce an already negative attitude.

Finally, it is important for the school-based professional to know that this group is at greater risk for mechanical implant failure (Chute, 2001). Often, these children fall frequently and are susceptible to head injury, thus creating the potential for damage to the implanted internal receiver. It is essential for the speech and hearing professional to know the signs of potential device malfunction so that it can be reported home or to the implant facility.

SUMMARY

As performance with the cochlear implant has improved, expansion of candidacy criteria has permitted individuals who were initially overlooked for implantation to now be considered. Children within all the "special populations" can be successful users of the device as long as parents and professionals are aware of the slow or limited progress that may occur commensurate with their "special-ness." Intervention strategies that accommodate these children and their unique needs will allow them to maximize the potential of the device given their unique circumstances. It is only through a collaborative effort that the benefits of implantation can be extended to this group.

Chapter 11

LISTENING IN NOISY CLASSROOMS

Room Acoustics, FMs, and Other Assistive Devices

The remarkable outcomes observed in children who utilize cochlear implants cannot be overemphasized. However, it is important to keep in mind that even though these children are capable of impressive perceptual performance, they do not hear normally. It is equally important to remember that the average classroom in the United States may be poorly structured acoustically, thus placing even the hearing child at a disadvantage. Successful classroom behavior encompasses myriad tasks that require students to listen, comprehend, write, and comment all within minutes or seconds. For a student to successfully take notes in a class, he or she must comprehend the message, simultaneously, or within a short period of time, look down from the teacher, and write it legibly so that it can be meaningful later. For children with cochlear implants, (especially those who only use unilateral cochlear implants), this ability to retrieve and record spoken lessons in the classroom becomes even more challenging if the room is not acoustically ideal. It is critical that children in classrooms, whether they are hearing or have hearing loss, be provided with the clearest signal. Accomplishing this requires a number of considerations. First, there is the classroom itself and how acoustically friendly it may or may not be. Second, there is the teacher output with respect to intensity and clarity. Lastly, there is the recipient of the signal who must bring to the task a series of capabilities ranging from detection to comprehension of the spoken material. A greater understanding of how these aspects interact with each other can assist the school professional in ensuring the best possible outcome for the child who uses a cochlear implant in the classroom.

CLASSROOM ACOUSTICS

For a classroom to be optimal for a child's listening ability, background noise should be at a low intensity and reverberation time minimal. Sources of background noise include heating or ventilation systems, activities within the classroom or neighboring classrooms, and environmental noise outside the classroom. Reverberation refers to the amount of time it takes for sound to decay. In large, hard-walled rooms there is an echo quality that indicates a slow sound-decay time. However, in most classrooms, reverberation issues that are not obvious to the average listener may create poor listening environments for the child with a cochlear implant or the hearing child with a learning or auditory-processing disorder. In addition to distorting the main signal in the room, long reverberation times can also exacerbate background noise.

Background noise is measured in units known as signal-to-noise ratios (SNR) that can vary from negative to positive. An SNR +5 indicates that the main speaker's output is 5 dB above the noise; an SNR 0 indicates speech and background noise at the same level; SNR −5 would mean that the speech is 5 dB below the noise. Perception, therefore, improves as SNR increases. It is easier for a child to listen to speech at an SNR +10 than it would be at an SNR −10. Typically the poorest SNR occurs when the teacher is at the back of the classroom behind the students or when he or she is speaking too close to the noise source (e.g., standing near a noisy air-conditioning unit). Generally, it is recommended that children with hearing loss have at least an SNR +15 (Seep et al., 2000). At this level speech perception increases substantially.

To overcome compromised signal-to-noise ratios, amplification of the speaker's voice to an appropriate level over the noise is necessary. This can be accomplished using a variety of technologies that are outlined in the sections to follow. Obviously, the better approach is to build classrooms that are initially constructed to reduce background noise. Recently, the American National Standards Institute (ANSI) recommended that new classrooms should be designed to have a background noise of no greater than 35 dBA (ANSI, 2002).

Assessing reverberation time (RT) is a bit more complicated but can be performed using a standard formula. This formula takes into account the size of the room, the areas of different surface materials, and the absorption levels of those materials at certain frequencies. Ultimately an RT of 0.4 to 0.6 seconds is desirable. Unfortunately, most classrooms have RTs greater than 1 second (Seep et al., 2000). Reverberant rooms are treated by either decreasing the size of the room or increasing the amount of absorption. For older classrooms with high ceilings, adding a "dropped ceiling" that uses sound absorption tiling effectively treats both issues simultaneously. This may not always be easily accomplished as windows and lighting may prevent its construction. When a "dropped ceiling" is not possible, adding absorbing materials such as fabrics, cork boards, and carpeting can offer some relief. Sound-absorption materials that are evenly distributed throughout the classroom are more effective than those that are concentrated in only one area. Often, adding sound-absorption materials will contribute to reduction in background noise. Well-placed carpeting or tennis balls on the bottom of chairs will substantially reduce the amount of noise that occurs in the classroom. It is important to remember that all sound should not be absorbed. In larger classrooms, the teacher's voice must be able to reach the back of the room before the sound-absorbing materials soak it up. For all these reasons, it is important that classrooms with children with cochlear implants be assessed for RT and noise to ensure the best signal delivery.

TECHNOLOGIC ACCOMMODATIONS

As noted previously, the speech output of the teacher is another major component of providing a good listening environment for the student. Teachers in acoustically advantageous classrooms who speak softly or with a heavy accent will be a challenge to even the hearing child. For the child with a cochlear implant, the ability to follow classroom content under these circumstances will be met with great frustration. Regardless of teacher speaking style, however, the child who uses a cochlear implant must have a signal that can be consistently detected by the implant microphone. Personal or sound-field FM systems have increased in popularity to meet this need.

SOUND-FIELD FM SYSTEMS

Sound-field amplification systems are the more traditional ones that have been used in large lecture halls for many years. They consist of a microphone into which the presenter speaks and well-placed acoustic receivers in the room which deliver the signal to the listener. These can be hard-wired, as is the case in most auditoriums, or they can use FM transmission to make them more portable from one room to the next. Placing a sound-field system in a classroom addresses two important aspects of the speaker/listener paradigm. By using such a system, the teacher's voice is amplified approximately 8 to 10 dB. This creates a more advantageous signal-to-noise ratio for the child. In addition, sound-field systems provide a more uniform signal throughout the classroom so that children seated in the back of the room have the same input as those in the front of the room.

Sound-field systems vary from compact, portable, battery-powered, single-speaker units to more permanently placed, multiple loudspeakers that can be situated in different portions of the classroom. In some cases, these loudspeakers can be placed on stands, mounted in the ceiling, or affixed to the walls. There are a variety of manufacturers of these systems. The reader is directed to Appendix C for a listing of distributors and their Web site addresses.

In survey studies of teachers who used sound-field systems, 96% found them to be effective. In addition, many of these same teachers reported reduced stress and vocal strain after their use. Similarly, 93% of students who use sound-field systems reported positive attitudes (Crandell, 1998). Educationally, this technology can enhance academic instruction through its use in oral reading and oral presentations.

FM systems cannot be used without attention to proper management. Calibration and output of the FM is critical to its delivery of the appropriate signal level. Systems that are set too low will have little effect; those that are set too high may be uncomfortable for some children. When FMs are set too high for children who use cochlear implants, they will be rendered essentially ineffective as the implant will detect the high-level input and automatically reduce it before delivering it to the child. Systems that are set too low will have reduced sound levels as they reach the implant microphone.

In addition to the calibration of the sound-field FM, the placement of the speakers is equally important. Speakers that are situated in the upper corners of the room will be less effective than those on speaker stands at a reasonable level relative to the child's ears. It is also important not to block the loudspeakers with pictures or posters as this will substantially distort and decrease sound output. Smaller portable desktop systems are more efficient in delivering the signal to the child, as they are placed in closer proximity to the user. However, to prevent them from abuse from falling, it is best to have some method of securing them such as the use of Velcro. Because these smaller systems can utilize both rechargeable and alkaline batteries, it is important to have a member of the school team who is responsible for their management.

Finally, as with any system, it is important for the speaker to wear the microphone in a manner that will be the most effective. For this reason, microphones that utilize a headband or occipital band and place the microphone directly in front of the mouth are the recommended technology of choice. Lapel microphones attached to garments are often too far from the speaker's mouth and are subject to clothing noise and interference from jewelry.

Evaluating the utility of any technology is important in determining its effectiveness. For children with cochlear implants, teachers can utilize the Screening Instrument for Targeting Educational Risk (SIFTER). This questionnaire focuses on observations of the teacher of the child's classroom performance related to good listening skills. A self-assessment inventory is available with the Listening Inventory for Education (LIFE). This inventory uses pictures of common classroom situations that could provide a listening challenge to the student. The student then indicates how much difficulty he or she experiences in each environment. Both these evaluations can be performed in a pre/post mode to assess the effects of the introduction of sound-field amplification.

It is important to understand, however, that sound-field systems do have their limitations. In excessively reverberant rooms, the 8- to 10-dB advantage may not be enough to overcome the poor acoustic environment. In very small classrooms there may be problems with feedback and benefit may be limited. Additionally, depending on speaker placement and the placement of the child relative to the speaker, the enhancement may still not be enough to overcome background noise. For this reason, personal FM systems may be a better method of choice for the implanted child.

PERSONAL FM SYSTEMS

Personal FM systems offer a more favorable signal-to-noise ratio as the input is directed to the child's assistive device. In the case of the child with a cochlear implant, FM coupling has evolved substantially over the past several years. Previously, when children used body-worn speech processors and FM systems were also body-worn, the equipment was extremely cumbersome. In addition, because the two devices required a direct coupling, problems with cable interface were frequent. Interference between the two devices and other systems in the class was also problematic. Thus, FM coupling was used in a much smaller percentage of children with cochlear implants. More recently as both cochlear implant speech processors and FM systems have decreased in size, some of these problems have subsided. However, it is important to note that they have not completely disappeared.

Although FM systems offer a greater advantage in noise than a sound-field system, FM systems have more working parts and their functionality cannot be as easily verified as a sound-field system. This makes it crucial for school professionals servicing children with cochlear implants to be knowledgeable about these personal devices to ensure proper functioning. An FM system that is not working properly may actually decrease signal input to the implant user, thereby making the recipient more susceptible to distortion and reducing benefit required in noisy situations.

In studies of children with cochlear implants in noise, researchers have found that performance can decrease by as much as 50% as the SNR goes from quiet to +5 dB. Fetterman and Domico (2002) studied 96 children with cochlear implants and found a consistent drop in performance as the sentences were delivered in quiet and at SNRs of +10 and +5 dB. Given that the average classroom functions well below this level, it is essential for children with implants to have additional sound input to ensure auditory access to school content. However, as noted previously, as these systems are not as easy to monitor as sound-field systems there are certain prerequisites for fitting personal FM systems to children with cochlear implants.

Children who utilize a cochlear implant and are being considered for an FM should have at least 3 to 6 months of cochlear implant experience prior to interfacing the FM system. Children should have adequate communication skills (either oral or sign) to be able to provide feedback about what they hear with the FM and cochlear implant. With some cochlear implant experience, the child should be able to demonstrate reliable, age-appropriate responses to auditory tasks to ensure that progress is being made. Finally, someone at school should be identified as the main monitor of the device so that troubleshooting and listening checks can occur on a regular basis.

The variety of FM-compatible systems is more numerous than in previous years. There are systems that can be readily connected to body-worn processors without the use of unwieldy equipment. Devices that piggyback onto the existing speech processor and can be held in place easily are state-of-the art (see Figures 11–1 and 11–2).

Teachers and speech and hearing professionals must be aware of the numerous configurations and the proper settings for the transmitter and the receiver. As these differ from one device to the next, the best approach is to contact the individual cochlear implant manufacturer along with the FM manufacturer to ensure proper control setting.

Behind-the-ear speech processors have made FM use cosmetically appealing with greater reliability. For these systems to work in tandem, they require proper adjustment. Programming adaptations for the implant are often necessary to ensure that the processor is

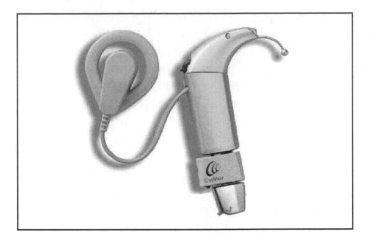

Figure 11–1. FM and Nucleus Cochlear Implant System

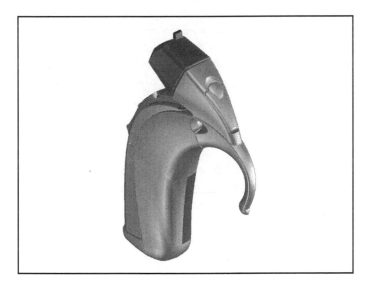

Figure 11–2. FM and Clarion Cochlear Implant System

set to receive the FM signal. School professionals must be aware that they cannot simply order equipment and connect it to the implant as it will not function appropriately. Knowledge of system battery requirements and rate of drain is necessary as these will vary among the different models. Failure to monitor this aspect of

FM usage may result in poor performance due to battery discharge that goes undetected.

Some systems can be monitored using headset earphones that are provided by the individual manufacturer. Again, the school professional should be in contact with the cochlear implant facility and/or the individual manufacturer to learn these procedures. Basic management of the FM should be performed daily by individuals who have been designated to fulfill this important role. This can be accomplished by using informal or iterative checks, versus more formal assessments.

Informal checks of the cochlear implant and FM system are quick and easy and can be performed by using a portable speaker, the monitoring headsets that accompany the implant, or standard behavioral listening tests. A small portable speaker purchased from a local radio store can provide the output for the speech and hearing professional to monitor the FM system. By plugging the FM receiver into the speaker and then speaking into the transmitter, the signal can be heard through the speaker to ensure that the FM is functioning appropriately. The monitor headphones that accompany some of the cochlear implant systems are quicker and easier in performing this function. All that is required is the manufacturer-supplied earphones plugged into the FM receiver as the school-based professional listens to the signal while speaking into the microphone. In addition, the cochlear implant recipient can be asked to respond to a variety of auditory-only stimuli.

Formal assessment of FM function can be performed using behavioral sound-field testing and/or electroacoustic measures. These tend to be more time-consuming and often must be completed on site. For behavioral assessment, the child's performance should first be determined in the cochlear implant-only mode and then with the cochlear implant and FM activated. When in the cochlear implant-only modality, the child's speech perception abilities should be measured in quiet and at a +5 dB SNR. Once completed, the FM system should be attached and the procedure repeated. Needless to say, this is a very time-consuming process and also presumes a certain level of performance from the child.

Electroacoustic assessment requires special equipment that is often available through the school system by the educational audiologist. This demands a certain level of skill and experience but does not necessitate any participation on the part of the child.

A standard hearing aid test box is required so that the monitor earphones can be connected to the coupler. (If a cochlear implant system does not have monitor earphones this cannot be done.) Various recordings are made and compared to ensure proper function. For educational audiologists interested in further information about this method of assessment they are directed to Thibodeau (2003).

In comparing the different methods of verifying proper FM and cochlear implant function, it is clear that the informal listening checks, which utilize the monitor earphones, are the quickest and most efficient. No feedback from the child is called for thereby making informal listening checks a technique that can be used by the entire school team. Behavioral listening checks that are basic and request minimal detection and discrimination are also easy and efficient to use. The more advanced behavioral testing under traditional soundproof conditions using stimuli in quiet and in noise can provide a wealth of information, but are time-consuming and necessitate a particular level of performance by the child. Finally, the electroacoustic check does not entail any feedback from the child but requires experience and additional equipment on the part of the educational audiologist.

SOUND FIELD VERSUS PERSONAL FM

The choice of which audio enhancement system is recommended depends on a number of very important criteria. As noted previously, children should have some experience with their implants alone before fitting any of these systems. For very young children in preschool settings or children who have multiple disabilities, sound-field systems will ensure the signal advantage without the question of FM and implant function. For older children who have limited experience with cochlear implants, sound-field systems should be used until there is a comfort level on the part of the implant facility and therapeutic professionals regarding the child's level of functioning. The opposite is often true for adolescent cochlear implant users who find the presence of a totable system on their desk to be too much of a stigma. What is important is that no child should be fitted with an FM system until there is agreement among all professionals working with the child that the implant recipient is capable of giving feedback to them regarding its sound clarity.

OTHER FM ISSUES

In addition to the FM being coupled to the cochlear implant, many children will also use a hearing aid or another cochlear implant on the opposite ear. Children can use FM systems coupled to the hearing aid or other implant successfully. These systems can be matched for frequency so that a single transmitter can be used by the teacher. Issues of implant recipient feedback remain the same.

ADDITIONAL AUDIO DEVICES

As we live in an age of cell phones, computers, iPods, and CD players, the bombardment of sound from each of these is often overwhelming to those of us with hearing. Interestingly, children with implants also appreciate these latest technologic gadgets and gravitate toward them in a similar manner. Cell phone use in the United States is at an all-time high with the age of getting one's first cell phone decreasing each year. There are now children's cell phones that can be preprogrammed with only a handful of telephone numbers so that the child can call home, school, or a relative with the push of only one button. A large percentage of cochlear implant recipients enjoy telephone conversational skills and they are able to easily access this technology without any additional equipment. Some manufacturers produce telephone adapter connectors to enhance the signal for users who require it. Most use the telephone in a manner similar to hearing individuals.

Computer usage among the deaf has risen extensively as it has opened up communication in a manner never thought possible. E-mail access and instant messaging have contributed to an ease of communication that the deaf have not previously known. In addition, Web sites and software that generate speech signals for listening practice make the home computer an extension of the therapy room. These can be accessed using traditional speakers that are connected to the computer or through more direct input from the computer to the implant. It is crucial that implant recipients who connect directly to any technology that is interfaced with standard AC current use a surge protector to guard against any random power spikes.

Portable, personal audio systems are in widespread use in both the hearing and implanted population. Each implant manufacturer offers a variety of interface cables that can often enhance listening through these devices. Experience suggests that it is an individual appreciation that drives the decision to use these special connectors. As music has become more accessible, many implant recipients (especially adolescents) are finding it enjoyable.

Music appreciation via a cochlear implant has only recently received some attention as initial studies of implant efficacy were focused on speech perception abilities. Presently, the majority of the research in this area has been performed in adult listeners, and, more specifically, postlinguistically deafened adult recipients (Gfeller et al., 2005). The implications for children who are raised using cochlear implants from a young age are unknown at the present time and warrant attention as these children progress through the educational system and are exposed to music.

Studies in adult implant recipients include anecdotal reports of music appreciation; however, group data demonstrate problems in pitch perception and subsequent poor perception of melody and harmony. As a group, studies show considerable variability among implant recipients on recognition of familiar melodies (Gfeller, Turner, et al., 2002) with no superiority of device or processing strategy. Interestingly, implant recipients have demonstrated significant improvement in timbre perception of instruments as a result of structured training after implantation (Fujita & Ito, 1999). Likewise, the implications of this for children are not yet known.

Additionally, it has been shown that the age of the adult cochlear implant user at the time of the testing is strongly related to music perception and enjoyment (Gfeller et al., 1998). Cognitive ability has also been shown to be predictive for some aspects of music perception. Some implant recipients report that music generally sounds like noise whereas others report some music as being acceptable and other music too complex. In recent studies that investigated "real world" music (Gfeller et al., 2005), cochlear implant recipients were compared to normal hearing listeners across three types of music: classical, pop, and country. The results indicated that the implant recipients rated music as less pleasant and more complex when compared to normal hearers. When listening to previously known musical pieces, the implant recipients were less accurate than their hearing counterparts. A weak correlation was found for age at time of testing and music appreciation with the younger listeners performing better. Additionally, performance on speech perception measures and the amount of focused music listening time after implantation was also correlated with musical enjoyment. Clearly these data suggest that earlier exposure to music may reflect better music identification and appreciation. It would also suggest that trained musical appreciation will foster this ability. As young children often use music as a learning tool it is important to continue to explore this ability in children with cochlear implants.

SUMMARY

The cochlear implant can provide its recipients with a wealth of information with respect to spoken language. To maximize benefit in a classroom setting, the use of an FM system is strongly recommended. These systems can take the form of sound-field devices from which the entire class can benefit or personal systems used by the individual. Decisions about which systems are most appropriate are based on criteria that depend on the child's experience with the cochlear implant and his or her ability to express verbally any problems that might arise.

It is essential that teachers receive in-service training on the use of FM systems to ensure proper use. The role of the educational audiologist is critical in the follow-up and maintenance of these devices. The school team is challenged to ensure the child's compliance in utilizing the FM appropriately to contribute to success. As FM systems become smaller and more accessible their use will continue to grow.

In addition to FM systems, there are a variety of accessories to enhance delivery of other signals to the cochlear implant recipient. These include interface cables that connect the recipient with cell phone, computer, or musical delivery devices. As musical delivery systems become more widespread, exposure to this type of stimuli is increasing among implant users. The level of appreciation for music is often individual but still falls short of that of the hearing person. As research continues in this area, information about children's perception of music will become available. The ramifications of training children with cochlear implants at young ages in the realm of musical perception are uncharted territory that needs further investigation.

Chapter 12

LISTENING WITH TWO EARS

Bilateral Cochlear Implants and Cochlear Implants and Hearing Aids

The ability to hear with two ears enables the listener to perform a number of critical tasks that makes communication easier and more efficient. Two ears allow the listener to hear softer sounds, perceive speech in a background of noise, and localize the direction from which sound is emanating. It is through the processing of sound in the central system that information from each ear is filtered and used to enhance perception. This task is performed through an intricate analysis by each ear as it examines features such as timing, intensity, and signal duration, to name a few. The time that a signal arrives at each ear provides the listener with information regarding loudness that can assist in the ability to determine directionality. Signal durations and intensities contribute to the capacity to filter out background noise and attend to the "main" speaker. Obviously, the fact that two ears can detect twice as much sound permits the listener to perceive softer sounds in the environment. For perception to be at its maximum, the ability to hear in both ears is required.

Hearing loss, as a rule, occurs most often similarly in both ears. However, unilateral hearing loss is a condition that can be present at birth or develop over time due to disease or sudden systemic problems. As hearing is normal in one ear and poor in the other, children who are born with unilateral hearing loss, often have delayed diagnosis as speech and language will generally evolve in a near-normal manner. Despite the efforts of universal newborn-hearing screening in this country, it is estimated that the average age of identification of children with unilateral hearing loss is approximately 8.7 years (Lee et al., 1998). This age coincides with third grade and marks a time when academic information begins to evolve into greater content-based, comprehension-driven curricula. It is at this point that teachers become suspicious of a child's learning abilities and further investigation may lead to diagnosis of unilateral hearing loss.

The incidence of unilateral hearing loss in the pediatric population is estimated to be 3 in 1,000 births (Lee et al., 1998). Among African-American, Cuban-American, Mexican-American, Puerto Rican, and non-Hispanic white children, it is estimated that approximately 391,000 school-aged children in the United States have unilateral hearing loss. As noted previously, unilateral hearing loss may not substantially impede the development of language in children, but the ramifications of hearing in only one ear on educational and social interactions have been demonstrated in numerous studies in the United States and abroad (Lee et al., 1998). Children from culturally and linguistically diverse populations may be at even greater risk. By making accommodations for these children, the speech and hearing professional can alleviate some of the difficulties they experience, but the multiplicity of factors involved may have an additive effect that can still disrupt learning. As children with unilateral hearing loss hear normally in one ear, they are treated not as children with hearing difficulties but more as children with learning difficulties. In some cases, this may be the correct approach; in others it may not.

The effects of unilateral hearing loss on an individual are related to the ability to hear effectively in a background of noise, perceive soft sounds, and localize the direction of sound. Clearly, these are the exact traits that are considered to contribute to bilateral hearing. If one ear is removed from the perceptual process, then each of these abilities will be compromised. In addition, children will be unable to receive signals of low-to-mid intensity if they are being generated from the side that has no hearing. However, functionally, the child with the unilateral hearing loss will appear to be "normal" as most forms of communication will be maintainable. This is in direct opposition to the child who presents with bilateral hearing loss.

Children with bilateral hearing loss may demonstrate degrees of impairment that range from mild to profound. In most cases, these losses will be symmetric in nature (i.e., the loss in each ear will be the same). The majority of children will be treated with bilateral amplification to ensure that signals are accessible to each ear. Depending on the degree of hearing loss, access to conversational speech may range from good to very poor. Regardless of degree of hearing loss, a hearing aid does not restore normal hearing. Data show that children with even mild degrees of hearing loss, will still fail to recognize 25 to 40% of the speech signal and have difficulty perceiving weak consonants and some vowels (Alpiner et al., 2000). This may have deleterious consequences on more complex syntactic development as well as vocabulary. As the degree of hearing loss becomes greater, the effects on speech, language, and learning will also be greater.

The cochlear implant has changed the landscape for children with severe-to-profound deafness. With approval by the FDA in 1990, implant technology has rapidly become the "best practice" standard for this pediatric group. As the outcomes of implantation have demonstrated continued improvement over the past 15 years in areas of speech, hearing, language, education, and socialization, attention has now turned to the prospect of providing this input in both ears.

Historically, implants were performed in one ear because of their comparative novelty in the field of hearing rehabilitation. As a cochlear implant requires surgery, its contribution as a hearing device brought with it greater risk. Unlike a hearing aid, it simply could not be changed without additional surgical intervention. As the results with cochlear implants improved and manufacturers were able to build system upgrades into the software, recipients were able to take advantage of subsequent technology without added surgery. Also, in some cases, cochlear implants were explanted and newer or similar models were implanted without any decrement and, in some cases, an increase, in performance. The fear of being unable to utilize an ear once it had been implanted began to fade rapidly.

BILATERAL IMPLANTATION

Armed with data from hearing aid studies that demonstrate improved benefit from bilateral sensory input, Gantz et al. (2002) embarked on a study of the safety and efficacy of bilateral cochlear implants in the adult population. The premise of the study was twofold. First, it was to determine the utility of bilateral implants as "best practice" for treating bilateral severe-to-profound sensorineural hearing loss. Second, it was an attempt to determine which ear to implant—the better or the poorer hearing ear. With this is mind, eight adults were enrolled in this study. One group consisted of individuals with bilaterally symmetric severe-to-profound hearing loss. The other group included individuals whose hearing loss was asymmetric (a severe hearing loss in one ear and a profound hearing loss in the other ear) but fell within the criteria of severe-to-profound. The results of this study laid the groundwork for subsequent studies in adults and children. Preliminary findings indicated improved speech perception in noise and better performance in quiet. Localization ability began to exhibit improvement as well. In addition, the study found that, although performance in the better hearing ear was superior to that of the poorer hearing ear initially, both ears effectively looked the same after 6 months of implant use.

In 2001, a more wide-scale study in adults and children was sponsored by Cochlear Americas to monitor bilateral implants in a larger population. This and subsequent studies by Firszt et al. (2005) supported the initial results of Gantz et al. Indeed, both children and adults demonstrated improved performance in noise and in quiet along with better performance in tasks requiring localization skills.

Groups of children and adults in these studies consisted of both simultaneous and sequentially implanted individuals. In the majority of cases, reports supported bilateral implantation as providing better signal perception. In the cases of sequential implantation, where the child or adult had used a cochlear implant for anywhere from a few months to 15 years or more, the results still supported the claims. In many cases of sequential implantation, the implant recipient used different generations of cochlear implant systems. For example, children or adults might have a Nucleus-22 in one ear and a Nucleus-24 in the other. Others might have a Clarion CII or 1.2 in one ear with a Clarion High Res 90K in the other. Interestingly, these individuals were able to utilize both devices despite the fact that very different types of speech-processing strategies were being delivered to each ear (Chute & Parisier, 2004).

Performance with a cochlear implant, whether unilateral or bilateral, varies across the population of recipients. In general, when implant surgery was performed simultaneously in children or adults with short durations of deafness, outcomes were maximal in a short period of time. When implants were received many years apart, the amount of time required to acclimate to the new signal could be as short as a month or as long as a year or more. What separates the performance of the recipients is still unknown and requires further study, but clearly, access to normal hearing at some time in life, coupled with hearing aid use in the opposite ear, may be contributing factors. The motivation to use both devices continuously, especially during the early days post bilateral implantation, is crucial to outcome.

In a study by Chute et al. (2005), speech production changes in a postlinguistically deafened adult who received bilateral sequential implants were reported. This adult had successfully used a cochlear implant system in one ear for more than 11 years before receiving the second implant and had speech that could be characterized as completely intelligible. Regardless, voice recordings obtained at baseline with one implant and compared later with bilateral implants on the day of initial activation and at the 3- and 6-month intervals, indicated improved voice onset time, more normal fundamental frequency, and better production of affricates. If this result can be observed in a postlinguistically deafened adult using bilateral implants, the implications for children who are developing spoken language skills are far reaching. More studies investigating the effects of bilateral implantation on speech production are required.

There are numerous concerns about bilateral implantation which parents and professionals often voice as they ponder that choice. It is important for school-based professionals to have a complete understanding of the issues to assist parents as the questions arise. It is not uncommon for parents to seek advice from school personnel as they grapple with some of these decisions. In an effort to provide this information in a coherent and cohesive manner, the following commonly asked questions are posed with potential answers.

MY CHILD IS DOING SO WELL WITH ONE IMPLANT, HOW WOULD TWO REALLY BE OF BENEFIT?

Recall that in the earlier discussion regarding bilateral hearing and its effects on speech perception, research demonstrates the advantage in background noise, localization, and the ability to hear soft sounds. In addition, severe-to-profoundly deaf children who use traditional amplification have limited or no access to the speech signal until after they receive their implants. However, under the best circumstances, the cochlear implant will transform a child with a bilateral severe-to-profound sensorineural hearing loss to one with a mild hearing loss. As noted earlier, children with mild hearing losses will continue to miss 25 to 40% of the speech signal.

If one views the difficulties encountered by children with perfectly normal hearing in one ear and a hearing loss in the other ear, one will see that children continue to have problems with: background noise, localizing sounds, input coming from the side of the ear with the hearing loss, and soft sounds at great distances. Consider that 48% of children with unilateral hearing loss have significant academic difficulty that may require grade repetition or resource assistance (Culbertson & Gilbert, 1986). Therefore, when a child receives a unilateral cochlear implant, that child has effectively been changed from one who is severe-to-profoundly bilaterally deaf to one who has a mild unilateral sensorineural hearing loss and a profound loss in the other ear. The listening challenges that face children every day in the classroom will be greatly improved by implantation but not completely remediated. As a large majority of children who receive unilateral cochlear implants are now being educated in mainstream classrooms, it behooves teachers to understand the continued limitations that these children demonstrate and how to accommodate them during classroom activities. This is reviewed in Chapter 11 on FM systems and classroom acoustics.

WHAT TYPE AND AMOUNT OF THERAPY DOES A CHILD WITH A COCHLEAR IMPLANT REQUIRE AND SHOULD THE IMPLANT ON THE FIRST EAR BE REMOVED TO "FORCE" THE NEWLY IMPLANTED EAR TO RESPOND?

The use of an auditory-oral approach that fosters listening in conjunction first with a visual signal is the foundation of good auditory work. Incorporation of an auditory-verbal approach once the child has knowledge of the vocabulary and task at hand solidifies the listening experience. A child who receives two implants does not require twice the amount of therapy. Instead, therapy should be a combination of training techniques that are utilized under various listening situations. It is not recommended that a child's first implant be removed for extended periods of time to "force" the hearing in the second implanted ear. However, it is recommended that therapy for children who receive implants sequentially include opportunities to challenge listening with each ear individually and then with both ears simultaneously. Standard therapeutic practice using hearing aids has always followed this paradigm. Children with cochlear implants should not be treated any differently.

SHOULD A CHILD'S EAR BE "SAVED" FOR FUTURE TECHNOLOGY?

Although it is difficult to determine exactly what the future holds with respect to issues such as all-implantable devices and hair cell regeneration, the fact remains that children who are being educated in mainstream classrooms require maximal auditory input *now*. As content becomes more demanding, it is important that the student with the cochlear implant is able to access the curriculum in the same manner as his or her hearing peers. This means listening with two ears. The sheer process of taking notes while a teacher is speaking is taxing enough for the hearing child. When a child with one implant must negotiate classroom noise, and/or attend to a teacher who is moving around the class while speaking, the disadvantages can mount logarithmically. Bilateral implants will not make these problems disappear but can certainly ameliorate them. For the child in the classroom, the future is now.

Although there are no guarantees, previous experiences with cochlear implants have demonstrated that different generations of these devices can be removed and replaced. This same process should hold true for other future technologies. By "saving" the child's ear today, we may be denying him or her valuable access for more immediate auditory needs.

WILL CHILDREN HAVE TO BE MAPPED TWICE AS MUCH?

Strategies for cochlear implant mapping are evolving continually. Manufacturers are developing more objective models based on physiologic responses to create a functional map quickly. These newer paradigms will cut mapping time in half. The fact that a child utilizes two implants will add to mapping time initially but once an optimal map has been reached there should be minimal change. For children receiving their second implant, knowledge of the mapping process will assist in the activation of the second device.

The most common initial response to sound after activation of the second device is one of overwhelming loudness. Programming often requires that processors be set slightly lower with small increases built into the maps or controls to ease the child into louder settings. Once again, if one refers to the processes that have been used with bilateral hearing aids, the similarities between fitting protocols are obvious. It is also apparent that programming two devices will not take twice as much time. As more audiologists gain experience with programming bilateral cochlear implants, the process will most likely undergo further refinement.

WILL INSURANCE COVER THE COST OF BILATERAL IMPLANTS?

Although it is not clear whether the majority of medical insurers will support bilateral implantation, many successful implant surgeries have been performed with full or partial coverage. As more data are generated on the cost-effectiveness of bilateral implants over the life span of the child, the issue of reimbursement may become less problematic. It is important for centers fitting bilateral implants to report their findings so that all deaf children can take advantage of the research that demonstrates their effectiveness. Best practice for children with hearing loss has always been binaural amplification. Deaf children who receive cochlear implants deserve the same consideration.

COCHLEAR IMPLANTS AND HEARING AIDS

In the opening chapter of this book, one of the changes reported in the field of cochlear implants over the past decade was the implantation of children with some residual hearing. Presuming that many of these children have symmetric hearing loss, the likelihood of their having some usable hearing on the side opposite the implant is high. Before bilateral implantation is even considered, the recommendation of placing a hearing aid on the opposite ear is important. Initially, there was skepticism about the cochlear implant, an electrical device, working in conjunction with a hearing aid, an acoustic device. However, research in this area has shown that both devices can and should be used satisfactorily (Ching et al., 2001).

Ultimately, the goal of the use of a cochlear implant in one ear and a hearing aid in the other (often referred to as bimodal stimulation) is to provide bilateral hearing and the benefits inherent thereof. These include localization and improved performance in quiet and in noise. A secondary goal would be to provide continuous stimulation to the unimplanted ear so that it can be "primed" to take advantage of future technology. To derive the benefit of hearing with the opposite ear, a properly fit hearing aid is required. As the cochlear implant is tuned differently from a hearing aid (although they both apply the same basic principles) it is important that the programming audiologist work in tandem with the hearing aid dispensing audiologist to ensure the best outcome. It is not a matter of merely placing the hearing aid back on the opposite ear after the implant has been activated. For these devices to work appropriately, prescriptive methods of fitting should be utilized.

Ching et al. (2003, 2004) implemented a fitting protocol for children and adults for proper programming of their hearing aid in conjunction with their implant. In her study of 23 children (2003) almost half of whom had previously discontinued hearing aid use prior to implantation, she was able to demonstrate improved performance for the entire group when using both devices. She also showed that no child exhibited a decrement in performance when using the hearing aid with the cochlear implant. She reported similar findings for 21 adults (2004) when they utilized their cochlear implant with their hearing aid as opposed to the cochlear implant alone or the hearing aid alone. The importance of proper fitting of the hearing aid was emphasized to ensure the best outcome.

Numerous other researchers confirmed Ching's findings when fitting a hearing aid in the opposite ear (Hamzavi et al., 2004; Tyler et al., 2002). However a number of factors should be considered when providing this type of stimulation. These include the age of the child, the duration of hearing aid use, the educational demands on the child, the amount of residual hearing, and the level of commitment on the part of the parents, recipient, and professionals.

The age of the child is more a factor for older children than younger ones. With prescriptive methods now available for both hearing aids and implants, the ability to derive a proper fit should be well within the reach of the audiologist. Young children who have worn hearing aids the entire time prior to implantation should be fitted with both devices immediately, before they make the decision that wearing one is more comfortable. Interestingly, children with residual hearing are more reluctant to relinquish the hearing aid and will use it successfully with the implant from the time of initial activation. Children who ceased wearing a hearing aid after implantation may be more hesitant to resume using a device in the opposite ear as it sometimes requires that listening be "retrained." Clearly then, duration of hearing aid use in the ear opposite the implant plays an important role.

In addition to the age of the child and duration of hearing aid use, the demands of the classroom must be taken into account. A child who has functioned only with a cochlear implant for a long period of time will require acclimation to wearing both devices. When children are under intense academic constraints, it is probably best to wait until the classroom situation is less demanding to ease transition to using both devices.

The amount of residual hearing in the ear opposite the implant will most certainly play an important role. Children with more residual hearing will have greater benefit and will tend to continue to use their hearing aid after implantation. Children whose hearing in the opposite ear is very limited may find the addition of a hearing aid bothersome with no real gain to be derived. The key to wearing both devices is the level of motivation and commitment on the part of the recipient, the parents, and the professionals involved with the recipient. School-based personnel should understand this commitment to reinforce simultaneous use of a hearing aid and cochlear implant.

Questions posed for issues concerning hearing with bilateral implants are quite similar to those addressing the use of a hearing aid with a cochlear implant.

MY CHILD IS DOING SO WELL WITH AN IMPLANT WON'T THE ADDITION OF A HEARING AID TO THE OTHER EAR CREATE A CONFUSING SIGNAL?

As noted in the research by Ching et al. (2003), no child demonstrated a decrement in performance when using a hearing aid in the opposite ear. In cases in which the hearing in the opposite ear is profound, there may be very little functional benefit in wearing the hearing aid. However, continued stimulation to the unimplanted ear could only act as a positive rather than a negative influence. Adults who have used a hearing aid on the opposite side all report a qualitative change even when a quantitative one is not evident (Chute et al., 1995; Tyler et al., 2002).

SHOULD A CHILD WITH SOME RESIDUAL HEARING IN THE OPPOSITE EAR CEASE WEARING THE HEARING AID FOR A PERIOD OF TIME TO "FORCE" THE IMPLANTED EAR TO LEARN TO LISTEN?

Again, the answer is similar to that discussed with bilateral implants. Children should use both devices simultaneously during all waking hours. During therapy sessions, activities can focus on using the cochlear implant alone, the hearing aid alone, and the cochlear implant and hearing aid together. As the goal in bimodal stimulation is bilateral hearing, children should use these devices together in primary listening conditions to gain valuable experience. Certainly for children in noisy classrooms the benefits of wearing both devices far outweigh any risk. There is a misconception by some school personnel that continuing use of the hearing aid in the opposite ear will prevent the child from learning to use the implant. Again, best practice with hearing aids would not support this claim. Besides, for some children who are reliant on their hearing aids, denying them access may actually set up a negative reaction to the implant. This is certainly not the goal.

IF A CHILD IS RECEIVING SOME BENEFIT FROM WEARING A HEARING AID IN THE OPPOSITE EAR, HOW WILL I KNOW IF AN IMPLANT IN THAT EAR WOULD BE BETTER?

This question can only be answered after a child undergoes a series of evaluations at the cochlear implant center. Speech perception tests performed in quiet and in a background of noise will provide the audiologist with a yardstick with which to make a recommendation. Any child wearing an implant and a hearing aid should be monitored yearly with a variety of assessments that include speech, language, audition, and educational tests. Continued communication with the cochlear implant center will assist families and recipients in making the best decision at the best time. Observations by teachers, school-based SLPs, and educational audiologists become invaluable in these circumstances as they provide input regarding the child's ability to function in school.

WILL A REFITTING OF THE HEARING AID BE REQUIRED EACH TIME THE CHILD IS MAPPED?

Studies that have assessed cochlear implants and hearing aids have not reported routine refitting of the hearing aid along with cochlear implant mapping. However, continued assessment by the programming audiologist coupled with information from the school may identify children who might require hearing aid refitting. This is most often a result of a decrement in hearing in the unimplanted ear requiring a change in the gain of the hearing aid. It is important that children with residual hearing in the opposite ear be monitored for any changes in hearing level in that ear over time. The role of the educational audiologist for these children is critical in the early identification of any changes in hearing acuity. Threshold shifts should be reported to the parent and the cochlear implant center to ensure that the child is receiving the best signal from both devices.

WHAT ROLE MIGHT SCHOOL-BASED PROFESSIONALS PLAY IN THIS PROCESS?

The major contributions that school-based personnel can make are threefold: evaluation, rehabilitation, and counseling. Teachers, SLPs, and audiologists with knowledge of the child can obtain baseline performance measures against which progress can be charted. These individuals can be supportive of the use of two devices whether they both are cochlear implants or one is an implant and one a hearing aid. Rehabilitation goals should be realistic and foster the use of both devices simultaneously. Information regarding the availability of bilateral implantation should be disseminated to parents considering implantation so that school professionals can play a proactive role.

SUMMARY

The state of the art of cochlear implantation has created a new landscape that requires professionals to understand the effects of implantation alone, implantation with a hearing aid in the opposite ear, and implantation in both ears. The effects of bilateral stimulation on listening in classrooms cannot be overlooked. With more demanding material being presented to school-aged children at younger ages, the ability to access language and vocabulary becomes even more critical. Acoustic situations that diminish good speech perception, such as background noise, soft speech, or speech signals that cannot be localized quickly enough to discriminate, create a need for better input to the auditory system. Even outside the classroom, children function in a noisy environment for day-to-day social interaction. For all these reasons, any device configuration, whether it is bilateral cochlear implants or a cochlear implant in one ear and a hearing aid in the other ear, that enhances listening ability should be fully explored.

Chapter 13

SOCIAL DEVELOPMENT AND THE COCHLEAR IMPLANT

When the cochlear implant was first introduced, it was studied in great depth from the perspective of its being an auditory prosthesis. As a result, researchers measured its effects on audition and, more specifically, speech perception. It was not until later that outcomes related to speech and language development were explored. Further in the process, research into the academic achievements of children with implants commenced. The last area to receive attention has been socialization. Interestingly, it is this most recent field of study that fueled much of the initial controversy around implantation.

The Deaf community has always believed that children who are born deaf are born into a culture that incorporates a linguistic, educational, political, and social complexity that defines it. A vital portion of this community is its close-knit interaction that relies on the common language of ASL. It embraces those with all levels of hearing loss (and hearing persons with ties to the Deaf community such as interpreters) making no judgment about an individual's ability to exist using more traditional communication modalities. Within the community, oral language is not necessary and, therefore, any societal stigma from using it less efficiently is unimportant. In the past, many children were given hearing aids in an attempt to acquire oral communication ability but were unable to access enough hearing through them to develop spoken language skills. Often these children were negatively labeled. There are accounts of children who were forced to try to use this nonfunctional hearing and, when they failed, were made to feel inferior. It was not until they later "discovered" ASL and communication success that they believe their lives began.

To some extent, the cochlear implant has changed this process. It is well documented that the majority of children, given certain profiles, can successfully use a cochlear implant to develop oral language skills. But, the question remains as to whether these children will be socially adept at negotiating a world that has certainly undergone some remarkable changes. An understanding of how children with cochlear implants grow up socially is still unclear as the research has been less immediate in this area. However, some studies have begun to shed some light on this evolving area of human development. Before addressing this research, it is important to understand what is generically categorized as "socialization" and the facets that it incorporates.

Socialization begins at birth and is a direct result of communication with society. For the infant, this communication begins with the immediate family and more directly, the mother. Research has shown that children who do not receive this type of attention often have difficulties in developing attachments later in life (Mellon, 2000). As socialization is so integrally based on language, children who cannot easily access the language of the home begin at a disadvantage that sometimes continues throughout their lives. But even the best communication at home does not necessarily ensure the best socialization skills outside the home. From birth to adulthood, individuals must learn to be able to interact with a variety of communication partners who will range from the very familiar (mom, dad, siblings) to the very unfamiliar (strangers). This progression in socialization building begins in the home, expands to the immediate extended family, the neighborhood, school, friends, the workplace, and finally to those totally unknown. In some cases, socialization will be facilitated by language; in other cases, it may be hindered by internal emotions that are completely unrelated to language.

Early communication begins in infancy when the newborn learns that even crying can be rewarded with actions that result in a positive reaction. Bonds between parent and child evolve over time as the child learns the social mores of the household. Positive reinforcement educates the child in behaviors that support general societal norms. Negative reinforcement may create an environment from which social skills become stunted or, in the worst case, result in antisocial behavior. As children leave the cocoon of the household, they expand their abilities to communicate among extended family members as well as neighborhood friends. If a child's ability to communicate in the language of this next circle of interaction is inefficient, then certain developmental, social milestones may not be met. Lack of communication can take many forms. It may not necessarily mean that the language skills of the child do not match the language requirements of this next layer of societal contact. It may also be a matter of other personality traits that inhibit the child's ability to fully relate to the outside world. As the circles of interaction expand, any inability to communicate within the previous circle will have deleterious effects on those that expand from the home base.

It would appear, then, that socialization is not just a function of the act of communication but the manner in which one communicates. Certainly, many of us know individuals who have perfect command of English and are still considered to be outside the social process due to other compounding factors. The manner of communication sets up circumstances that contribute to, or detract from, the development of personality.

PERSONALITY AND SELF-ESTEEM

Personality is also a multifaceted aspect of human nature that is tied to the socialization process. Personality traits have been measured using various scales and questionnaires, and attempts to pigeonhole individuals into one personality type have not met with success. Personality consists of myriad other traits that contribute to the manner in which an individual responds to daily life.

From the ability to communicate and interact with others, images of self-esteem and feelings of self-worth evolve. When parents and teachers communicate with their children in a manner that "build[s] inner confidence, a sense of purpose and involvement, meaningful constructive relationships with others, [and] success at school" (Corkille-Briggs, 1970, p. 2), children are more likely to have a positive self-image. As an adult, feelings of self-worth may be related to a person's ability to be employed at a level representing an income that can support a particular lifestyle. Employment is often tied to an individual's ability to communicate either orally or in the written form. Data on the writing and reading skills of children from schools for the deaf indicate that many children who graduate from these programs will approach adulthood with marked employment disadvantages (Kasen et al., 1990). Proponents of implantation will cite this literature, which notes the poor reading and writing level of children who use manual communication, as proof to support implantation as a vehicle to improve these skills. Opponents of cochlear implantation will suggest that children who are unable to reap the potential of the implant and develop only limited communication ability via spoken language will harbor feelings of resentment and poor self-worth. Most recently, data on employment and quality of life offered by the hearing aid industry demonstrate that the degree of hearing loss affects income over the lifetime of the hearing impaired individual (*Hearing Journal,* 2005). Many parents are seeking implantation with long-term goals of employment equity for their child in mind. The larger question remains as to whether a cochlear implant can contribute to personal fulfillment and happiness. Will the increased potential for language competence with the cochlear implant influence social and emotional development in a positive way?

Research coming from the University of Maryland's (UMD) Child Development Lab may soon help in understanding the impact that implantation has in the social and emotional development of the young child. Researchers at UMD are looking at the functioning of several key aspects of the social and emotional development of children with cochlear implants in an effort to identify "specific areas of social or emotional difficulty [that] could enable targeted intervention" for children with cochlear implants (Schorr, 2005, p. 31). In addition, identification of potential areas of concern may trigger more proactive intervention for children receiving implants. Because language acquisition is closely associated with identity, social development, and social integration, perhaps the social impact of implantation may be inferred from gains in language development.

Quittner et al. (2004) reported changes in cognitive, social, and behavior development postimplantation that were related to the improved communication ability enjoyed by these young children. They identify a synergistic effect that enables the child to respond to his or her environment in a more naturalistic manner. The belief is that this will lead to better parent-child relationships, better communication, and increased self-image. Quittner's study utilized a very young implant recipient in an effort to demonstrate these early improvements. Clearly longitudinal studies will be required before any definitive conclusions can be made.

AN HISTORICAL PICTURE

It may also be helpful to consider the historical research on the social-emotional development of deaf children that was accomplished in the decade of the 1980s prior to the availability of the cochlear implant for the pediatric population. In so doing, we may be able to get a picture of the impact of hearing loss without implantation. The reader is cautioned, however, to review the following information with an understanding that the effects of profound deafness can never be viewed in isolation; results of investigations into the social and emotional development of deaf youngsters may be influence by factors that are a byproduct of the deafness (Moores, 1996). In fact, it may very well be that it was the inadequate coping behaviors of the significant others in the child's life that affected adequate social development of the deaf child (Levine, 1981). The confounding effects of language skill in understanding tasks and examiners' queries cannot be overlooked. That being said, it makes intuitive sense that auditory access provided by the cochlear implant may change the "coping behaviors of the significant others in the child's life" thereby limiting negative caregiver reaction in the equation of social skill development for the deaf child.

Many deaf children have been labeled with behavioral characteristics which include immaturity, impulsivity, and lack of empathy (Schlesinger & Meadow, 1972) that can have a deleterious effect on social functioning. Clearly, children who have good language ability, regardless of communication modality, tend to demonstrate better interpersonal skills (Spenser, Koester, & Meadow-Orlans, 1994).

Unfortunately, the majority of the population of deaf children is born to hearing parents whose dominant language modality is oral. As the implant closes the gap on language development, especially in children who are implanted early, it may likewise produce fewer children with behavioral traits that impede socialization.

With that in mind, three scenarios are offered to the reader as examples of differences and similarities that exist in social contexts. Imagine two deaf teens in animated conversation, signing to each other and laughing about the topic. Simultaneously, picture two other teens who have cochlear implants speaking with each other in a different conversation. A third group consists of hearing children talking about the party that occurred yesterday. Which group of the three would you consider to be "happier" or more socially adept? Obviously, the answer is "all three" as each dyad is communicating within a monocentric group with similar wants and needs. Consider, however, a slight change. The first deaf teen leaves his or her deaf classmate and walks into the local grocery store. The student is then met there by one of the implant recipients and one hearing adolescent. Which child now would you perceive as "happier" or more socially adept? The answer, once again, is "all three." If we look at the child as an entity who has self-image so that he or she is able to function with a sense of character, no hearing loss will stand in the way. Imagine one last scenario. This time take a look at the hearing child and know that this child has very poor self-image and has few, if any, friends. A walk to the local grocery store for this child may be more daunting than for anyone who may have difficulty communicating.

But, for a moment, let us take a closer look at a child who uses only manual communication and feels self-conscious in communication settings with hearing persons because of it. Clearly, an inability to communicate with others outside those that use sign language will create more challenges for this child. Intuitively then, one asks "Does the child with the cochlear implant socialize better because of the ability to communicate?" It has been noted that even hearing individuals face challenges when placed in social situations. Therefore, the cochlear implant may assist the child in getting as close as possible to the social constructs of society but may still not be fully integrated simply because of other constraints superfluous to the implant. The questions are then "What's a teacher to do? What's a parent to do?"

Teachers and school professionals can begin the process of adding to their knowledge base of children with implants by evaluating them with respect to their social development. School personnel should observe the implanted child's behaviors in small- group academic activities as well as small-group play events. Likewise, these observations should be made during large group activities in the respective areas. Analysis of one-on-one interactions with other children and adults can also add valuable information to the findings of the speech and hearing professional who is monitoring a child with a cochlear implant. The question of changes in social behavior can only be answered if school personnel systematically evaluate its development. As changes occur in the classroom, they are often seen at home.

The literature suggests that good communication among family members is the cornerstone of good social functioning. However, the exact nature of the communication may also be at the root of the problem. Often, in a parent's quest to ensure academic competitiveness, the child is left with little time for other social activities. Similarly, some tasks may be too demanding for the child's listening skills due to the excessive background noise that accompanies them. Finally, children who are placed in mainstream activities without any precounseling of the leader, or of other participants, may find themselves outside the communicative interactions that are integral to successful participation.

School professionals can assist children with implants by ensuring that they are supportive of the child's participation in activities outside the classroom. Sometimes a suggestion by the teacher or the SLP for a child to join a particular club is all that is takes. But, once the suggestion is made, school personnel must be prepared to follow up by providing much needed information to those who are unfamiliar with a deaf child with a cochlear implant. It may take some reconfiguration of the lunchroom tables to ensure that the implanted child is not left sitting alone. Likewise, teachers can provide the positive support that so many children crave as they pass through their educational experiences.

Parents should be wary of filling the child's day with therapy as opposed to other sports or social events. Recognizing an individual child's strengths and weakness will also assist in the choice of activities that might be best. Encouragement and continued support arc critical especially for the child during the middle school years.

As more children with implants have entered mainstream classrooms, it is easier to identify other children who also have these devices. Many cochlear implant centers have support groups and activities for children with implants. Web sites have been set up for young implant recipients so that they can correspond via the Internet. The Internet has changed the face of how we all communicate. A deaf child on the Internet is no different from a hearing child as communication is through the written word. In fact, the Internet and its resources for communication have been the impetus behind children's learning to write and read more effectively. Despite its power, parents are urged to use caution with their child's use of the Internet; the inherent risk of free and open communication requires that parents continuously monitor their child's correspondences.

SUMMARY

The benefits of cochlear implantation have expanded far beyond the areas of auditory perception as these devices have improved over time. Through improved audition, access to spoken language skills has become an attainable goal for a large number of implanted children. With these new spoken language skills, children can begin to gain entry into hearing society in a more seamless and natural manner. This access has created opportunities for deaf children to socialize within the larger society. This not only provides deaf children with the potential for gaining insight into hearing society but also allows for hearing society to gain insight into deaf children. This unprecedented exchange may be the beginnings of social growth for all that evolves from mutual communication and understanding.

Chapter 14

A GLIMPSE INTO
THE FUTURE

Over the past 50 years, the manner in which we rehabilitate those with hearing loss has seen enormous change. These changes have resulted in the birth and growth of the fields of audiology, speech-language pathology, and deaf education. Like all growth, it is not without some pain that has, at times, stalled progress by polarizing those treating and those being treated. No doubt, those who continually question technology, treatment paradigms, and philosophical orientation regarding hearing loss will remain. Instead of waging a persistent battle over who is right, professionals must be able to embrace all technologies, treatment options, and philosophies in a manner that respects individual choice. The remarkable changes that have occurred during the last half of the previous century are nothing compared to what lies ahead. The question remains whether we, as professionals, will be ready for them and what role we will play in their effectiveness.

As we saw in Chapter 1, the evolutions in the technologic arena have brought us from very rudimentary, first-generation hearing aids to the cochlear implant. Treatments essentially moved from devices used outside the body of deaf and hard-of-hearing individuals to those that required surgical intervention, thus bringing physicians into an area that was often foreign to their practice and knowledge. As a rule, deafness was a diagnosis provided by the physician and audiologist and turned over to the hearing aid dispenser and teacher. Deaf culture was virtually unknown to the medical world before the birth of the implant. It is now an integral part of their understanding about implantation and its effects on a community. Clearly, this aspect of treating (or not treating) deafness will continue to be part of the fabric that makes up the lives of those with hearing loss. Likewise, methods by which diagnostic and treatment protocols evolve will present new challenges to professionals who provide long and short-term solutions.

As we take a glimpse into the future of treating hearing loss, several "players" need to be considered. Each has a role that will change with time. To conceive of what lies ahead entails consideration of how manufacturers (and their researchers), professionals, and the individual with hearing loss will contribute to this process. The future is not strictly about technology and what will be available. It is also about the professionals who dispense the technology and the people who receive it. A closer look and some "thinking outside the box" is what this chapter represents. For the reader, it is important to understand that these are notions that may or may not ever come to be. But, it is also important to understand that once, a long time ago, man envisioned being able to fly like a bird in the air. Without being able to dream of what might be, we are immobilized in a present without perspective of tomorrow. It is with those dreams that the reader is cautioned so as not to think that what is being suggested *will* occur but only to think about the possibilities that *might* occur.

To look into the future, it is necessary to spend a bit of time in the past to see how we have arrived at where we are today. We know that cochlear implants have gotten smaller and more efficient, offer better speech perception, and now can be used in infants and those with residual hearing. Clarke (2004) sees the future as one that technologically will offer improved speech processing strategies, totally implantable devices, hybrid devices, and smarter programming systems. As we explore each of these areas from a technologic point of view, we must also understand them within the context of the professionals in the field and the individual with hearing loss.

FUTURE TECHNOLOGY

For those with hearing loss, regardless of degree, the goal of any technology from hearing aids to cochlear implants is to attempt to restore as much function as possible. To do this, we have seen hearing aids evolve from simple analog models to digital ones that can better deliver sound to the damaged auditory system. The overall goal is to improve speech perception ability and communicative function to the person with hearing loss. With the cochlear implant, the issue of what features to codes and send to the electrodes can be the difference between a system that works and one that does not. To simplify matters about speech processing strategies, it is sufficient to say that we are still implanting electrodes into a badly damaged system and must not only select those features of sound that we believe to be important but deliver them into a physiologically inferior structure. We also know that the auditory system, when damaged, is often unable to control its own ability to handle loudness growth and, therefore, requires some type of optimization of this important aspect of sound. Present day systems now have some type of "dynamic range optimization" but these still remain rudimentary. It may very well be that some other aspect of sound must be emphasized to provide better speech perception.

There has been much emphasis placed on the "speed" of the speech processing strategy. In some cases, this may be a more effective method of providing a better signal, but it may not be true in other cases. Stimulating nerves faster does not necessarily mean that they are able to function more effectively as there is a time period where the nerve needs to "rest" and then "regain" function. If the signal is being delivered at consistently high rates, the nerve may be unable to "fire" quickly enough to take advantage of it. One is reminded at this point of the classic comedy routine from the show "I Love Lucy" when a conveyor belt of candies to be wrapped passes in front of Lucy. She is quite able to perform the task when the belt is moving at a reasonable pace but as it speeds up she is unable to keep up with the delivery of the candy thereby making the process fruitless. In some respects, we should think about the speeding conveyor belt of candy as the delivery speed and the auditory nerve as poor Lucy trying to capture as many pieces of candy (i.e., signal) that she can. In some cases, it is totally impossible. But let us take the analogy farther. Maybe with training her speed will increase. Maybe someone else is more proficient than Lucy (could it be Ethel?) and she or he is able to handle a more rapid conveyor belt. Rate is an unknown variable at the present time that may have far-reaching effects postimplantation. Would it not be wonderful to be able to predict either ahead of time or at the time of device activation which speed is optimal for an individual implant recipient? In a similar manner, would it not also be wonderful to be able to estimate better the neural survival for each cochlea, thus making the mapping process more individualized?

One should also be reminded that different speech features are more discernible at different rates. For example, high rates deliver information about manner of articulation more effectively; low rates tend to be better for place of articulation (Grayden & Clark, 2000). As the ultimate goal is to make speech more intelligible, future systems will need to take this information into account in a more effective manner. But it may not only be about the "speech." There is no reason to assume that a deaf individual who receives a cochlear implant should only be interested in hearing someone speak. We fill our days with music. No one is free from watching the millions of individuals worldwide connected to their iPods as they hum, sing, or just listen to whatever variety of music makes them happy. The music industry is so aware of this phenomenon that lawsuits have erupted over "shareware," which allows computer-savvy individuals the ability to download just about anything they want for their listening pleasure. Somewhere in the midst of trying to make speech more perceptible, we ignored the fact that individuals with hearing loss would like to participate in all aspects of life—including musical perception. The challenge of making music more distinct for cochlear implant recipients is an area of growing research. The finer timing cues along with the neural responses in the cochlea will have to be overcome before music can really sound better for the implant recipient.

To deliver all the important information to the cochlear nerve, the electrode itself has always been a critical part of the system. Recall that the auditory nerve is made up of thousands of fibers that run through the center core of the cochlea. Previous research has shown that electrodes situated closer to the center portion (known as the modiolus) can deliver the signal more efficiently to the neural tissue. But, remember that the electrode is never able to reach the most apical portion of the cochlea and despite improved electrode models that tend to coil around the modiolus, there is still a need to develop better designs. This is where the newest scientific techniques that incorporate nanotechnology may become important. Nanotechnology for those not aware is known as the "science of the small" (Clark, 2004). It permits scientists to build replicas of human anatomy down to the cellular level to allow for better modeling of systems. The average size of present-day electrodes is approximately 17 mm. The average length of the basilar membrane in the cochlea is 35 mm. Clearly, if we are ever to attempt to get more discrete firing of the neural elements, we will have to be able to introduce an electrode that is similar in size to the cochlea in which it sits. Clark (2004) suggests the use of hydrogels, which would curl as they meet the cochlear fluids. He has also suggested thin film technology that can be used with the hydrogels to introduce finer electrodes closer to the modiolus. Lastly, there is some thought that electrodes that act at auditory intraneural arrays whereby there is a direct interface between the electrode and the nerve may be possible (Clark, 2004).

Undoubtedly, there can be no discussion about the future of implantation without mention of the all-implantable device. Major questions still remain about the position and type of microphone that could sustain daily wear and exposure. Many possibilities are being investigated from using the natural anatomy of the ear as a microphone to the use of infrared light that is reflected off the eardrum. Certainly, the issue of power to the all-implantable device must be considered. Whether there will be a rechargeable battery that will require replacement over time or a system that could be externally charged while sleeping are both possible scenarios.

The future of hair cell regeneration and genetic engineering are also part of the expectations of those with hearing loss. Although hair cell regeneration has been successful in lower animals (the chick), and newer models of identifying some of the genes appear promising, there are still numerous setbacks in this effectively reaching the population in the very near future. The question of the use of neural growth hormones that can be "pumped" into an implanted electrode array combines the use of electrical stimulation with some form of regeneration. These techniques may have greater ramifications for the more long-term or congenitally deafened individual (Clark, 2004).

Genetic engineering has now begun as several of the genes associated with deafness have been identified. The issue of manipulating these genes in utero remains an untapped aspect of science that will bring the ethicists and scientists into some contentious discussion. The outcomes of genetic engineering have already been observed for some other syndromes. There is no doubt that similar reconstruction of genes for deafness may be on the horizon.

EFFECTS OF TECHNOLOGY ON SCHOOL PROFESSIONALS

If we think back to the days of the Wright brothers, no one would have ever thought of the growth of the air industry itself and the many other industries outside of aeronautics that would develop. The opportunities for employment and expansion of services within any new industry are logarithmic in the initial stages. If the industry is to sustain itself over time, it must continually evolve, invent, and expand. This requires skills in individuals to support that industry. The airlines would be nowhere today without their own staff of pilots, flight attendants, travel agents, schedulers, air traffic controllers, and so forth. Likewise, industries that are tangentially related to, but nonetheless dependent upon the airlines include everything from recreational activities at Disney World to sending a Fed Ex package to someone across the country (when it positively has to be there). That being said, what does the future hold for professionals presently working in the field of implantation and how might that change?

First and foremost, the key to real change is the recognition that it is occurring and a willingness to adapt to it. Those of you who have read *Who Moved My Cheese* (Johnson, 1998) are aware that some individuals find change difficult. For a variety of reasons that have paralyzed the world of deafness for decades, many individuals are reluctant to embrace philosophies that may not be those that were sufficient at the start of their careers. The evolution of technology will require a revolution in the way we educate professionals and the children who are the recipients of the new technology. Let us explore the future for each of the professionals for whom this book has been written.

THE AUDIOLOGIST

The sheer manpower that will be required as cochlear implants (and hearing aids for that matter) will increase substantially as devices become more widely distributed. In a survey of graduate programs in the United States, it was found that 40% of the audiologists and 30% of the speech-language pathologists had no exposure to implantation on the graduate level (Chute, 2003). In a survey of cochlear implant centers performed that same year, there were fewer than two audiologists in 60% of the centers. If the field is to expand at all, the number of audiologists who are capable of fitting an implant must grow. Service delivery models must change as well. New skills will be required on the part of audiologists in the field and cochlear implants must expand outside the surgical centers so that more individuals can receive services. For this to occur, two issues must be addressed. The first is mapping; the second is the location of the mapping audiologist.

Mapping the cochlear implant has progressed substantially so that it has become demystified over time. Newer software packages combine electrophysiologic responses that can be obtained while the child is undergoing the surgery, to those that can be adjusted later using similar paradigms along with some optimized or streamlined protocols. More recent programming models are researching the use of "genetic algorithms" that essentially have the recipient listening to several selections of speech and choosing which sounds best. This is done repetitively until a sampling has been obtained (while more automatic adjustments are made to the maps) and until a target level of performance is reached. Obviously, this can only be done with individuals who can provide the appropriate type of feedback.

In addition to changes in the mapping of the cochlear implant, the professional who is performing the mapping and the expertise and location of the mapping procedure will also evolve. There are now more courses and opportunities for audiologists in the field to learn how to map. Mapping may very well come under the purview of the educational audiologist as more children enter mainstream school programs. This will not only require training but funding to make it possible.

The concept of remote mapping may also become more conventional for individuals who are not geographically close to an audiologist with implant knowledge. Videostreaming permits an audiologist in one center to assist the programming audiologist at a more remote location with fitting the map (Franck, 2005). The question has always been raised as to whether mapping can be effectively performed via traditional telephone lines. Undoubtedly, as telemedicine progresses, both the clinical and ethical issues of utilizing these methods for audiologic purposes needs further exploration.

Other technologies that will be further explored may be commonly used items such as PDAs or memory sticks to allow for downloads of maps to other forms of technologies that may be at the recipient's disposal. Certainly, even today, as cochlear implant recipients travel around the world, it is worthwhile for them to be in possession of the specifications of the map should they require a remapping while traveling. This can easily be accomplished through the use of a memory stick. But more, importantly, a national database that houses all maps that can be retrieved at any time, anywhere, is already being developed.

Issues of what constitutes the "best" map, and whether there is some method of predicting performance preimplantation, still eludes us. Likewise, postimplantation mapping should not require the amount of upkeep that present systems seem to demand. This may be more of a counseling change than anything else. To continue to map cochlear implant recipients frequently, even after years of use, is counterproductive and not cost-effective. With many implant centers facing financial constraints, it is important for all professionals involved in the cochlear implant (re)habilitation of individuals to understand what mapping can and cannot do.

As the possibilities of hybrid devices (part hearing aid and part cochlear implant) evolve, the dispensing audiologist must become integral to the process of implantation. Up to now, this group has remained outside the implant world as hearing aid dispensers who follow a different type of client. Certainly issues of reimbursement for all types of services that are audiologic in nature will continue to drive the cochlear implant dispensing process.

THE SPEECH-LANGUAGE PATHOLOGIST

The SLP remains the most qualified provider of postimplant (re)habilitative services for children with cochlear implants. They are trained in eliciting language, speech, and voice in children with and without hearing loss. With some retraining and retooling, their role in the postimplantation process is critical to the success of any single child. Training paradigms, however, have continued to change as children gain more knowledge of computers at younger ages and their exposures to other technologies is greater. To return to the issue of the iPod, it is not unusual to see hearing children, teens, and adults patched into these devices for very long periods of the day—whether it is when they are walking, exercising, or just sitting around. Use of this technology in conjunction with cochlear implant (re)habilitation has not yet occurred, but with very little adaptation can provide the child with continuous listening opportunities outside of therapy. This is not to suggest that this is the only type of listening therapy to which a child should be exposed, but it offers an opportunity to reinforce the activities that were part of the session. Learning to listen with a cochlear implant is a matter of overlearning what has been heard and overlaying it onto real life experiences. Separate from those experiences, however, listening to specially designed downloads that permit multiple exposures can only add to the process.

Home computers and software programs are beginning to make their way into carryover therapy experiences; however, more of these listening opportunities need to be individually tailored to the child. This will require technology (and training) that will permit the therapist to easily download lessons. In this manner, contextualized lessons can be played repetitively so that the child has the listening experience after leaving the therapy room. An interactive I-Pod may eventually do the programming?!

THE TEACHER OF THE DEAF OR MAINSTREAM TEACHER

The classrooms of the future will not remotely resemble those of today. Technology has already made its way into the self-contained classroom via infrared and loop systems, smart boards, computerized real-time captioning, and amplification. Paperless classrooms in which each student has a laptop networked to the teacher's will be commonplace. Assessment of student learning will take place through immediate computerized polling that allows the teacher to determine whether concepts are being understood. Real-time speech-to-print capability will make auditory access to the teacher's voice an option. Virtual field trips will be accomplished without ever leaving the school. Vast networks of communication will link schools to one another.

SUMMARY

As we began this book, we looked back on the two decades of cochlear implant work and how the winds of change have propelled this technology to where it is today. There is no doubt that technology will continue to evolve; however, it is important for professionals to be prepared as this transformation occurs. It is also important to understand that despite the brightness of the future, deaf children require cochlear implants now. Waiting for the next generation of devices will not help today's children.

The purpose of this final chapter is to empower professionals working with children with cochlear implants to be contributors to the process as it continues to evolve. It is true that the future is an unpredictable thing. Einstein once said, "I never think of the future—it comes soon enough." But if we do not look to the future or think about it, then we are but passive recipients rather than active participants. As professionals we are in the most prominent place to shape the future of how we address the needs of children and adults with hearing loss. However, it is only through continually changing our beliefs that we will be able to actively participate. Sara Ban Breathnach (2002, p. 113) put it best when she wrote ". . . change your beliefs, you change your behaviors. Change your behaviors, change how you make choices. Change your choices get more chances. Get more chances, take more risks. Take more risks" . . . and find more possibilities. The possibilities remain endless.

References

Adams, M. J. (1990). *Beginning to read: Thinking and learning about print.* Cambridge, MA: MIT Press.

Allen, T. (1986). A study of the achievement patterns of hearing-impaired students:1974–1983. In A. Schildroth & M. Karchern (Eds.), *Deaf Children in America* (pp. 161–206). San Diego, CA: College-Hill Press.

Alpiner, J., Hansen, E., & Kaufman, K. J. (2000). Transition: Rehabilitative audiology into the new millennium. In P. McCarthy & J. Alpiner (Eds.), *Rehabilitative audiology: Children and adults* (3rd ed.). Baltimore: Lippincott, Williams & Wilkins.

American National Standards Institute (ANSI). (2002). *Acoustical performance criteria, design requirements, and guidelines for schools.* S12.60. New York: Author.

Ban Breathnach, S. (2002). *Romancing the ordinary.* New York: Scribner.

Bellis, T. J. (2003). *Assessment and management of central auditory processing disorders in educational settings: From science to practice.* Clifton Park, NY: Delmar Learning.

Berlin, C., Hood, L., & Rose, K. (2001). On renaming auditory neuropathy as auditory dys-synchrony. *Audiology Today, 13*, 15–17.

Berlin, C., Morlet, T., & Hood, L. (2003). Auditory neuropathy and dyssynchrony: Its diagnosis and management. *Pediatric Clinics of North America, 50*, 331–340.

Bertram, B., Lenarz, T., & Lesinski, A. (2000). Cochlear implants for multihandicapped children pedagogic demands and expectations. In S. Waltzman & N. Cohen (Eds.), *Cochlear implants* (pp. 254–255). New York: Thieme.

Bilger, R. C., Black, F. O., & Hopkinson, N. T. (1977). Evaluation of subjects presented fitted with implanted auditory prostheses. *Annals of Otology, Rhinology and Laryngology, 86*(suppl 38), 1–16.

Bowen, C., & Cupples, L. (1998). A tested phonological therapy in practice. *Child Language Teaching and Therapy, 14*, 1, 29–50.

Calvert, D., & Silverman, S. R. (1975). *Speech & deafness.* Washington, DC: AG Bell.

Carney, A. (1986). Understanding speech intelligibility in the hearing impaired. *Topics in Language Disorders, 6,* 47–59.

Chall, J. (1979). The great debate: Ten years later, with a modest proposal for reading stages. In L. B. Resnick & P. A. Waever (Eds.), *Theory and practice of early reading.* Hillsdale, NJ: Erlbaum.

Chall, J. (1983). *Learning to read: The great debate.* New York: McGraw-Hill.

Ching, T. Y., Incerti, P., & Hill, M. (2004). Binaural benefits for adults who use hearing aids and cochlear implants in opposite ears. *Ear & Hearing, 25*(1), 9–21.

Ching, T. Y., Psarros, C., Hill, M., Dillon, H., & Incerti, P. (2001). Should children who use cochlear implants wear hearing aids in the opposite ear? *Ear & Hearing, 22*(5), 365–380.

Chute, P. M. (2001, February). *Children with multiple handicaps: Implications for implantation.* Paper presented at the 8th Symposium on Cochlear Implants in Children, Los Angeles, CA.

Chute, P. M. (2001, June). *Cochlear implants in children with multiple handicaps.* Presentation at the Northeast Regional Family Retreat, Sturbridge, MA.

Chute, P. M. (2003, April). *Manpower issues affecting cochlear implantation.* Paper presented at the 8th Conference on Cochlear Implants in Children. Washington, DC.

Chute, P. M., Fallon, M., & Marvin, L. (2005, May). *Speech and voice changes following bilateral cochlear implantation.* Paper presented at the 10th Symposium on cochlear implants in children, Dallas, TX.

Chute, P. M., Gravel, J. S., & Popp, A. L. (1995). Speech perception abilities of adults using a multichannel cochlear implant and frequency transposition hearing aid, *Annals of Otology, Rhinology and Laryngology Supplement, 166,* 260–263.

Chute, P. M., Kretschmer, R. E., Popp, A. L., & Parisier, S. C. (1995). Cochlear implants performance in a deaf child of deaf parents: A case study. *Annals of Otology, Rhinology and Laryngology Supplement, 166,* 316–318..

Chute, P. M., & Nevins, M. E. (1995). Cochlear implants in people who are deaf/blind. *Journal of Visual Impairment and Blindness, 89,* 297–301.

Chute, P. M., & Nevins, M. E. (2002). *The parents' guide to cochlear implants.* Washington, DC: Gallaudet University Press.

Chute, P. M., & Parisier, S. C. (2004). The simultaneous use of ACE and SPEAK in a bilaterally implanted adult. *International Congress Series, 1273,* 439–442.

Clark, G. M. (1975). A surgical approach for a cochlear implant. An anatomical study. *Journal of Laryngology and Otology, 89,* 9–15.

Clark, G. M. (1995). Cochlear implants: Historical perspective. In G. Plant & K. E. Spens (Eds.), *Profound deafness and communication* (pp. 165–218). London: Whurr.

Clark, G. M. (2004). *Cochlear implants: Fundamentals and applications* (pp. 381–442). New York: Springer-Verlag.

Clark, G. M., Busby, P. A., & Dowell, R. C. (1992). The development of the Melbourne/Cochlear multiple-channel cochlear implant for profoundly deaf children. *Australian Journal of Oto-Laryngology, 1,* 3–8.

Clark, G. M., Busby, P.A., & Roberts, S. A. (1987). Preliminary results for the Cochlear Corporation multi-electrode intracochlear implants on six prelingually deaf patients. *American Journal of Otology, 8,* 234–239.

Cleary, B. (1984). *Dear Mr. Henshaw.* New York: HarperCollins.

Corkille-Briggs, D. (1970). *Your child's self-esteem.* New York: Doubleday.

Cowan, R., DelDot, J., & Barker, E. J., et al. (1997). Speech perception results for children with implant with different levels of preoperative residual hearing. *American Journal of Otology, 18,* 125–126.

Crandell, C. (1998). Using sound field FM amplification in the education setting. *The Hearing Journal, 51,* 10–19.

Culbertson, J. L., & Gilbert, L. E. (1986). Children with unilateral sensorineural hearing loss: cognitive, academic and social development. *Ear & Hearing, 7,* 38–42.

Cummins, J. (1984). *Bilingualism and special education: Issues in assessment and pedagogy.* San Diego, CA: College-Hill Press.

Davis, B., & MacNeilage, P. (1995). The articulatory basis of babbling. *Journal of Speech and Hearing Research, 38,* 1199–1211.

Dayton, K. K. (1970). Oculomotor and visual problems in deaf children. *American Orthoptics Journal, 20,* 75–80.

DeFillipo, C., & Scott, B. (1978). A method for training and evaluating the reception of ongoing speech. *Journal of the Acoustical Society of America, 63,* 1186–1192.

Erber, N. (1982). *Auditory training.* Washington, DC: AG Bell.

Fetterman, B. L., & Domico, E. H. (2002). Speech recognition in background noise of cochlear implant patients. *Otolaryngology-Head and Neck Surgery, 126,* 257–263.

Firszt, J., Reeder, R., Wackym. A., & Barco, A. (2005). *Initial experiences of a 5-year multicenter study on bilateral implantation in children.* Paper presented at the 10th Symposium on cochlear implants in children, Dallas, TX.

Fountas, I., & Pinnell, G. S. (2001). *Guiding readers and writers.* Portsmouth, NH: Heinemann.

Fryauf-Bertschy, H., Tyler, R. S., Kelsay, D. M., & Gantz, F. J. (1992). Performance overtime of congenitally deaf and postlinguistically deafened children using a multichannel cochlear implant. *Journal of Speech, Language and Hearing Research, 35,* 913–920.

Franck, K. (2005). Cochlear Implant programming using telemedicine at the Childrens' Hospital of Philadelphia, *Volta Voices, 13.*

Fujita S., & Ito, I. (1999). Ability of Nucleus cochlear implantees to recognize music. *Annals of Otology, Rhinology and Laryngology, 108,* 634–640.

Gallaway, C. (1998). Early interaction. In S. Gregory, P. Knight, W. McCracken, & S. Powers, (Eds), *Issues in deaf education.* Clevedon, UK: Multilingual Matters.

Gantz, B. J., Tyler, R. S., Rubinstein, J. T., Wolaver, A., Lowder, M., Abbas, P., Hughes, M., & Preece, J. P. (2002). Binaural cochlear implants placed during the same operation. *Otology Neurotology, 23*(2), 169–180.

Garber, A., & Nevins, M. E. (2005, October 6). *Push-in or pull-out: Models for 1 on 1 services.* Cochlear Americas HOPE OnLine Seminar.

Gardner, H. (1983). *Frames of mind: The theories of multiple intelligences.* New York: Basic Books.

Geers, A. (2002). Factors affecting the development of speech, language and literacy in children with early cochlear implantation. *Language, Speech & Hearing Services in the Schools, 33,* 173–184.

Geers, A. (2003). Background and educational characteristics of prelingually deaf children implanted by 5 years of age. *Ear and Hearing, 24*(1, suppl.), 59S–68S.

Geers, A., & Moog, J. (1987). Predicting spoken language acquisition in profoundly deaf children. *Journal of Speech and Hearing Disorders, 52*(1), 84–94.

Geers, A., Nicholas, J., Tye-Murray, N., Uchanski, R., Brenner, C., Davidson, L., Toretta, G., & Tobey, E. (2000). Effects of communication mode on skills of long-term cochlear implant users. *Annals of Otology, Rhinology, and Laryngology Supplement, 185,* 85–92.

Geers, A., Tobey, E., & Moog, J. (2005). *Cochlear implantation and literacy.* Paper presented at the 10th Symposium on Cochlear Implants in Children; Dallas, TX.

Gfeller K. E., Knutson, J. F., Woodworth, G., Witt, S., & DeBus, B. (1998). Timbral recognition and appraisal by adult cochlear implant users and normal hearing adults. *Journal of American Academy of Audiology, 9,* 1–19.

Gfeller, K., Olszewski, C., Rychener, M., Sena, K., Knutson, J., Witt, S., & McPherson, B. (2005). Recognition of "real world" musical excerpts by cochlear implant recipients and normal hearing adults. *Ear & Hearing, 26,* 237–250.

Gfeller, K., Turner, C., Woodworth, G., Mehr, M., Feran, R., & Knutson, J. (2002). Recognition of familiar melodies by adult cochlear implant recipients and normal hearing adults. *Cochlear Implants International, 3*(1), 29–53.

Goldstein, M. (1939). *The acoustic method for the training of the deaf and hard of hearing.* St. Louis, MO: Laryngoscope Press.

Grayden, D. B., & Clark, G. M. (2000). The effect of rate stimulation of the auditory nerve on phoneme recognition. In M. Barlo (Ed.), *Proceedings of the 8th Australian International Conference on Speech Science and Technology* (pp. 356–361). Canberra, Australia: Australian Speech Science and Technology Association.

Guiberson, M. M. (2005). Children with cochlear implants from bilingual families: Considerations for intervention and a case study. *The Volta Review, 105*, 29–40.

Gunning, T. (1996). *Creating literacy instruction for all students.* Boston: Allyn & Bacon.

Hamzavi, J., Pok, S. M., Gstoettner, W., & Baumgartner, W. D. (2004). Speech perception with a cochlear implant used in conjunction with a hearing aid in the opposite ear. *International Journal of Audiology, 43*(2), 61–65.

Harker, L. J., Vanderheider, S., Veazey, D., Gentile, N., & McCleary, E. (1999). Multichannel cochlear implantation in children with large vestibular aqueduct syndrome. *Annals Otology, Rhinology, Laryngology, 108*, 39–43.

Harrington, M., & Powers, A. (2004). Cochlear implants and teacher preparation programs: A national survey. *Teacher Education and Special Education (TESE), 27*(4), 360–372.

Hearing Journal. (2005). Report. *Hearing Journal, 10*(6).

Hodson, B., & Paden, E. (1991). *Targeting intelligible speech: A phonological approach to remediation* (2nd ed.). Austin, TX: Pro-Ed.

House, L. R. (1987). Cochlear implants: The beginning. *Laryngoscope, 97*, 996–997.

House, W. F., & Urban, J. (1973). Long term results of electrode implantation and electronic stimulation of the cochlea in man. In W. S. Fields & H. Leavitt (Eds.), *Neural organization and its relevance to prosthetics* (pp. 273–280). New York: Intercontinental Medical Books.

Hudgins, C. V., & Numbers, F. (1942). An investigation of the intelligibility of speech of the deaf. *Genetics Psychology Monographs, 25*, 289–392.

Jensen, J. (1969). Malformations of the inner ear in deaf children. *Acta Radiology, 286*(suppl.), 1–97.

Johnson, D. (2001). *Vocabulary in the middle and elementary school.* Boston: Allyn & Bacon.

Johnson, S. (1998). *Who moved my cheese?* New York: G. Putnam & Sons.

Kasen, S., Ouellette, R., & Cohen, P. (1990). Mainstreaming and postsecondary educational and employment status of a rubella cohort. *American Annals of Deaf, 135*, 22–26.

Kirk, K. I. (2000). Challenges in the clinical investigation of cochlear implant outcomes. In J. K. Niparko (Ed.), *Cochlear Implants: Principles and practice* (pp. 269–290). Philadelphia: Lippincott, Williams and Wilkins.

Kirk, K., Miyamoto, R. Ying, E. Perdew, A. & Zuganelis, H. (2002). Cochlear implantation in young children: Effects of age at implantation and communication mode. *The Volta Review, 102,* 127–144.

Kretschmer, R., & Kretschmer, L. (1978). *Language development and intervention with the hearing-impaired.* Baltimore: University Park Press.

Lee, D. J., Gomez-Marin, O., & Lee, H. M. (1998). Prevalence of unilateral hearing loss in children: The National Health and Nutrition Examination Survey II and the Hispanic Health and Nutrition Examination Survey. *Ear and Hearing, 19*(4), 329–332.

Leguire, L., Fillman, R., Fishman, D., Bremer, D., & Rogers, G. (1992). A prospective study of ocular abnormalities in hearing impaired and deaf students. *Ear, Nose and Throat Journal, 12,* 643–646.

Levine, E. (1981). *The ecology of early deafness.* New York: Columbia University Press.

Ling, D. (1976). *Speech and the hearing impaired child: Theory and practices.* Washington, DC: AG Bell.

Ling, D. (1986). *Foundations of spoken language for hearing-impaired children.* Washington, DC: AG Bell.

Lof, G. (2004). *Confusions about speech sound norms and their use.* On-Line Language Conference available from: http://www.thinking publications.com/LangConf04/PosterSessions/PostersessionsPDFs/ LofPart1.pdf

Luetke-Stahlman, B., & Luckner, J. (1991). *Effectively educating students with hearing impairments.* New York: Longman.

Mangiari, A. (1991). *A child with a hearing loss in your classroom? Don't panic!* Washington, DC: AG Bell.

Markides, A. (1970). The speech of deaf and partially hearing children with special reference to factors affecting intelligibility. *British Journal of Disorders of Communication, 5,* 126–140.

Marschark, M., & Harris, M. (1996). Success and failure in learning to read: The special case of deaf children. In C. Cornoldi & J. Oakhill (Eds.), *Reading comprehension difficulties: Process and intervention* (pp. 279–300). Hillsdale, NJ: Erlbaum.

Mayne, A., Yoshinaga-Itano, & C. Sedey, A. (2000b). Receptive vocabulary development of infants and toddlers who are deaf or hard of hearing. *The Volta Review, 100,* 29–52.

Mayne, A., Yoshinaga-Itano, C., Sedey, A., & Carey, A. (2000a). Expressive vocabulary development of infants and toddlers who are deaf or hard of hearing. *The Volta Review, 100,* 1–28.

McCaffrey, H. A., Davis, B., MacNeilage, P., & von Hapsburg, D. (1999). Multichannel cochlear implantation and the organization of early speech. *The Volta Review, 101,* 5–29.

McClatchie, A., & Therres, M. K. (2003). *AUSPLAN: Auditory Speech and Language*. Oakland, CA: Children's Hospital & Research Center.

Mellon, N. (2000). Psychosocial development of children in deafness. In J. K. Niparko (Ed.), *Cochlear implants; Principles and practice* (pp. 319–321). Philadelphia: Lippincott, Williams and Wilkins.

Meyer, T. A., Svirsky, M. A., Kirk, K. I., & Miyamoto, R. T. (1998). Improvements in speech perception by children with profound prelingual hearing loss: Effects of device, communication mode, and chronological age. *Journal of Speech, Language and Hearing Research, 41*, 846–858.

Miyamoto, R., Kirk, K., Svirsky, M., & Sehgal, S. (1999). Communication skills in pediatric cochlear implant recipients. *Acta Otolaryngologica, 119*, 219–224.

Miyamoto, R. T., Osberger, M. J., & Robbins, A. M. (1994). Variables affecting performance in children *Laryngoscope, 104*, 1120–1124.

Moeller, M. P. (1998). *The deafness early intervention project: Strategies and outcomes*. Paper presented at the annual International Pediatrics Conference, Denver, CO.

Moog, J. S., & Geers, A. E. (1999). Speech and language acquisition in young children after cochlear implantation. *Early Identification and Intervention of Hearing Impaired Infants. 32*(6), 1127–1141.

Moores, D. (1996). *Educating the deaf: Psychology, principles and practices*. Boston: Houghton-Mifflin.

Nelson, K. (1986). *Event knowledge*. Hillsdale, NJ: Erlbaum Associates.

Nevins, M. E., & Chute, P. M. (1996). *Children with cochlear implants in educational settings*. San Diego, CA: Singular Publishing Group.

Niparko, J. K., Cheng, A. K., & Francis, H. W. (2000). Outcomes of cochlear implantation assessment of quality of life and economic evaluation of the benefits of cochlear implant in relation to costs. In J. K. Niparko (Ed.), *Cochlear implants: Principles and practice* (pp. 269–290). Philadelphia: Lippincott, Williams and Wilkins.

Osberger, M. J., & Fisher, L. (1998, June). *Preoperative predictors of postoperative implant performance in children*. Paper presented at the 7th Symposium on Cochlear Implants in Children; Iowa City, IA.

Osberger, M. J., Fisher, L., & Kalberer, A. (2000a). Speech perception results in children implanted with the CLARION multi-strategy cochlear implant. *Advances in Otorhinolaryngology, 57*, 417–420.

Osberger, M. J., Todd, D. S. L., Berry, S. W., Robbins, A.M., & Miyamoto, R. T. (1991). Effect of age at onset of deafness of children's speech perception abilities with a cochlear implant. *Annals Otology, Rhinology, and Laryngology, 100*, 883–888.

Osberger, M. J., Zimmerman-Phillips, S., & Fisher, L. (2000b). Relationship between communication mode and implant performance in pediatric

Clarion patients. In S. Waltzman & N. Cohen (Eds.), *Cochlear implants* (pp. 254-255). New York: Thieme.

Otto, J. W., & Kozak, V. (1998). *Questions teachers ask: A guide for the mainstream teacher with a hearing impaired student.* Washington, DC: AG Bell.

Peterson, A., Shallop, J., Driscoll, C., Breneman, A., Babb, J., Stoekel, R., & Fabry, L. (2003). Outcomes of cochlear implantation in children with auditory neuropathy. *Journal of American Academy of Audiology, 14*, 188-201.

Pollack, D. (1964). Acoupedics: A unisensory approach to auditory training. *The Volta Review, 66*, 400-409.

Quigley, S. P., & Kretschmer, R. E. (1982). *The education of deaf children.* Baltimore: University Park Press.

Quinn, M. A. (2005). *Speech goal selection and potential causes of breakdown.* Presentation for WI Department of Public Instruction: Evaluating Speech, Langauge and Auditory Competencies in Children who are Deaf/Hard of Hearing; Waukesau, WI.

Quittner, A., Leibach, B., & Marciel, K. (2004). The impact of cochlear implants on young deaf children. *Archives of Otolaryngology/Head and Neck Surgery, 130*, 547-554.

Robbins, A. M. (2000). Language development. In S. Waltzman & N. Cohen (Eds.), *Cochlear implants* (pp. 269-283). New York: Thieme.

Robbins, A. M. (2002). *How does total communication affect cochlear implant performance in children?* Paper presented at the 4th ACOF International Conference: The Impact of Scientific Advances on the Education of Deaf Children; Paris, France.

Robbins, A. M., Bollard, P. M., & Green, J. (1999). Language development in children implanted with the Clarion cochlear implant. *Annals Otology, Rhinology, and Laryngology Supplement, 177*, 113-118.

Robbins, A. M., Svirsky, M. A., Miyamoto, R.T., & Kessler, K. S.. (1995). Language development in children with cochlear implant. *Advances in Otorhinolaryngology, 50*, 160-166.

Rumelhart, D. E. (1982). Schemata: The building blocks of cognition. In J. Guthrie (Ed.), *Comprehension and teaching: Research reviews.* Newark, DE: International Reading Association.

Schlesinger, H., & Meadow, K. (1972*). Sound and sign: Childhood deafness and mental health.* Berkeley: University of California Press.

Schoor, E. (2005, Summer). Social and emotional development of children with cochlear implants. *Hearing Health*, pp. 31-33.

Schopmeyer, B., Dobaj, H., & Niparko, J. (1997, February). *Emergence of spontaneous expressive vocabulary in children with cochlear implants.* Paper presented at the Fifth International Cochlear Implant Conference; New York.

Schopmeyer, B., Mellon, N., Dobaj, H., & Niparker, J. (2000). Emergence of expressive vocabulary in children with cochlear implants. In S. Waltzman & N. Cohen (Eds.), *Cochlear implants* (pp. 287-288). New York: Thieme.

Seals, B. (2003). Interpreting for students with cochlear implants. *RID Views*, pp. 6-7.

Seep, B., Glosemeyer, R., Hulce, E., Linn, M., & Aytar, P. (2000). *Classroom acoustics: A resource for creating environments with desirable listening conditions.*. Melville, NY: Acoustical Society of America.

Shriberg, L. (1993). Four new speech and prosody voice measures for genetics research and other studies in developmental phonological disorders, *Journal of Speech and Hearing Research*, *36*, 105-140.

Spencer, L., Barker, B., & Tomblin, B. (2003). Exploring the language and literacy outcomes of pediatric cochlear implant users. *Ear & Hearing*, *24*, 236-247.

Spencer, P., Koester, L. S., & Meadow-Orlans, P. (1994). Communicative interactions of deaf and hearing children in a day care center. An exploratory study. *American Annals of the Deaf*, *139*, 512-518

Spencer, L., Tomblin, B., & Gantz, B. (1997). Reading skills in children with multichannel cochlear implant experience. *The Volta Review*, *99*, 193-202.

Staller, S. J., Beiter, A. L., Brimacombe, J. A, Mecklenberg, D., & Arndt, P. (1991). Pediatric performance with the Nucleus 22-channel cochlear implant system. *American Journal of Otology*, *12*, 126-136.

Stanovich, K. E. (1986). Matthew effects in reading: Some consequences of individual differences in the acquisition of literacy. *Reading Research Quarterly*, *22*, 360-407.

Stern, R. E., Yueh, B., Lewis, C., Norton, S., & Sie, K. C. (2005). Recent epidemiology of pediatric cochlear implantation in the United States: Disparity among children of different ethnicity and socioeconomic status. *Laryngoscope*, *115*(1), 125-131.

Svirsky, M. A., & Chin, S. B. (2000). Speech production. In S. Waltzman & N. Cohen (Eds.), *Cochlear implants* (pp. 293-309). New York: Thieme.

Svisrky, M. A., & Holt, R. (2005, May). *Speech perception and language in congenitally deaf children implanted in the first year of life.* Paper presented at the 10th Symposium on cochlear implants in children; Dallas, TX.

Thibodeau, L. (2003, November). *Electroacoustic assessment of cochlear implants and FM systems.* Paper presented at the American Speech Language and Hearing Association Convention; Chicago.

Tobey, E., Geers, A., Douek, B., Perrin, J., Skellett, R., Brenner, C., & Torretta, G. (2000). Factors associated with speech intelligibility in children with cochlear implants. *Annals of Otology, Rhinology & Laryngology Supplement*, *185*, 28-30.

Tyler, R. S., Parkinson, A. J., Wilson, B. S., Witt, S., Preece, J. P., & Noble, W. (2002). Patients utilizing a hearing aid and a cochlear implant: Speech perception and localization. *Ear & Hearing, 23*(2), 98–105.

United States Census Bureau. (2000). *United States Dept of Commerce, Economics and Statistics Administration.* Washington, DC: Government Printing Office.

Waltzman, S. (2000). Variables affecting speech perception in children. In S. Waltzman & N. Cohen (Eds.), *Cochlear implants* (pp. 199–214). New York: Thieme.

Waltzman, S., Cohen, N., & Gomolin, R. (1997). Perception and production results in children implanted between 2 and 5 years of age: Cochlear implant and related sciences update. *Advances in Otorhinolaryngology, 7,* 177–180.

Waltzman, S. B., Robbins, A. M., Green, J. E., & Cohen, N. L. (2003). Second oral language capabilities in children with cochlear implants. *Otology & Neurototology, 25,* 757–763.

Wilbur, R. (1987). *American Sign Language: Linguistic and applied dimensions.* Austin, TX: Pro-Ed.

Wilkes, E. (1999). *Cottage acquisition scales for listening, language and speech.* San Antonio: Sunshine Cottage for Deaf Children.

Zwolan, T. A., Zimmerman-Phillips, P. S., Aschbaugh, C. J., Hiefer, S. J., Kileny, P. R., & Telian, S. (1997). Cochlear implantation of children with minimal open set speech recognition. *Ear & Hearing, 18,* 240–251.

Appendix A

ORGANIZATIONAL RESOURCES AND WEB SITES PROVIDING INFORMATION ON DEAFNESS OR COCHLEAR IMPLANTS IN CHILDREN

Alexander Graham Bell Association for the Deaf and Hard of Hearing (AG Bell)
3417 Volta Place, NW
Washington, DC 20007
202-337-5220
http://www.agbell.org

American Academy of Audiology
11730 Plaza America Drive, #300
Reston, VA 20190
703-790-8466
http://www.audiology.org

American Academy of Otolaryngology–Head and Neck Surgery
One Prince Street
Alexandria, VA 22314
703-836-4444
http://www.entnet.org

American Society for Deaf Children
P.O. Box 3355
Gettysburg, PA 17325
717-334-7922
http://www.deafchildren.org

**American Speech-Language-
Hearing Association (ASHA)**
10801 Rockville Pike
Rockville, MD 20852
800-638-8255
http://www.asha.org

**Auditory-Verbal International
(AVI)**
2121 Eisenhower Avenue, #402
Alexandria, VA 22314
703-7391049
http://www.auditory-verbal.org

Advanced Bionics Corporation
12740 San Fernando Road
Valencia, CA 91342
800-678-2575
http://www.bionics.com

Beginnings for Deaf Children
P.O. Box 17646
Raleigh, NC 27619
919-850-2746
http://www.beginningssvcs.com

**Boystown National Research
Hospital**
Omaha, NE 68131
My Baby's Hearing Web site:
http://www.babyhearing.org

Cochlear Americas
400 Inverness Parkway, Suite 400
Englewood, CO 80112
800-523-5798
http://www.cochlearamericas.com

**Cochlear Implant Association,
Inc. (formerly CICI)**
5335 Wisconsin Avenue, Suite 440
Washington DC 20015
202-895-2781
http://www.cici.org

**Deafness Research
Foundation**
2801 M Street NW
Washington DC 20007
http://www.drf.org

The Ear Foundation
Marjorie Sherman House
83 Sherwin Road
0115 942 1985
Nottingham, UK
NG7 2FB
http://www.earfoundation.org.uk

Hearing Exchange
http://www.HearingExchange.com

John Tracy Clinic
806 West Adams Blvd.
Los Angeles, CA 9007
800-522-4582
http://www.johntracyclinic.org

**Laurent Clerc National Deaf
Education Center**
Gallaudet University
800 Florida Avenue
Washington, DC 20002-3695
202-651-5638
http://clerccenter.gallaudet.edu

**Learning to Listen
Foundation**
Phillips House
10 Buchan Court
Toronto, Ontario, Canada
M2J 1V2
Phone: +1-416-491-4648, ext. 8221
Fax: +1-416-491-7215
http://www.learningtolisten.org

Listen–Up
http://www.listen-up.org

Med El Corporation
2222 East Highway 54
Beta Building Suite 180
Durham, North Carolina 27713
888-655-3524
http://www.medel.com

National Association of the Deaf
814 Thayer Avenue
Silver Spring, MD 20910
301-587-1788 (V)
301-587-1789 (TTY)
http://www.nad.org

National Institute on Deafness and Other Communication Disorders (NIDCD)
National Institutes of Health
1 Communication Avenue
Bethesda, MD 20892-3456
301-241-1044
http://www.nidcd.nih.gov
nidcdinfo@nidcd.nih.gov

Network of Educators of Children with Cochlear Implants (NECCI)
Hearing and Speech Center
Long Island Jewish Hospital
New Hyde Park
718-470-8910
http://http://www.northshorelij.com/NECCI

Oral Deaf Education Website
http://www.oraldeaf.org

The Oberkotter Foundation
877-672-5332
http://www.oraldeafed.org

RNID of Deaf and Hard of Hearing People
London, UK
EC1Y 8SL
0808 808 0123
http://www.rnid.org.uk

Appendix B

SAMPLE DAILY LOG

Date: ————————————

Auditory Behavior. Indicate child's response to the following:

Name
Environmental Sounds (ready to listen)
Environmental Sounds (spontaneously)
Speech Sounds (ready to listen)
Speech Sounds (spontaneously)
Are any of these responses different from previous behavior?

Speech. Indicate child's production of the following:

Speech in imitation of a model
Spontaneous speech production
Degree of intelligibility
Are any of these productions different from previous behavior?

Language. Indicate the child's expressive/receptive language skills:

Child understood spoken words/phrases/sentences/connected speech
Was comprehension of language in a structured or unstructured context?
Child produced spoken (used simultaneous communication) words/
   phrases/sentences/connected speech
Was production of language spontaneous or in imitation to a model?
Was the child's language behavior different from previously noted?

Social. Indicate child's social behavior in the following settings:

Small-group academic activity
Small-group play activity
Large-group academic activity
Large-play activity
One-on-one with another child
One-on-one with an adult
Was the child's social behavior different from previously noted?

Concerns/Questions. Please note any concerns or questions about the child related to his/her use of the cochlear implant.

————————————————————————————

————————————————————————————

————————————————————————————

Appendix C

FM MANUFACTURER RESOURCES

Phonic Ear Inc.
Corporate Headquarters
3880 Cypress Drive
Petaluma, CA 94954-7600
Toll-free: 800-227-0735
Vox: 707-769-1110
Fax: 707-769-9624
Web site: http://www.phonicear.com

Phonak Inc., USA
4520 Weaver Parkway
Warrenville, IL 60555-3927
Phone:630-821-5000 or 800-679-4871
Fax: 630-393-7400
E-mail: info@phonak.com
Web site: http://www.phonak-us.com

Lightspeed Technologies
11509 SW Herman Road
Tualatin, OR 97062
Education Phone: 800-732-8999
Wireless Sound Solutions Phone: 866-840-3662
Website: http://www.lightspeed-tek.com

Index

A

ACE (advanced combined encoders), 5
Acoustics, classroom, 166-167
Adolescent users, 79
Adult implant recipients, 176-177
Advanced Bionics Corporation, 3, 222
AG Bell, 58, 221
Age of implantation
  infants
    acoustic environment creation, 91-92
    connected discourse, 89-90
    experience processing/spoken language, 90
    home language learning routines, 92-93
    language content building, 90
    language functionality, 91
    skill activity selection, 91
    speech development, 105
    spoken language input needs, 89-91
  overview, 101-102
  preschoolers
    chronologic/listening ages assessment, 111

    listening activities/games, 94-97
    overview, 93-94
  school-aged children
    connected discourse, 97-100
    No Child Left Behind, 98
    overview, 97-98
  teenagers
    congenital deafness, 100-101
    motivating listening, 100
    reading selections, 101
    rhythm/beat, 100-101
    speech tracking, 101
  toddlers
    acoustic environment creation, 91-92
    connected discourse, 89-90
    experience processing/spoken language, 90
    home language learning routines, 92-93
    language content building, 90
    language functionality, 91
    selecting skill activities, 91
    skill activity selection, 91
    spoken language input needs, 89-91
Alexander Graham Bell Association for the Deaf and Hard of Hearing, See AG Bell

American Academy of Audiology,
    221
American Academy of
    Otolaryngology-Head and
    Neck Surgery, 221
American Society for Deaf
    Children, 221
Anatomy, cochlear, 28–29
APD (auditory processing
    disorders), 22, 26, 75
ASHA (American Speech-Language-
    Hearing Association), 222
Assessment
    articulation, 111–112
    CALP (Cognitive and Academic
        Language Proficiency), 37
    Listening Inventory for
        Education (LIFE), 169–170
    materials, 64
    preschoolers at implant age, 111
    Screening Instrument for
        Targeting Educational Risk
        (Sifter), 169
    skill development, 7–8
    Suprasegmental Recognition and
        Production Test (SRAPT),
        109
Audiology
    cochlear implantation impact,
        7–8
    future of, 207–208
    mapping, 207
Auditory learning, 37–38
Auditory management, 137–138
Auditory neuropathy/dys-
    synchrony, 159
Auditory perception, 6, 85, 88
Auditory processing disorders
    (APD), 22, 26, 75
Auditory skill development
    and auditory comprehension,
        87–88
    cues, suprasegmental/segmental,
        85–87

and detection, 84–85
and discrimination, 85
hierarchies, 84–88
and identification, 85, 87
jump-starting postimplantation,
    137–138
pattern perception, 85, 88
and segmental identification,
    85–87
Auditory Training (Erber), 84
Auditory-Verbal International
    (AVI), 222
Auditory verbal therapists, 62

B

Beginnings for Deaf Children, 222
BICS (Basic Interpersonal
    Communication Skills), 37
Bilateral implantation
    auditory-oral approach, 185
    benefits of, 184
    concerns, 183–187
    early implementation, 182–183
    insurance coverage, 186–187
    mapping needs of, 186
    and "saving" of unimplanted ear,
        185–186
    therapeutic practice, 185
Boystown National Research
    Hospital, 222

C

CALP (Cognitive and Academic
    Language Proficiency), 37
Cell phones, 175
*A Child with a Hearing Loss in
    Your Classroom? Don't
    Panic!!* (Mangiari), 63
CICI, *See* Cochlear Implant
    Association, Inc.

CIS (continuous interleaved sampling), 5
Clarion implants, 6, 71, 72, 172
Classrooms
    acoustics, 166-167
    additional amplification, 63
    ANSI (American National Standards Institute) background noise limit, 167
    background noise, 167
    buddy systems, 64
    cell phones, 175
    computers, 175
    consistency, 64
    FM systems, 175
        personal, 49, 170-174
        sound-field, 168-170, 174
    gauging student understanding, 64
    listening/speaking curricula, 138
    personal audio systems, 175-176
    RT (reverberation time), 167
    SC (simultaneous communication), 136, 139, 141, 157
    self-contained, 135-136
    small-instruction, 135-136
    TC (total communication), 136
    technology, 61-62, 167-168
    visual augmentation, 64
Cochlea
    anatomy of, 28-29
    malformation, 29
    ossified, 28-29
Cochleae, abnormal, 29, 157-159
Cochlear Americas, 3, 4, 6, 182, 222
Cochlear Implant Association, Inc., 222
Cochlear implantation, 1-2, *See also* Cochlear implants; History
    and abnormal cochleae, 157-159

age of implantation, *See main heading* Age of implantation
all-implantable devices, 205
and audiology field, 7-8
auditory management postimplantation, 137-138
auditory neuropathy/dys-synchrony, 159
bilateral, 182-187, *See also main heading* Bilateral implantation
and children with disabilities, 159-162
and cognitive handicaps, 161-162
and concurrent signing, 133-134
    premises based on, 136-143
deaf children of deaf families, 155-157
education field impact, 9
employment equity desire, 196
frontloading services, 38
helping literacy, 121-122
intervention zone
    age at implantation, 27-28
    and candidacy factors, 26-35
    and cochlear anatomy, 28-29
    communication modality, 37-38
    deafness duration, 27-28
    device management, 35-38
    and disabilities, 31-32
    educational environment, 34
    and families, 32-34, *See also main heading* Families
    and formal language system use, 30-31
    habilitation, 36-38
    implant process, 35-38
    residual hearing use, 29-30
    and second language in house, 31, 37

Cochlear implantation,
intervention zone *(continued)*
support service availability,
35, 38
working within, 23–26
and Ling's hierarchy, 106
and listening age concept, 110
and lower socioeconomic
households, 153–155
and low muscle tone, 161
noncognitive handicaps,
160–161
and nonnative-English speakers,
148–153, *See main
heading* Nonnative-English
speakers *for details*
parental choice for, 137
physiologic zone, 24
neural survival, 22
outcome predictability, 22–23
and outcome predictability,
22–23
positive outcome domino effect,
122
post-babbling stage, 110
and self-esteem, 199–200
single-channel, 2–3
skepticism/criticism of, 10
and SLP (speech-language
pathology) field, 8–9
and social development, *See
main heading* Social
development
speech assessment, 111–112
suprasegmental
rhythm/intonation, 109
12-month mark, 132
visual problems, 161
Cochlear implants, *See also*
Cochlear implantation
adolescent users, 79
and APD (auditory processing
disorders), 16
behavior challenges, 78–79

bilateral, 182–187, *See also
main heading* Bilateral
implantation
device adjustment, *See* Mapping
device management, 77
duration of use, 79
and ESD (electrostatic
discharge), 81
habilitation, 36–38
with hearing aids
concerns, 189–191
and evaluation of hearing
success, 190
overview, 187–189
and remapping, 190–191
should be simultaneous?,
189–190
will two signals be
confusing?, 189
and helmet use (sports and
such), 82
Ling six sounds listening checks,
80
listening checks, 80
maintenance, 80
monitoring, 80
noncompliance, 78–79
performance, classroom, 17–40,
See main heading
Performance *for details*
population changes, 13–14
proper functioning, 79–81
sensitivity control, 76
and sound detection, 85
and sports, 66–67, 82
user controls, 76
volume control, 76
wear time, 78–79
Cognitive handicaps, 161–162
Collaborative teams, *See* Teams
Computers
classroom, 175
home, 208
Cued speech, 159

D

Daily Log Sample, 225-226
Deaf children of deaf families,
        155-157
Deaf Culture, 142, 202
    optionality of implants, 156
    and skepticism/criticism of
        implantation, 10, 144, 155
    and social development,
        193-194
Deafness
    abnormal cochleae, 29, 157-159
    congenital, 100-101, 205-206
    history, 2
    literacy skills, 118
    profound, 103, 109, 123
    social development, 197-198
Deafness Research Foundation,
        222
Deaf President Now (DPN)
        movement, 155
Deaf speech
    variability deficits, 109
    vowel clarity, 110
Disabilities, children with,
        159-162
Dys-synchrony, auditory, 159

E

EA (educational audiologists),
        61-62
    and mapping, 73, 207
The Ear Foundation, 222
Early interventionists (EI), 13
Educational audiologists, See EA
        (educational audiologists)
Educational interpreters, See
        Interpreters, educational
Educational programs, See also
        Speech services
    assistive devices, 49

characteristics
    academic accommodation,
        49-50
    administrative professional
        support, 51-52
    audition valued, 46-47
    auditory instruction
        prioritized, 48
    challenging instruction, 48-49
    extracurricular communication
        needs met, 50-51
    implant assistive technology
        potential recognized, 45
    listed, 43
    parental choice respected,
        45-46
    spoken language valued, 47
    unconditional implant
        acceptance, 42-44
    and English vocabulary
        complexity, 60-61, See also
        vocabulary *under main
        heading* Literacy
IDEA (Individuals with
        Disabilities Education Act),
        49
IEP (Individualized Education
        Plan), 50, 88, 141, 144
implants with hearing aids, 191
LRE (least restrictive
        environment), 49
mainstreaming, 11, 12, 44, 57-58,
        63-65, 143-144, 200
overview, 41-42
and personal FM systems, 49,
        170-174
simultaneous communication
        (SC), 59, 60, 157
Education field
    cochlear implantation impact,
        9-12
    cochlear implant education
        center, Gallaudet University,
        11

Education field *(continued)*
and hearing impaired
classrooms, 10
and mainstream classrooms, 11,
12, *See also main heading
Mainstreaming*
mixed classroom messages, 10-11
and multiple learning
challenges, 12
and oral programs, 10
sign language, 11-12
Electrostatic discharge, *See* ESD
(electrostatic discharge)
English as second language
resources, 152
ESD (electrostatic discharge), 81
Evan-Moor Corporation, 100

F

Families
ASL-only, 157
and child self-esteem, 199-200
and cognitive handicaps, 162
counseling of, 9
deaf children of deaf families,
155-157
and educational program
characteristics, 45-46
generalization skills, show 114
and habilitation, 36-37
home language learning
routines, 92-93
and intervention
parent-child mutual
expectations, 33-34
structure/support, 32-33
and literacy, 122
lower socioeconomic
households, 154-155
maintenance, external
hardware, 80

as mapping information sources,
73
and maximal wear time, 78
and noncognitive handicaps,
160-161
nonnative-English speakers,
149-151
rationale for implantation, 137
reporting by, 7-8
scheduling mapping, 74
special education habits, 64
FM systems, 175
implant compatible devices,
171-173
interface, 6
personal, 170-174
sound-field, 168-170, 174
Future
and audiologists, 207-208
genetic engineering, 205-206
hair cell regeneration, 205
mainstreaming, 209-210
of mapping, 207-208
SLP (speech-language
pathologists), 208-209
teachers of children who are
deaf or hard of hearing
(TOD), 209-210
of technology
all-implantable devices, 205
and electrodes, 204-205
hybrid devices, 208
and music, 204
nanotechnology, 205
overview, 202-204
and school professionals, 206

G

Gallaudet University
cochlear implant education
center, 11

Laurent Clerc National Deaf
     Education Center, 11, 222
Guiding Readers and Writers
     (Fountas & Pinnel)s, 129,
     See also Literacy

H

Hearing aids with implants
  concerns, 189–191
  and evaluation of hearing
     success, 190
  overview, 187–189
  and remapping, 190–191
  should be simultaneous?,
     189–190
  will two signals be confusing?,
     189
Hearing Exchange, 222
Hearing loss
  age of identification, 180
  bilateral, 180, 181
  mild to moderate, 1
  mild-to-moderate, 1
  sensorineural, 184
  severe-to-profound, 1–2, 184
  speech development models,
     106–108, *See also main
     heading* Speech
     development
  unilateral, 180–181
High resolution coding, 5
History
  body-worn processors, 6
  BTE (behind-the-ear) devices, 6
  Clarion device, 6
  and deafness, 2
  electrode design, 4
  external hardware modification,
     5–7
  of hearing aid technology, 1–2
  of implant numbers, 181–182

manual communication, 1–2, 44
multichannel implants, 3–4, 5
program storage capacity, 6
receiver design, 4–5
single-channel implants, 2–3
social development of Deaf,
     197–198
of speech processing strategies,
     5
House Ear Institute, 2

I

IDEA (Individuals with Disabilities
     Education Act)
  cochlear implantation, 147
  educational programs, 49
Interpreters, educational, 143
  and child's emerging language
     skills, 145
  and postimplant child attention
     to, 144–145
  vocabulary sophistication,
     145–146

J

John Tracy Clinic, 222

L

Laurent Clerc National Deaf
     Education Center, Gallaudet
     University, 11, 222
Learning to Listen Foundation, 222
Lightspeed Technologies, 227
Ling, Daniel, 106
Ling six sounds listening checks, 80
Listening Inventory for Education
     (LIFE), 169–170

Listening skills, *See* Auditory skill development
Listen-Up, 222
Literacy
  and acoustic environment, 127
  aided *versus* implanted, 126–127
  basal readers, 124
  challenges, 129–130
  Chall's critical third stage, reading, 125
  cochlear implantation assistance, 121–122
  code breaking, 124
  comprehension monitoring, 129
  and figurative, nonliteral language, 128–129
  inferential skills, 120
  intentional instructions, 127–128
  language experience approach, 123–124
  and linguistic competence, 120
  Matthew Effect, 119
  overview, 117–118, 130
  and parents, 122
  phonics instruction, 122–123
  prerequisites, 118–122
  reading to learn, 124–126
  and spoken language, 120, 121–122
  syntax knowledge, 120, 121–122, 128–129
  variability, 125–126
  vocabulary, 126–128
  and vocabulary, 119, 121, 124, 126–128
Lower socioeconomic households, 153–155

M

Mainstreaming, 11, 12, 44
  child participation enhancement, 63–65
  future, 209–210
  and sign language, 135, 143–144
  and SLPs, school-based, 57–58
  social development, 200
  team teaching, 58
Manual communication, 1–2, 44
Mapping
  and APD (auditory processing disorders), 75
  assessment, 72–73
  baseline performance measures, 76
  C-level, 72, 73
  collaboration, 76–77
  comfort, 70–72
  daily session logs, 76–77, 225–226
  and device management, 77
  device switch on, 70
  dynamic range, 73
  electrode activation, 71–72
  goals, 75
  infants, 72
  information sources, 73
  M-level, 72, 73
  NRI (neural response imaging), 72–73
  NRT (neural response telemetry), 72–73
  programming audiologist, 70, 71, 72, 73, 77, 80
  programs, 73
  progress in, 207
  remote, 207–208
  schedules, 73–74
  and speech intelligibility, 77
  suboptimal, 74–75
  system specificity, 71
  thresholds, 70–72
  T-level, 72, 73
  toddlers, 72

videostreaming, 208
Med El Corporation, 223
Meningitis, 28
Minimed Technologies, *See*
    Advanced Bionics
    Corporation
Mondini deformities, 29, 158-159
Multidisciplinary teams, *See* Teams
Music perception/appreciation,
    176-177

N

NAD (National Association for the
    Deaf), 10, 11, 155-156, 223
National Institute on Deafness and
    Other Communication
    Disorders (NIDCD), 223
Network of Educators of Children
    with Cochlear Implants, 58
Network of Educators of Children
    with Cochlear Implants
    (NECCI), 223
Neuropathy, auditory, 159
No Child Left Behind, 98
N of M coding strategies coding, 5
Nonnative-English speakers
    and advocacy, 153
    child communication, 151-152
    culture differences, 150
    English as second language
        resources, 152
    family communication, 149-151
    overview, 148-149
    therapeutic intervention, 153
Nucleus implants, 71, 172

O

The Oberkotter Foundation, 223
Oral Deaf Education Web site, 223

P

Performance
    auditory, 18
    educational achievement, 20
    and expectation disconnect, 17
    and habilitation, 18
    language development, 19
    outcomes, overall, 20-21
    speech production, 19-20
    zones
        benchmarks, 38-40
        intervention, 23-38, *See also*
            intervention zone *under*
            Cochlear implantation
        overview, 21
        physiologic, 21-23, *See also*
            physiologic zone *under*
            Cochlear implantation
Phonak Inc., USA, 227
Phonic Ear, Inc., 227
Psychologists, 12-13

Q

Questions Teachers Ask (Otto and
    Kozak), 63

R

Reading, *See* Literacy
Registry of Interpreters for the
    Deaf (RID), 143
Research
    auditory perception, 6-7
    overview, 6
Retinitis pigmentosa, 160-161
RNID of Deaf and Hard and
    Hearing People, 223
RT (reverberation time),
    classroom, 167

S

Schools for the deaf, 135, 142–143
Screening
  newborn, 9
  Universal Newborn Hearing
      Screening, 14
Screening Instrument for Targeting
      Educational Risk (Sifter), 169
Sign language, 11–12
  and concurrent implantation,
      133–134
    premises based on, 136–143
  long term, 134–135
  oral-only transition, 134
  overview, 131–132
  short term, 132–134
SLP (speech-language
      pathologists), 63, 64, 65
  assessment by, 57
  case management by, 57–58
  future, 208–209
  and mapping, 73, 76–77
  school-based, 57–59, 141–142
SLP (speech-language pathology),
      8–9
SNR (signal-to-noise ratios),
      classroom, 166–167
Social development
  and Deaf Culture, 193–194
  and implantation, 196–197
  mainstreaming, 200
  personality, 195–197
  self-esteem, 195–197
  socialization and
      communication, 194–195
Social workers, 12–13
Sound and Fury (film
      documentary), 156–157
*Speech and the Hearing-Impaired
      Child: Theory and
      Practices* (Ling), 106
Speech clarity
  overview, 103–104

speech and language
  speech development,
      104–108, *See main
      heading* Speech
      development *for details*
Speech development
  assessment, implant recipients,
      111–112
  babbling, 105
  childhood hearing loss models
    aided *versus* implanted,
      106–107
    categorical
      phonemes/consonants,
      106–107
    Ling's hierarchy, 106
    Shriberg's classification,
      106–107
  physiology/anatomy, 104–105
  postimplantation, 105–106
  speech foundations, 108–111
    and auditory access, human
      voice, 110
    chronologic/listening ages, 111
    jargoning age, 110–111
    listening age concept, 110
    vowel clarity, 108–109
Speech reading, 79
Speech services, 112–113
  intervention plans, 112–113
  listening/speaking relationship,
      112
Suprasegmental Recognition and
      Production Test (SRAPT),
      109

T

Teachers, classroom, 62–63, *See
      also* Classrooms; Education
      field; Teams
  FM systems
    personal, 49, 170–174

sound-field, 168–170, 174
Teachers of children who are deaf
    or hard of hearing (TOD),
    59–61, 63, 64
  and future, 209–210
  itinerant, 60, 65
Teams
  art teachers, 66
  auditory verbal therapists (AVT),
    62
  building custodians, 67–68
  chorus teachers, 65
  classroom teachers, 62–63, 114
  collaborative intervention,
    58–59
  EA (educational audiologists),
    61–62
  and English vocabulary
    complexity, 60–61
  mainstreaming, 57–58
  music teachers, 65
  observing device mapping, 70
  overview, 55–56
  physical educational teachers,
    66–67
  pullout services, 114
  push-in intervention, 58–59, 114
  school secretaries, 67–68
  and simultaneous
    communication (SC), 59, 60
  SLP, school-based, 57–59
  SLP (speech-language
    pathologists), 63, 64, 65
  and speech services, 114

teachers of children who are
    deaf or hard of hearing
    (TOD), 59–61, 63, 64, 65
technology and classrooms,
    61–62
Therapy
  for learning sounds, 77
TOD, *See* Teachers of children
    who are deaf or hard of
    hearing (TOD)

U

United States Cochlear
    Corporation, *See* Cochlear
    Americas
Universal Newborn Hearing
    Screening, 14

V

*Vocabulary in the Elementary
    and Middle School*
    (Johnson), 128, *See also*
    vocabulary *under* Literacy

W

Walt Disney rehabilitation
    Research Institute, *See*
    House Ear Institute